Business Spelling and Word Power

by A. H. Lass

Donald Publishing Co., Inc.
New York, N.Y.

TABLE OF CONTENTS

USES
of the Dictionary

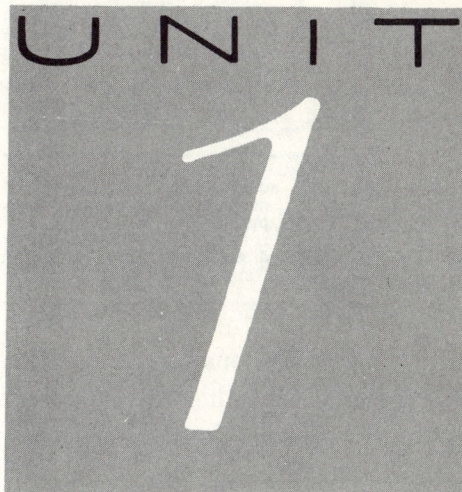

UNIT 1

Your dictionary is one of the most useful books at your disposal. In your everyday reading, writing and speaking there are many occasions when you must consult the dictionary.

In the business world, it is an indispensable tool — your key to communication. Use it properly and you will become aware of the many different types of information available from it. In fact, you will find it a truly fascinating book.

In this unit, the wealth of information available to you in the dictionary is clearly illustrated. See how much pleasure and knowledge you will derive from becoming familiar with this wonderful book.

The actual dictionary entries on the following pages are from Webster's New World Dictionary of the American Language.

SPELLING

How many g's are there in **exa—erate**? Is it **superintend*a*nt** or **superintend*e*nt**? Your dictionary tells you.

> **ex·ag·ger·ate** (ig-zaj'ə-rāt'), *v.t.* [EXAGGERATED (-id), EXAGGERATING], [< L. *exaggeratus*, pp. of *exaggerare*, to heap up, increase, exaggerate; *ex-*, out, up + *aggerare*, to heap up < *agger*, a heap, mound], 1. to think, speak, or write of (something) as greater than it is; magnify beyond the fact; overstate. 2. to increase or enlarge to an abnormal degree; overemphasize; intensify. *v.i.* to give an exaggerated description or account of something; use exaggeration.

> **su·per·in·tend·ent** (sōō'pĕr-in-ten'dənt, sū'pĕr-in-ten'dənt), *n.* [OFr. *superintendant* < LL. *superintendens*, ppr. of *superintendere*, to superintend], a person in charge of a department, institution, project, etc.; director; manager; supervisor. *adj.* superintending. Abbreviated **Supt.**, **supt.**

Some words have more than one possible spelling. In your dictionary the spelling considered most correct is featured *first;* alternative spellings are mentioned later in the entry. Throughout this book we have given *only* the preferred spelling of a word. It is this preferred spelling that you should learn. Consider all alternative spellings as being incorrect. For example, always write **judgment** although the dictionary says: *"Also spelled* **judgement."**

PRONUNCIATION

Through the use of a stress mark ('), the dictionary tells you which syllable of a word is accented—that is, spoken a bit more strongly or forcefully than the other syllables. The *diacritical marks* (ā, ă, ä, etc.) tell you how to sound various vowels and consonants in the word. (The *key words* at the bottom of each page furnish a key to the use of diacritical marks.) Some words have two acceptable pronunciations. The first one listed is the preferred pronunciation. Let's try a word like:

at ten u ate

What syllable is accented? One look at the dictionary and you have your answer. The ' (called *acute accent*) indicates the syllable to be accented.

> **at·ten·u·ate** (ə-ten'ū-āt'), *v.t.* [ATTENUATED (-id), ATTENUATING], [< L. *attenuatus*, pp. of *attenuare*, to make thin < *ad-*, to + *tenuare* < *tenuis*, thin], 1. to make slender or thin. 2. to dilute; rarefy. 3. to lessen or weaken in severity, value, etc. 4. in *bacteriology*, to make (a virus, etc.) less deadly. *v.i.* to become thin, weak, etc. *adj.* (ə-ten'ū-it), attenuated.

Now, how is the **u** pronounced? The key words at the bottom of the page tell you.

fat, āpe, bâre, cär; ten, ēven, hêre, ōver; is, bīte; lot, gō, hôrn, tōōl, look; oil, out; up, ūse, fûr; get; joy; yet; chin; she; thin, *then*; zh, leisure; ŋ, ring; ə for *a* in *ago*, *e* in *agent*, *i* in *sanity*, *o* in *comply*, *u* in *focus*; ʼ as in *able* (ā'b'l); Fr. bal; ä, Fr. coeur; ö, Fr. feu; Fr. mon; ô, Fr. coq; ü, Fr. duc; H, G. ich; kh, G. doch. See pp. x–xii. ‡ foreign; * hypothetical; < derived from.

The **u** in **attenuate** is pronounced like the **u** in **use**. How do you pronounce: **advertisement, comparable, pianist, inquiry**?

ad·ver·tise·ment (ad'vẽr-tīz'mənt, əd-vûr'tiz-mənt), *n.* [Fr. *avertissement*, advertisement; see ADVERTISE], a public notice or announcement, usually paid for, as of things for sale, needs, etc.: also spelled **advertizement**: abbreviated **ad, ad., adv., advt.**

com·pa·ra·ble (kom'pẽr-ə-b'l), *adj.* [L. *comparabilis*], 1. that can be compared; having characteristics in common. 2. worthy of comparison.

pi·an·ist (pi-an'ist, pyan'ist, pē'ə-nist), *n.* [Fr. *pianiste*; It. *pianista*], a person who plays the piano.

in·quir·y (in-kwīr'i, in'kwə-ri), *n.* [*pl.* INQUIRIES (-iz. -riz)], [earlier *enquery* < ME. *enquere*], 1. the act of inquiring. 2. an investigation or examination. 3. a question; query. Also **enquiry**.

DERIVATIONS

Perhaps you are interested in the origins of words. If you wish to know from which language a word comes and what it originally meant in that language, you can find this information in the dictionary. Where do we get the words **boycott** or **boysenberry**?

boy·cott (boi'kot'), *v.t.* [after Captain *Boycott*, land agent ostracized by his neighbors during the Land League agitation in Ireland in 1880], 1. to join together in refusing to deal with, so as to punish, cause to do something, etc. 2. to refuse to buy, sell, or use: as, they *boycotted* the newspaper. *n.* a boycotting.

boy·sen·ber·ry (boi's'n-ber'i, boi'z'n-ber'i), *n.* [*pl.* BOYSENBERRIES (-iz)], [after Rudolph *Boysen*, Am. horticulturist who developed it], a berry, dark red or almost black when ripe, resulting from crossing varieties of raspberry, loganberry, and blackberry.

From what language do we get **biography**?

> **bi·og·ra·phy** (bī-og′rə-fi, bi-og′rə-fi), *n.* [Gr. *biographia* < *bios*, life + *graphein*, to write], 1. the histories of individual lives, considered as a branch of literature. 2. [*pl.* BIOGRAPHIES (-fiz)], an account of a person's life, described by another; life story. Abbreviated **biog.**

Gr here means *Greek.* Note, too, that **biography** comes from two Greek words:

Bios—life

Graphein—to write.

CAPITALIZATION

Should you capitalize **first aid, indian?** Check with your dictionary.

> **first-aid** (fūrst′ād′), *adj.* of or used for first aid.
> **first aid,** emergency treatment for injury or sudden illness, given before regular medical care is available.

> **In·di·an** (in′di-ən), *adj.* [LL. *Indianus* < L. *India*], 1. of India or the East Indies, their people, or culture. 2. of the American aboriginal races (American Indians) or the West Indies, or their cultures. 3. of a type used or made by Indians. 4. made of maize, or Indian corn. *n.* 1. a native of India or the East Indies. 2. a member of any of the aboriginal races of North America, South America, or the West Indies: originally so named from the belief, held by early explorers, that these regions were part of Asia. 3. popularly, any of the languages spoken by the American Indians. Abbreviated **Ind.**

ABBREVIATIONS

Consult your dictionary to find the meanings of abbreviations like **e.g.,** and **i.e.**

> **e.g.,** *exempli gratia,* [L.], for the sake of example; for example.

> **i.e.,** *id est,* [L.], that is.

GRAMMAR and USAGE

Do you know that your dictionary contains much of the information found in a grammar text-book, that it can help you express yourself correctly? You can find the answers to the following questions just by using a dictionary:

Which is correct? **The mumps (is, are) unpleasant.**
The mumps is unpleasant is correct.

> **mumps** (mumps), *n.pl.* [construed as sing.], [pl. of obs. *mump*, a grimace: prob. from patient's appearance], an acute communicable disease, usually of childhood, caused by a virus and characterized by swelling of the salivary glands, especially the parotid, or, occasionally in adults, by inflammation of the testes, breasts, etc.

Mumps, as indicated in the dictionary, is a singular noun even though it *looks* like a plural noun because it ends in **s.** It therefore takes a singular verb **is.** What is the plural of **mongoose?**

> **mon·goose, mon·goos** (mon'gōōs, muŋ'gōōs), *n.* [pl. MONGOOSES (-iz)], [Marathi *mangūs*], a ferretlike, flesh-eating animal of India, known for its ability to kill rats, poisonous snakes, etc.

The dictionary says: *pl. -gooses* indicating that the plural is **mongooses.** How about the plurals of **mosquito, notary public, summons,** and **cupful?**

> **mos·qui·to** (mə-skē'tō), *n.* [pl. MOSQUITOES, MOSQUITOS (-tōz)], [Sp. & Port., dim. of *mosca*, L. *musca*, a fly], any of a large group of two-winged insects, the females of which have skin-piercing mouth parts used to extract blood from animals, including man: some varieties are carriers of certain diseases, as malaria and yellow fever.

> **no·ta·ry** (nō'tēr-i), *n.* [pl. NOTARIES (-iz)], [ME. *notarye*; OFr. *notaire*; L. *notarius* < *notare*, to note], an official authorized to certify or attest documents, take depositions and affidavits, etc.
> **notary public,** [pl. NOTARIES PUBLIC], a notary: abbreviated N.P., n.p.

> **sum·mons** (sum'ənz), *n.* [pl. SUMMONSES (-iz)], [ME. *somounce, somons*; Anglo-Fr. *somonse*; OFr. *sumunse* < base of *somondre, semondre*; see SUMMON], a call or order to come, attend, appear, or perform some action; specifically, *a*) in *law*, an official order to appear in court; also, the writ containing such an order. *b*) a call, command, knock, or other signal that summons. *v.t.* [Colloq.], to serve a court summons upon.

> **cup·ful** (kup'fool'), *n.* [pl. CUPFULS (-foolz')], 1. as much as a cup will hold. 2. in *cookery*, half a pint.

What part of speech is **ahoy?**

> **a·hoy** (ə-hoi′), *interj.* [interj. *a* + *hoy*, var. of *hey*], in *nautical usage*, a call used in hailing a person or a vessel: as, ship *ahoy!*

The dictionary says: *interj.*, meaning an *interjection.*

SPECIAL INFORMATION

Information about famous persons and places, real and fictional, is included in all good dictionaries. Who is **Hercules? Charlemagne?** Where is **Blarney?**

> **Her·cu·les** (hŭr′kyoo-lēz′), *n.* [L.; Gr. *Hērakleēs* < *Hēra,* Hera + *kleos,* glory],   1. in *Greek & Roman mythology,* the son of Zeus and Alcmene, renowned for feats of strength, particularly the twelve labors imposed on him by Hera.   2. [h-], any very large, strong man.   3. a northern constellation: see **constellation,** chart.

> **Char·le·magne** (shär′lə-mān′), *n.* (*Charles I*), king of the Franks (768–814 A.D.); emperor of the West (800–814 A.D.); lived 742–814 A.D.; established Holy Roman Empire: called *Charles the Great.*

> **Blarney stone,** a stone in Blarney Castle in the county of Cork, Ireland, said to impart skill in blarney to those who kiss it.

IDIOMS

Idioms and idiomatic expressions are defined in most large dictionaries. What is meant by **crocodile tears? an ivory tower? a red herring? blue Monday?**

> **crocodile tears,** insincere tears or a hypocritical show of grief: from an old belief that crocodiles shed **tears** while eating their prey.

> **ivory tower,** figuratively, a place of mental withdrawal from **reality** and action: used as a symbol of escapist tendencies, especially in art and literature.

> **red herring,** 1. a smoked herring.   2. something used to confuse, or to divert attention from something else: from the practice of drawing a herring across the trace in hunting, to distract the hounds.

> **blue Monday,** [? after D. *blaaw maandag*: orig. a minister's term, from the excessive work done on Sunday], [Colloq.], any Monday. so called because considered depressing as the beginning of **a week** of work contrasted with the pleasures of the weekend.

SYLLABIFICATION

By the use of a dot (sometimes, a hyphen) the dictionary tells you at just what point a word may be split into syllables. If, for example, you had to divide the word **fascinate** at the end of a line, where would you place the hyphen? Consult your dictionary to find out.

> **fas·ci·nate** (fas′′n-āt′), *v.t.* [FASCINATED (-id), FASCI-
> NATING], [L. *fascinatus*, pp. of *fascinare*, to bewitch,
> charm < *fascinum*, an enchanting, witchcraft], 1.
> originally, to bewitch; put under a spell. 2. to attract
> or hold motionless, as by a fixed look or by inspiring
> terror. 3. to attract by delightful qualities; charm.
> —*SYN.* see attract.

LEVELS of USAGE

Your dictionary tells you whether words are *colloquial, slang, archaic,* and the like.

> **ain't** (ănt), [early assimilation, with lengthened and
> raised vowel, of *amn't*, contr. of *am not;* later confused
> with *a'nt* (are not), *i'nt* (is not), *ha'nt* (has not, have not)],
> [Colloq.], am not: also a dialectal or substandard con-
> traction for *is not, has not,* and *have not: ain't* was
> formerly standard for *am not* and is still defended by
> some authorities as a proper contraction for *am not* in

> **wack·y** (wak′i), *adj.* [WACKIER (-i-ĕr), WACKIEST (-i-ist)],
> [? < *whack* (a blow) + *-y;* cf. SLAP-HAPPY], [Slang],
> erratic, eccentric, or irrational: also **whacky.**

> **me·thinks** (mi-thinks′), *impersonal v.* [past tense
> METHOUGHT (-thôt′)], [ME. *me thinketh;* AS. *me thyncth;*
> *me,* me, to me + *thyncth,* it seems < *thyncan,* to seem],
> [Archaic], it seems to me.

OTHER VALUABLE FEATURES

In addition, the dictionary serves a number of miscellaneous but important purposes. In it you can find historical and geographical information, a list of proofreading symbols, rules for punctuation, and a wealth of other matter. Of course, the smaller the dictionary you use, the less likely it is to contain all of this information. So be sure to have with you at school, on the job, or at home, a complete and authoritative dictionary. You will find it your most useful aid to correct writing, spelling, and vocabulary building.

On the next page is a sample of a complete dictionary page. Study this sample carefully and note the many different types of information it contains.

CATCHWORD, a guide to the first entry on the page — **lb.**

lynx-eyed — CATCHWORD, a guide to the last entry on the page

ABBREVIATION

GEOGRAPHICAL ENTRY

SPOT MAP, showing location in relation to other places

SYLLABIFICATION, indicated by centered dots

PART-OF-SPEECH LABEL

PRONUNCIATION

FOREIGN PHRASE, indicated by double dagger (‡)

DERIVED FORM

ETYMOLOGY

USAGE LABELS (see p. xiii)*

EXAMPLES of the word in context

USAGE NOTE

INFLECTED FORMS, principal parts of the verb (see p. xiii)*

SUFFIX (see p. ix)*

NOTE ON SPELLING

VARIANT SPELLING (see p. ix)*

INFLECTED FORMS, comparative and superlative (see p. xii)*

SYNONYMY (see p. xiv)*

lb., [L.], *libra*, pound; *librae*, pounds.

Li·ber·i·a (lī-bêr′i-ə), ***n.*** a country on the western coast of Africa, founded in 1847 by freed American Negro slaves: area, 43,000 sq. mi.; pop., 1,600,000 (est. 1947); capital, Monrovia: abbreviated **Lib.**

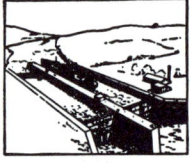

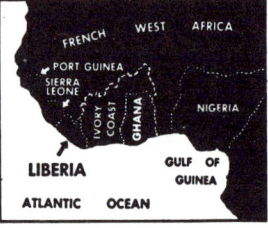

LIBERIA

Li·ber·i·an (lī-bêr′i-ən), ***adj.*** of Liberia, its people, or their culture. ***n.*** a native or inhabitant of Liberia.

lib·er·tar·i·an (lib′ẽr-târ′i-ən), ***n.*** [< *liberty* + *-arian*], 1. a person who believes in the doctrine of the freedom of the will. 2. a person who advocates full civil liberties. ***adj.*** of or upholding either of these principles.

‡li·ber·té, é·ga·li·té, fra·ter·ni·té (lē′ber′tā′ ā′gà′lē′tā′ frà′ter′nē′tā′), [Fr.], liberty, equality, fraternity: the motto of the French Revolution of 1789.

lik·a·ble (līk′ə-b'l), ***adj.*** having qualities that inspire liking; worthy of being liked; attractive, pleasant, genial, etc.: also spelled **likeable.**

like (līk), ***adj.*** [ME. *lik, lich* < AS. type **lic*, shortened < *gelic*, similar, equal, lit., of the same form or shape; akin to G. *gleich* (OHG. *gilih*), AS. *lic*, body, form (see LICH)], 1. having almost or exactly the same qualities, characteristics, etc.; similar; equal: as, a cup of sugar and a *like* amount of flour. 2. [Rare], alike. 3. [Dial.], likely. ***adv.*** 1. in the manner of one that is: as, he works *like* mad. 2. [Colloq.], likely: as, *like* as not, he is already there. ***prep.*** 1. similar to; somewhat resembling: as, she is *like* a bird. 2. in a manner characteristic of; similarly to: as, she sings *like* a bird. 3. in accord with the nature of; characteristic of: as, it was not *like* him to forget her birthday. 4. in the mood for; desirous of: as, I feel *like* sleeping. 5. indicative or prophetic of: as, it looks *like* a clear day tomorrow. *Like* was originally an adjective in senses 1, 3, 4, 5, and an adverb in sense 2, and is still considered so by conservative grammarians. ***conj.*** [Colloq.], 1. as: as, it was just like you said. 2. as if: as, it looks *like* he is signaling to us. ***n.*** a person or thing regarded as the equal or counterpart of another or of the person or thing being discussed: as, I have never seen the *like* of it. ***v.t.*** [LIKED (līkt), LIKING], [Obs.], to compare; liken. ***v.i.*** [Dial.], to come near (*to* doing something): in this use the verb is equal to the adverb *almost*.
and the like, and others of the same kind.
like anything (or **blazes, crazy, the devil, mad, etc.**), [Colloq. or Slang], with furious energy, speed, etc.
nothing like, not at all like; completely different from.
something like, almost like; about.
the like (or **likes**) **of**, [Colloq.], any person or thing like.

like (līk), ***v.i.*** [LIKED (līkt), LIKING], [ME. *liken*; AS. *lician* (akin to G. *leikan*) < base of *lic*, body, form (cf. LIKE, *adj.*); sense development: to be of like form—be like—be suited to—be pleasing to], 1. [Obs.], to please; be agreeable to: with the dative, as, it *likes* me not. 2. to be so inclined; choose: as, you may leave whenever you *like*. ***v.t.*** 1. to have a taste or fondness for; be pleased with; have a preference for; enjoy. 2. to wish: as, I should *like* to go there. ***n. pl.*** preferences, tastes, or affections: as, we know nothing of his *likes* and dislikes.

-like (līk), [AS. *-lic* < *gelic*; see LIKE, *adj.*, -LY], a suffix added to nouns: 1. to form adjectives meaning *like, characteristic of, suitable for*, as in *doglike, manlike, homelike*. 2. to form adverbs meaning *in the manner of*. Words formed with *-like* are usually written as one word, but are hyphenated if three *l's* fall together (e.g., *ball-like*).

like·a·ble (līk′ə-b'l), ***adj.*** likable.

like·li·hood (līk′li-hood′), ***n.*** [ME. *liklihode*; see LIKELY & -HOOD], 1. probability. 2. something that is likely to happen; a probability.

like·ly (līk′li), ***adj.*** [LIKELIER (-li-ẽr), LIKELIEST (-li-ist)], [ME. *likly, likliche*, after AS. *geliclic* or cognate ON. *likligr*; see LIKE, *adj.* & -LY], 1. apparently true to the facts; credible; probable: as, a *likely* account of the brawl. 2. seeming as if it would happen or make happen; reasonably to be expected; apparently destined: as, it is *likely* to leave at any minute. 3. such as will probably be satisfactory or rewarding; suitable: as, a *likely* place to find deer. 4. promising: as, a *likely* lad. ***adv.*** probably: as, he will very *likely* go.
SYN.—**likely** suggests probability or an eventuality that can reasonably be expected (he's not *likely* to win); **liable** and **apt** are loosely or informally used as equivalents of **likely**, but in strict discrimination, **liable** implies exposure or susceptibility to something undesirable (he's *liable* to be killed playing with firearms) and **apt** suggests a natural or habitual inclination or tendency (such people are always *apt* to become frightened); **prone** also suggests a propensity or predisposition to something that seems almost inevitable (he's *prone* to suspect others' motives). See also **probable.**—*ANT.* unlikely, indisposed.

line·back·er (līn′bak′ẽr), ***n.*** in *football*, any of the players stationed directly behind the line in a defensive formation.

lis·some, lis·som (lis′əm), ***adj.*** [altered < *lithesome*], 1. supple; limber; flexible. 2. nimble; agile.

Loch·in·var (lok′in-vär′, lokh′in-vär′), ***n.*** the hero of a ballad in Scott's *Marmion*, who boldly rides off with his sweetheart just as she is about to be married to another.

lo·ci (lō′sī), ***n.*** plural of **locus.**

lock (lok), ***n.*** [ME. *lokke*; AS. *loc*, a bolt, bar, enclosure, prison; akin to G. *loch*, a hole, ON. *lok*, a lid; prob. IE. base **leug-*, to bend, seen also in AS. *lucan*, to close (cf. LEEK)], 1. a mechanical device furnished with a spring and bolt, for fastening a door, strongbox, etc. by means of a key or combination. 2. anything that fastens something else and prevents it from opening, turning, etc. 3. a locking together; jam. 4. an enclosed part of a canal, waterway, etc. equipped with gates so that the level of the water can be changed to raise or lower boats from one level to another. 5. the mechanism of a firearm used to explode the ammunition charge. 6. in *engineering*, an airtight room opening into a compartment where the air is under compression. 7. in *wrestling*, any of several holds: as, an arm *lock*. ***v.t.*** 1. to fasten (a door, trunk, etc.) by means of a lock. 2. to shut (*up, in*, or *out*); confine: as, he was *locked* in the closet. 3. to fit; link; intertwine: as, we *locked* arms. 4. to embrace tightly. 5. to jam together so as to make immovable: as, the gears are *locked*. 6. to equip (a canal, etc.) with a lock or locks. 7. to move or pass (a ship) through a lock. ***v.i.*** 1. to become locked. 2. to be capable of being locked. 3. to intertwine or interlock; link together. 4. to close tightly and firmly: as, his jaws *locked*. 5. to jam, as gears.

LOCK IN CANAL

lock away, to store or safeguard in a locked box, container, etc.
lock out, 1. to shut out by or as by locking the door against. 2. to keep (workers) from a place of employment in an attempt to make them accept the employer's terms.
lock, stock, and barrel, [Colloq.], completely.
lock up, 1. to fasten the doors of (a house, etc.) by means of locks. 2. to enclose or store in a locked container. 3. to put in jail.
under lock and key, locked up; safely put away.

lock (lok), ***n.*** [ME. *lokke*; AS. *loc* (akin to G. *locke*); basic sense "a bend, twist"; IE. base as in prec. *lock*], 1. a curl of hair; ringlet; hence, 2. ***pl.*** [Poetic], the hair of the head. 3. a tuft of wool, cotton, etc.

Long·fel·low, Henry Wads·worth (wädz′wẽrth lôŋ′fel′ō), 1807–1882; American poet.

long green, [Slang], paper money.

long·hair (lôŋ′hâr′), ***adj.*** [Colloq.], designating or of intellectuals or intellectual tastes; specifically, playing or preferring classical music rather than jazz or popular tunes. ***n.*** [Colloq.], an intellectual; specifically, a longhair musician.

look-see (look′sē′), ***n.*** [Slang], a quick look; brief inspection.

lynx (liŋks), ***n.*** [*pl.* LYNXES (-iz), LYNX; see PLURAL, II, D, 1], [ME.; L.; Gr. *lynx*], 1. any of a group of wildcats found throughout the northern hemisphere and characterized by a ruff on each side of the face, long legs, a short tail, long, tufted ears, and keen vision: the North American species are the *Canada lynx* and the *Bay lynx*, or *bobcat*. 2. the long, silky, tawny fur of the lynx, sometimes dyed black. 3. [L-], a northern constellation lying between Auriga and Ursa Major.

LYNX (3 ft. long)

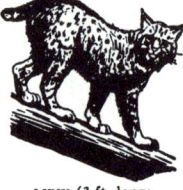

lynx-eyed (liŋks′īd′), ***adj.*** having very keen sight.

ANTONYMS

VARIANT SPELLINGS (see p. ix)*

VARIANT PRONUNCIATIONS (see pp. x, xi)*

IRREGULAR PLURAL

ETYMOLOGY, traced back to Indo-European base

FIELD LABELS, showing specialized senses

IDIOMATIC USAGE

IDIOMATIC PHRASES

BIOGRAPHICAL ENTRY

COMPOUND ENTRY

USAGE LABELS (see p. xiii)*

INFLECTED FORMS, plurals

ILLUSTRATION, size indicated

CAPITALIZATION indicated (sense 3)

HYPHENATED WORD

KEY TO PRONUNCIATION

fat, āpe, bâre, cär; ten, ēven, hêre, ovẽr; is, bīte; lot, gō, hôrn, tōōl, look; oil, out; up, ūse, fũr; get; joy; yet; chin; she; thin, *then*; zh, leisure; ŋ, ring; ə for *a* in *ago*, *e* in *agent*, *i* in *sanity*, *o* in *comply*, *u* in *focus*; ′ as in *able* (ā′b'l); Fr. bàl; ë, Fr. coeur; ö, Fr. feu; Fr. mon; ô, Fr. coq; ü, Fr. duc; H, G. ich; kh, G. doch. See pp. x–xii. ‡ foreign; * hypothetical; < derived from.

*refers to Introductory pages in Webster's New World Dictionary

This composite page is from WEBSTER'S NEW WORLD DICTIONARY of the American Language, College Edition, copyright 1958 by the World Publishing Company.

1 | Homonyms

If you write: "I'm a little **horse** today," don't be surprised if your reader wonders how you ever were graduated from elementary school or high school. Of course, *you* don't make this kind of error. You know the sentence should read: "I'm a little **hoarse** today."

In the first sentence, you are the only talking and writing **horse** (the four-legged animal) in captivity. In the second sentence, all you need is a gargle or some throat lozenges.

What makes the difference in these two sentences? Just a single letter—a: **horse** or **hoarse**.

Words like **horse** and **hoarse** are fairly common in our language. They are called *homonyms* —words that are *pronounced* alike but have different spellings and meanings. As a secretary you will generally write such words with the same shorthand outline, and will have to transcribe in terms of their context. That's why it's so important for you to learn what each of these homonyms means, how to tell homonyms apart, and how to use them correctly.

In this course are over 300 of the most commonly-used homonyms. We don't expect that you will cover all the words in this list at once. This isn't the best way to learn them. Rather, we have divided the big job—the 300 words—into a series of small easy jobs. Complete each of the small jobs—about 10 groups of words at a time—and before long you'll have the whole job done—successfully, permanently, painlessly.

ad—add

    ad—short form of *advertisement*

    add—to combine together to form a sum: *Add two and two.*

aid—aide

    aid—(verb) to help: *Will you aid the party of your choice?*; (noun) assistance: *Your aid is appreciated.*

    aide—an assistant: *The colonel's aide arrived on horseback.*

ail—ale

ail—to be ill: *What ails you?*

ale—a type of beer.

air—heir

air—the Earth's atmosphere.

heir—one who inherits: *The Duke's son is heir to his fortune.*

aisle—isle—I'll

aisle—a passageway between seats in a theater or other meeting room.

isle—an island.

I'll—contraction of *I will.*

aloud—allowed

aloud—spoken at an audible level: *He read his poems aloud.*

allowed—permitted: *Only invited guests are allowed to enter the theater this evening.*

altar—alter

altar—a raised structure used in religious ceremonies: *The bride approached the altar.*

alter—to vary; to modify: *The rise in unemployment did not alter our production plans.*

all—awl

all—entire, the whole of, without exception.

awl—a pointed instrument used to pierce holes in leather: *The shoemaker used an awl to add two lace holes to my boots.*

arc—ark

arc—part of a circle: *The plane flew in a wide arc around the mountain peak;* a high voltage electric spark: *The arc leaped from one electrode to the other.*

ark—Noah's boat.

ascent—assent

ascent—act of rising: *Elvis Presley's ascent to stardom was meteoric.*

assent—(noun) agreement; act of giving consent: *The City Council has given its assent to the new project.*

bail—bale

bail—security given to obtain release of a prisoner while awaiting trial: *To be out on bail;* To use a bucket or other vessel to remove water from a flooded area: *To bail out a leaking boat.*

bale—a large, closely-pressed package of merchandise: *A bale of cotton.*

ball—bawl

ball—a round, bouncy toy; a large, formal dance.

bawl—to cry loudly.

bare—bear

bare—naked: *a bare head;* empty: *a bare room;* unadorned: *the bare truth.*

bear—(verb) to carry or support: *to bear a load;* to give birth to: *to bear children;* (noun) a large animal: *a polar bear.*

base—bass

base—the bottom, the foundation; morally low: *He acted from base motives.*

bass—a deep sound or tone: *a bass cello.*

baron—barren

baron—a nobleman.

barren—incapable of producing offspring; bare of vegetation: *a barren desert;* unprofitable, empty: *a barren scheme.*

beat—beet

beat—(verb) to hit repeatedly: *to beat a drum;* to defeat: *to beat your opponents;* (noun) a repeated sound or motion: *the heart beat.*

beet—a vegetable.

Score_____

1 | Assignments

1. Do you know the meaning of the following limerick?
   (You couldn't possibly know it without using a dictionary!)

   > **A tiger by taste anthropophagous**
   > **Felt a yearning within his esophagus.**
   > **He spied a fat Brahmin**
   > **And said, "What's the harm in**
   > **A peripatetic sarcophagus?"**

   Look up each of the strange words in the Dictionary Section at the back of this book.
   Then write a brief definition in the space provided:

   anthropophagous: _flesh-eating; as a lion or tiger_

   esophagus: _A passageway for food to get to the stomach_

   Brahmin: _A haughty, cultured person from an upper-class family_

   peripatetic: _A person or object that moves from place to place._

   sarcophagus: _Something causing rapid disintegration of an object._

   Can you guess what became of the "fat Brahmin"? Can you see why he would be in
   a "peripatetic sarcophagus"?

2. On what level of usage (colloquial, slang, archaic, etc.) is each of the following
   words? Write your answer in the space at the right of each word.

   a. **bossy** _Colloquial_   d. **enthuse** _Colloquial_

   b. **bust** (to burst) _Slang_   e. **flabbergast** _Colloquial_

   √c. **zounds** _Slang (archaic)_   f. **ope** (to open) _Poetic_

3. Write in the spaces provided the language from which the following words are derived:

strength *Middle-English and Anglo-Saxon*   anthology *Latin and Greek*

4. Cross out the incorrectly spelled word in each of the following pairs:

develop ~~develope~~   ~~bankrupcy~~ bankruptcy   ~~stubborness~~ stubbornness

5. What is the meaning of the prefix **tele** as in **telegraph?** *Operating at a distance*
6. What or who was **Tantalus?** *a He was a king, the son of Zeus in Greek mythology.*
7. Rewrite these words in the spaces provided, dividing them into syllables and marking the accented syllables:

ignominy *ig'-no-min'-y*   acumen *a-cu'-men*

discourse *dis'-course*   deference *def'-er-ence* ✓
(the verb)

8. Circle the preferred spelling:

(theater) theatre   judgement (judgment)

9. Divide the following words into syllables:

distance *dis-tance*   dissolution *dis-so-lu-tion* ✓

disappoint *dis-ap-point*   disillusion *dis-il-lu-sion*

10. Who was **Moliere?** *a French writer of comedies*
11. What is the population of **Indiana?** *3,934,000.*
12. What does **carpe diem** mean? *make the most of today*
13. Should **SOS** have periods? *No*
14. How is the word **never** syllabicated? *nev-er*
15. For what does each of the following abbreviations stand?

anon. ✓ *anonymous*

C/A *Capital accountant, credit account, or current account*

FCIC *Federal Crop Insurance Corporation*

M. Ed *Master of Education*

Que. *Quebec*

Zn *Zinc*

Score_____

1 | Homonym

Assignments

A Select from the following words the one that correctly fits into the blank in each of the sentences below. Then write it in the space provided.

ail	all	aisle
ale	awl	isle
air	aide	I'll
heir	aid	

1. Brewery figures show that ___ale___ normally is outsold by beer. . . . . _ale_

2. With the coming of warm weather, sales of ___air___ conditioners begin to rise. . . . . _air_

3. Tourists love to travel to an ___isle___ in the South Pacific. _isle_

4. The Declaration of Independence states that ___all___ men are created equal. . . . . _all_

5. The eldest son was __heir__ to his father's fortune. . . . . . . _heir_

6. The doctor wondered what could ___ail___ the sick man. . . _ail_

7. The bride looked lovely as she came down the ___aisle___. _aisle_

8. A cobbler cannot work without an ___awl___. . . . . _awl_

9. ___I'll___ let you borrow it if I can spare it. . . . . _I'll_

10. Everyone rushed to ___aid___ the injured man. . . . . _aid_

13

B

In the following sentences underline the word in parentheses that makes the sentence correct. Then write it in the space provided.

1. In New York City no one under eighteen is (aloud—allowed) to drive an automobile. . . . . *allowed*
2. A good dressmaker can (alter—altar) this dress. . . . . *altar alter*
3. He indicated his (ascent—assent) by nodding. . . . . *assent*
4. The accused was released in $1,000 (bale—bail). . . . . *bail*
5. Place an (ad—add) in the Sunday paper. . . . . *ad*
6. After a period of silent study, the pupils read the story (aloud —allowed). . . . . *aloud*
7. The flowers were banked on the (alter—altar) for the wedding. . . . . *altar*
8. A rainbow is a colorful (arc—ark) in the sky. . . . . *arc*
9. Many (bails—bales) of hay are required to feed an elephant. . . *bales*
10. Hundreds of curious people watched the (assent—ascent) of the balloon. . . . . *ascent*

C

In some of the following sentences an incorrect word is used; cross it out and write the correct word in the space provided. Where there is no error, put a **C** in the space.

1. The polar bare is native to the Arctic region. . . . . *bear*
2. An oasis is a welcome sight in the otherwise baron desert. . . *barren*
3. It was surprising to hear a base voice coming from such a small boy. . . . . *bass*
4. I have just hired Johnson as my personal aid. . . . . *aide*
5. The children began to ball because they were scared. . . . . . *bawl*
6. After the Easter sale, the shelves were bear. . . . . *bare*
7. A baron has a seat in the House of Lords. . . . . *C*
8. The statue rested on a beautiful marble bass. . . . . *base*
9. We expect eight hundred guests at the annual ball. . . . . . . *C*
10. The beet of the jungle drums had an ominous sound. . . . . . *beat*

The Deadly Dozen

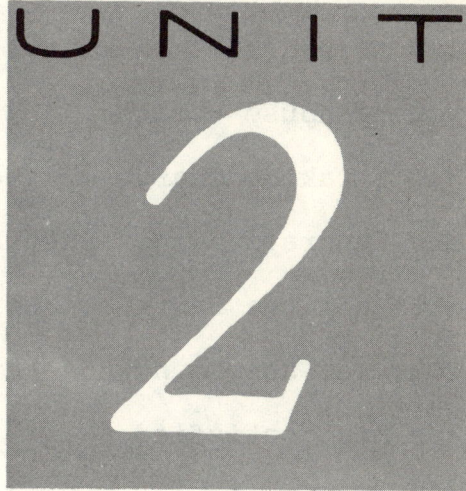

Here they are—twelve of the most troublesome words in our language, misspelled from kindergarten through college! Not everybody misspells them—but enough people do to give these words a reputation for being difficult.

it's	your	their	to	whose
its	you're	there	too	who's
		they're	two	

Are you surprised? These words look so simple. Each has only one syllable. They are often called "baby" words. But appearances are certainly deceiving. Many adults have trouble with this list.

Let's see what you can do with *The Deadly Dozen.* Try your hand at these five sentences. We have deliberately "loaded" them. Cross out the misspelled words in each sentence and then, in the space provided, write them spelled correctly. If there are no spelling errors in the sentence, mark it *C* for *Correct*.

1. ~~Its~~ ~~to~~ bad that ~~there~~ not coming to ~~you're~~ house tonight.   *It's, too, they're, your*

2. Who's taking charge of ~~they're~~ account?   *their*

3. ~~Its~~ imperative that they be ~~their~~ with all the facts at their disposal.   *It's there*   *C*

4. ~~Your~~ the salesman whose customers are most satisfied.   *you're*   *C*

5. ~~They're~~ accountants sat for days trying to discover ~~who's~~ error was responsible for the confusion.   *Their*   *whose*

Just a moment ago we said these twelve words are really "baby" words even though they tend to confuse many adults who should know better. Here's a simple way to approach them and make them yours once and for all:

It's = it is. It's is really *two words in one*—what we call a *contraction*.
Its indicates possession: **The bird hurt its wing.** (The wing belongs to the bird.)

If you have the slightest doubt about whether to use **it's** or **its**, try this foolproof device. Write out the sentence completely: **The bird hurt (it's, its) wing. It's = it is.** You would never say: The bird hurt **it is** wing. This doesn't make sense. So **it's** (the contraction) is not what you want. **Its** (possessive) is the correct word.

If you're sure about when to use **it's** — you're automatically sure of **its.** Learn one word and you have *two!*

What is true for **it's** and **its** holds true for **you're** and **your.**

You're = **you are** (two words in one — a *contraction*).
Your indicates *possession.* **Is this your house?** (Does the house belong to you?)

Again, test yourself by writing out the contraction within the sentence. Is this **you're** house? means: Is this **you are** house? Silly isn't it? The correct word has to be **your. Is this your house?**

They're = **they are** (a contraction). **They're not coming** = **They are not coming.**
There indicates *place* (over there). **Put it there.**
Their indicates *possession* (their books, their pencils, their house).

Who's = **who is; who has**
Whose indicates *possession:* **Whose friend are you?**
Follow the same rule. **Who's** your friend? means: **Who is your friend?**
Whose would be wrong here, wouldn't it?

Two means the *number* (2).
Too means *also, more than enough, beyond what is right or desirable.* (Think of the *double-o* as adding *more*—which is the general meaning of *too.*)
To is used for all cases not covered by **two** or **too.**
Study these sentences. All of them are correct.

```
There are two more days before we take inventory.

The workers found the factory too hot.

I'm coming too.

Go to the bank.
```

Spelling Aid: Note the similar spelling of the following words: **here, there, where.** All three of these words refer to *place.*

Homonyms

beer—bier

beer—a mildly alcoholic drink made from malt and hops.
The man enjoyed drinking a glass of beer after a hard day's work.

bier—a coffin
The bearers carried the bier to the cemetery.

berth—birth

berth—job or position: *He earned a berth on our team;* place to sleep on a ship or train: *a lower berth.*

birth—being born: *to give birth.*

berry—bury

berry—small juicy fruit with many seeds: *blackberry, raspberry,* etc.

bury—place a body or an object into the earth or a tomb.

blew—blue

blew—past tense of the verb *blow: The wind blew all night.*

blue—the color: *Jane has blue eyes.*

bloc—block

bloc—group of persons united for a common purpose:
In France, the Socialist bloc opposed the government measure.

block—(noun) a rectangular solid: *a block of wood;* a city square: *a city block;* (verb) to obstruct or blockade: *to block progress;* to shape out: *to block a hat.*

board—bored

board—piece of wood: *a board of oak;* meals provided for pay: *room and board;* group of persons managing a firm: *board of directors;* on a ship or train: *on board.*

bored—uninterested, wearied by something dull or tiresome:
The audience was bored with the new picture.

boarder—border

boarder—person who gets his room and meals regularly for pay.

border—dividing line between two countries: *the Canadian border;* an edge: *the border of a picture.*

bolder—boulder

bolder—more courageous: *The bolder of the two boys saved the day.*

boulder—a large rock.

born—borne

born—brought into life: *A child is born;* able by nature: *a born singer, a born athlete.*

borne—carried: *The ship was borne along by the breeze;* given birth to: *She had borne three children.*

bough—bow

bough—branch of a tree or shrub: *a hanging bough.*

bow—(rhymes with *how*) the front part of a ship; a bending from the waist to show respect.

brake—break

brake—(noun) device for slowing a machine or vehicle: *a car's brake;* (verb) to slow down: *The new government policy will brake the inflationary trend.*

break—(verb) to separate into parts by force: *break a bone;* (noun) an opening: *a break in the skin.*

breach—breech

breach—failure to observe the terms of a law or agreement: *breach of contract;* an opening made by breaking something: *a breach in a wall.*

breech—the part of a firearm behind the barrel: *He held the rifle by the breech.*

bred—bread

bred—(past tense of the verb *breed*) was the source of, produced: *In his case, familiarity bred contempt. The ranchman bred longhorn cattle.*

bread—food made from flour or meal: *rye bread, white bread,* etc.

bridal—bridle

bridal—pertaining to a bride or wedding: *bridal veil, bridal party.*

bridle—the head part of a horse's harness: *Attach the reins to the horse's bridle;* to hold back, curb: *He tried to bridle his temper;* to hold the head high to express scorn, anger, pride: *The attorney bridled in anger at the judge's remarks.*

but—butt

but—except, otherwise, yet, only, just, etc.

butt—(noun) the thick end of anything: *the butt of a gun;* the stub or stump: *a cigarette butt;* an object of ridicule or criticism: *the butt of a joke;* (verb) to thrust or strike against: *to butt with the head.*

buy—by—bye

buy—to purchase.

by—near at hand: *by the stream;* through the medium of: *made by hand,* etc.

bye—as in *good-bye.*

2 | Assignments

A In each of the blanks in the following sentences, insert the proper word from the following list. (Note: In some instances, more than one word may be correct.)

it's	your	their	to	whose
its	you're	there	too	who's
		they're	two	

1. _____It's_____ entirely up to you to decide _____whose_____ products you will buy.

2. _____There_____ are _____too_____ many organizations competing for the consumer dollar.

3. Do _____your_____ members understand _____their_____ responsibility for helping the community?

4. Labor representatives will meet tomorrow to present _____their_____ problems to management representatives.

5. _____It's_____ about time you learned to check _____your_____ own records.

6. Are you the man _____whose_____ place I'm taking?

7. You. _____Two_____ men will have to stay a bit later tonight.

8. _____Who's_____ covering the assignment for the girl who is ill?

√9. Our government must choose _____their_____ diplomatic agents with great care.

10. Are _____there_____ any of the fall models on exhibit at the appliance show?

In the following sentences underline the word in parentheses that makes the sentence correct.

1. (Its—<u>It's</u>) about time you sent us (<u>your</u>—you're) order for next spring.

2. When we call, we find (their—there—<u>they're</u>) always busy.

3. (<u>Who's</u>—Whose) going to take his place in (<u>your</u>—you're) organization?

4. (Your—<u>You're</u>) reports to the buyers do not meet with (<u>their</u>—there—they're) approval.

5. After studying (<u>their</u>—there—they're) financial reports, we feel that (your—<u>you're</u>) quite right in questioning the way they have managed (<u>their</u>—there—they're) affairs over (their—<u>there</u>—they're).

6. You'll find all (<u>your</u>—you're) tax forms over (their—<u>there</u>—they're).

7. (Your—<u>You're</u>) the kind of person who should be doing personnel work.

8. The managers' group will inform you when (<u>your</u>—you're) application is brought (<u>to</u>—too—two) (<u>their</u>—there—they're) attention.

9. (<u>Who's</u>—Whose) been calling you lately?

10. (<u>It's</u>-Its) much (to-<u>too</u>-two) late for the members of (<u>your</u>-you're) staff to correct (<u>their</u>-there-they're) errors now.

Score_____

2 | Homonym

Assignments

A Select from the following words the one that correctly fits into the blank in each of the sentences below. Then write it in the space provided.

beer	bury	berth	blue	board
bier	berry	birth	blew	bored

1. Most people prefer a lower to an upper _berth_ on a train.   _berth_
2. The _bier_ of the dead hero was draped with a flag. ..   _bier_
3. It was a moving moment when the bugler _blew_ taps.   _blew_
4. A landslide can _bury_ a village or turn the course of a river. . . . .   _bury_
5. A nurse's pay often includes room and _board_. . . . .   _board_
6. The colors of our flag are red, white, and _blue_. . . . . . .   _blue_
7. The people rejoiced at the _birth_ of the new prince. ..   _birth_
8. Americans prefer to drink _beer_ ice cold. . . . .   _beer_
9. The audience became _bored_ and restless as the speaker droned on and on. . . . .   _bored_
10. Her lips were as red as a _berry_. . . . .   _berry_

B In the following sentences underline the word in parentheses that makes the sentence correct. Then write it in the space provided.

1. A faulty (break—brake) in his car was the cause of the accident. .... *brake*

2. A tourist must show his passport at the (boarder—border). .... *border*

3. A (bolder—boulder), more aggressive policy will increase business. .... *bolder*

4. The cost of the repairs was (born—borne) by the insurance company. .... *borne*

5. (Bred—Bread) is the staff of life. .... *Bread*

6. The pre-Easter sale was expected to (break—brake) all previous records. .... *break*

7. Poor service made the (border—boarder) seek new lodgings. *boarder*

8. Abraham Lincoln was (borne—born) in a log cabin. .... *born*

9. Most mink coats are made from animals (bread—bred) on ranches. .... *bred*

10. Watch out for a falling (boulder—bolder) when you drive in mountainous country. .... *boulder*

C In some of the following sentences an incorrect word is used; cross it out and write the correct word in the space provided. Where there is no error write **C** in the space.

1. George was the but of all their jokes. .... *butt*

2. The bridle party arrived at the church on time. .... *bridal*

3. Attractive displays will tempt people to by more merchandise. *buy*

4. A lover of horses carefully selects the proper saddle and bridle. .... *C*

5. A smoldering cigarette but was the cause of the fire. ...... *butt*

6. A snowstorm can completely bury a car. .... *C*

7. The parents were overjoyed at the berth of their first son. ... *birth*

8. Faulty breaks have caused many automobile accidents. .... *brakes*

9. The carpenter placed the bored across the table. .... *board*

10. He was found guilty of breech of contract. .... *breach*

Say
What You See

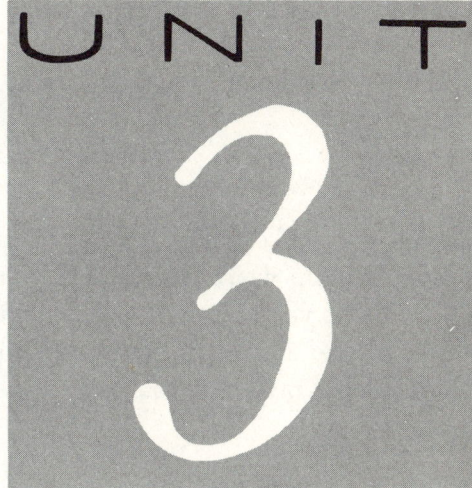

UNIT
3

In the following sentences you'll find a number of misspelled words. (You will be told how many after you have gone through these sentences.) Cross out each misspelled word and, above it, write the word correctly spelled.

1. The ~~Secertary~~ *Secretary* of State stood under a ~~tremenjous~~ *tremendous* ~~umberella~~ *umbrella*.

2. It will ~~probaly~~ *probably* come as no ~~suprise~~ *surprise* to you to learn that our ~~libary~~ *library* will open promptly.

3. The president of the college ~~attackted~~ *attacked* ~~athaletics~~ *athletics* as a ~~barbarious~~ *barbarous* form of activity.

4. No ~~modren~~ *modern* ~~goverment~~ *government* would tolerate religious ~~predujice~~ *prejudice*.

5. For a man of his ~~temperment~~ *temperament*, the Florida ~~temperture~~ *temperature* was too high in ~~Febuary~~ *February*.

In these five sentences, there are fifteen misspelled words. Did you get them all? Here's the correct spelling of each one.

1. Secretary   tremendous   umbrella

2. probably   surprise   library

3. attacked   athletics   ~~barbarous~~

4. modern   government   prejudice

5. ~~temperament~~   temperature   February

These words—and many like them—are misspelled mainly because they are mispronounced. The correct pronunciation won't *always* lead you to the correct spelling of a word. A great many English words, as you very well know by now, are not spelled as they sound. But some words, like those above, are usually misspelled only by people who do not pronounce them correctly. These people make the following types of pronunciation errors:

> Drop syllables or letters
> Add syllables or letters
> Switch syllables or letters
> Mispronounce syllables or letters

Here's a list of words people commonly misspell because they are careless. They just don't say what they see. The trouble spot in each word is underscored.

DON'T BE AN "ADDER"

att<u>a</u>cked	(2 syllables, *not* 3)	hind<u>r</u>ance*	(2 syllables, *not* 3)
<u>ath</u>letics	(3 syllables, *not* 4)	ligh<u>tn</u>ing	(2 syllables, *not* 3)
barb<u>arous</u>*	(3 syllables, *not* 4)	mischie<u>vous</u>*	(3 syllables, *not* 4)
chi<u>mn</u>ey	(2 syllables, *not* 3)	remem<u>br</u>ance	(3 syllables, *not* 4)
disast<u>r</u>ous	(3 syllables, *not* 4)	um<u>br</u>ella	(3 syllables, *not* 4)
heig<u>ht</u>	(no **th** at the end)		

DON'T BE A "DROPPER"

Ar<u>c</u>tic	(Pronounce the **c**)	pro<u>bab</u>ly	(3 syllables, *not* 2)
cam<u>e</u>ra	(3 syllables, *not* 2)	prom<u>pt</u>ly	(Pronounce the **pt**)
can<u>di</u>date	(Pronounce *both* **d**'s)	reco<u>g</u>nize	(Pronounce the **g**)
di<u>a</u>mond	(3 syllables, *not* 2)	san<u>d</u>wich	(Pronounce the **d**)
Feb<u>r</u>uary	(Pronounce the **r** after **b**)	sec<u>re</u>tary	(Pronounce the **r**)
gover<u>n</u>ment	(Pronounce the **n**)	stric<u>t</u>ly	(Pronounce the **t**)
hundre<u>d</u>th	(Pronounce the **d**)	su<u>r</u>prise	(Pronounce the **r** after **u**)
lib<u>r</u>ary	(Pronounce the **r** after **b**)	temper<u>a</u>ment*	(4 syllables, *not* 3)
pos<u>t</u>pone	(Pronounce the **t**)	temper<u>a</u>ture	(4 syllables, *not* 3)

DON'T BE A "SWITCHER"

envi<u>ron</u>ment*	<u>per</u>spiration
int<u>ro</u>duce	<u>per</u>spire
mod<u>er</u>n	pre<u>j</u>udice*
patt<u>er</u>n (**er** as in **baker**)	tra<u>g</u>edy
<u>per</u>form	

SAY WHAT YOU SEE

accum<u>u</u>late	pron<u>un</u>ciation
champ<u>ion</u>	pro<u>t</u>ection
d<u>i</u>vide (**i** as in **pit**)	sepa<u>r</u>ate
d<u>i</u>vine (**i** as in **pit**)	simil<u>ar</u>
pam<u>ph</u>let (**ph** = **f**)	tre<u>mend</u>ous

MEMORY AIDS These sentences will help you remember the correct spelling:

1. A good <u>secret</u>ary keeps her employer's <u>secret</u>s.

2. The job of a <u>govern</u>ment is to <u>govern</u>.

3. Scientists <u>labor</u> in the <u>labor</u>atory.

4. In colloquial speech, some people say "<u>congrat</u>s" when they mean <u>congrat</u>ulations.

5. At some beach picnics, the careless picnickers find <u>sand</u> in their <u>sand</u>wiches.

6. There is <u>a rat</u> in sep<u>arat</u>e.

3 | Homonyms

Know the difference between the two.

canon—cannon

canon—a law or body of laws of a church: *the Anglican canon.*

çannon—a large weapon of war.

canvas—canvass

canvas—strong cloth widely used to make tents and sails.

canvass—to go through a district or area soliciting votes for a candidate or orders for a product: *McFadden's supporters thoroughly canvassed the Eighth District to obtain every possible vote for him.*

capital—capitol

capital—city where the government of a country or state is located: *Washington, D.C., is the capital of the United States;* money or property a company uses in carrying on business: *Four thousand dollars of capital was invested in the firm;* an upper-case letter: *capital A.*

capitol—building in which a state or national legislature meets. When we refer to the building where our American Congress meets, we use a capital C: *The Capitol has a domed central roof.*

carrot—caret—carat

carrot—a vegetable.

caret—a proofreading mark (∧) to show where something has been left out.

carat—unit of weight for precious stones: *John gave his fiancée a two-carat diamond.*

cast—caste

cast—(verb) to throw or fling with a quick motion: *to cast a fishing line;* (noun) the players in a theatrical company; that which is formed in a mold: *a plaster cast.*

caste—exclusive social system having class distinctions based on rank, wealth, position: *Many Hindus would like to see the caste system abolished in India.*

ceiling—sealing

ceiling—the top of a room.

sealing—fastening or closing tightly: *Plaster is used for sealing cracks.*

cell—sell

cell—a small, bare room: *a prison cell;* unit of living matter: *a blood cell;* a small electric battery: *a dry cell;* a small subversive group: *a Communist cell.*

sell—to exchange for money or other payment: *to sell a house.*

cellar—seller

cellar—underground room: *a wine cellar.*

seller—one who sells.

cent—scent—sent

cent—a copper coin (penny).

scent—an odor: *the scent of violets.*

sent—past tense of *send: Johnson sent flowers to his wife.*

cereal—serial

cereal—grain used as food: *Oatmeal is a cereal.*

serial—story published or broadcast one part at a time at regular intervals: *a radio serial.*

chased—chaste

chased—ran after or caused to run away: *The hounds chased the hare.*

chaste—virtuous, modest: *a chaste woman.*

cheap—cheep

cheap—not expensive; not worth much: *cheap clothes.*

cheep—(verb) to make a sound like a young bird; (noun) the short, shrill sound of a young bird.

choir—quire

choir—a group of singers, most commonly in a church: *a boy's choir, the Norman Luboff Choir.*

quire—a set of 24 or 25 sheets of paper of the same size and stock: *Mary took a quire of Lindcroft stationery with her.*

chord—cord

chord—combination of musical notes in harmony: *A-major chord;* an emotional response: *to strike a sympathetic chord.*

cord—thick string; a measure of wood cut for fuel: *(128 cubic feet equals one cord of wood);* a small insulated electric wire fitted with a plug.

chute—shoot

chute—an inclined passage to slide things down: *a coal chute, a laundry chute.*

shoot—to let fly: *shoot an arrow, bullet,* etc.; to photograph: *shoot a picture;* (noun) a young outgrowth from a shrub or tree: *bamboo shoot.*

3 | Assignments

A There are misspelled words in some of the following sentences. Cross out each misspelled word and write the correct spelling in the space provided. If there are no misspelled words, write **C** in the space next to the sentence.

1. The enemy ~~attackted~~ under cover of darkness. . . . .   *attacked*
2. Boys generally enjoy ~~athaletics~~ more than girls. do. . . . .   *athletics*
3. During a war, armies are often guilty of many barbarous practices. . . . .   *C*
4. During the storm, the wind blew the chimney down. . . . . . .   *C*
5. The Great Depression had a disastrous effect on our country. . . .   *C*
6. The average height of men is about 5 feet 8 inches. . . . . . .   *C*
7. You are more of a ~~hinderance~~ than a help. . . . .   *hindrance*
8. ~~Lightening,~~ it is said, does not strike twice in the same place. . . .   *lightning*
9. Most healthy children are inclined to be ~~mischievious.~~ . . . . .   *mischievous*
10. The sale of ~~umberellas~~ has fallen off sharply. . . . .   *umbrellas*
11. The ~~Artic~~ still lures the adventurous soul. . . . .   *arctic*
12. Smith is a ~~canidate~~ for the governorship. . . . .   *candidate*
13. Anyone can operate the new cameras. . . . .   *C*
14. Do you know that the ~~dimond~~ is pure carbon? . . . .   *diamond*
15. Why do so many people misspell ~~Febuary?~~ . . . .   *February*
16. The ~~goverment~~ will issue new tax regulations next week.   *government*
17. We ~~reconize~~ the necessity for keeping all our records up to date. . . . .   *recognize*
18. All rules must be strictly observed. . . . .   *C*

19. Today's ~~tempeture~~ is 80°. . . . . *temperature*

20. The library will be open all day. . . . . *C*

21. There is an opening for an executive ~~secertary~~ in our organization. . . . . *secretary*

22. Please accept our congratulations on the fine new store you have opened. . . . . *C*

23. By this time, you have ~~probaly~~ had a chance to go over the figures. . . . . *probably*

24. We were ~~suprised~~ to learn that you had moved to Chicago. . . . *surprised*

25. Under seperate cover, we are sending the pamphlets that you ordered. . . . . *C*

B Cross out the misspelled word or words in each of the following groups of words and spell them correctly in the space at the right. If there are no errors, mark **C** in the space.

1. hundredth   postpone   surprise   diamond   *C*

2. probably   secretary   ~~temprament~~   postpone   *temperament*

3. ~~enviorment~~   introduce   perform   recognize   *environment*

4. pattern   hundred   ~~modren~~   separate   *modern*

5. perspire   prejudice   ~~tradegy~~   surprise   *tragedy*

6. ~~accumalate~~   February   divide   environment   *accumulate*

7. pamphlet   protection   similar   pattern   *C*

8. champion   ~~mischievious~~ divine   introduce   *mischievous*

9. ~~pronounciation~~ sandwich   tremendous   temperature   *pronunciation*

10. divide   barbarous   ~~probaly~~   perspire   *probably*

3 | Homonym
Assignments

A Select from the following words the one that correctly fits into the blank in each of the sentences below. Then write it in the space provided.

carrot	canvas	capital	cast	cellar
caret	canvass	capitol	caste	seller
carat				

1. The salesman sold the young man a modest diamond weighing less than one _____. .... _carat_

2. Lawn furniture made of _____ iron is fashionable and attractive. .... _cast_

3. Wine is at its best when it is aged and stored in a _____. _cellar_

4. The manufacturer decided to _____ the market before launching his new product. .... _canvass_

5. The state _____ has a gleaming white dome. .... _capital_

6. It is every novelist's ambition to write a best _____. ... _seller_

7. Insert a _____ to show omission of a word or letter. ... _caret_

8. Tennis shoes are made of _____. .... _canvas_

9. Most Americans consider the _____ system to be a social evil. .... _caste_

10. The underdeveloped nations of the world are trying to attract foreign _____. .... _capital_

B   In the following sentences underline the word in parentheses that makes the sentence correct; then write it in the space provided.

1. Some years ago, (sealing—ceiling) wax was used to fasten envelopes. . . . . _____

2. It is not easy to (cell—sell) luxury merchandise in times of depression. . . . . _____

3. When you buy anything, remember that (cheap—cheep) merchandise generally does not last long. . . . . _____

4. The recordings of the Trinity Church (Quire—Choir) are considered collectors' items. . . . . _____

5. The detectives traced the stolen car through its (cereal—serial) number. . . . . _____

6. The (scent—cent) of orange blossoms floated through the open window. . . . . _____

7. The mimeographing job will take about ten (choirs—quires) of paper. . . . . _____

8. She was a woman whose thoughts were (chased—chaste) and simple. . . . . _____

9. This has been a good year for our new breakfast (serial—cereal). . . . . _____

10. Have you (scent—sent—cent) in your spring orders? . . . . _____

C   In some of the following sentences an incorrect word is used. Cross it out and write the correct word in the space provided. Where there is no error write **C** in the space.

1. Thousands of customers were attracted to the store's one-~~sent~~ sale. . . . . _cent_

2. Reversing the traditional order of things, the cat ~~chaste~~ the dog down the street. . . . . _chased_

3. The ~~quire~~ practiced over a month for the Christmas Concert. ___choir___

4. The ~~Capital~~ in Washington, D. C., is a must for all sightseers. . . . . _Capitol_

5. He placed a ~~carat~~ in the sentence where he wanted the word *and* added. . . . . _caret_

Doubling
the Final Consonant

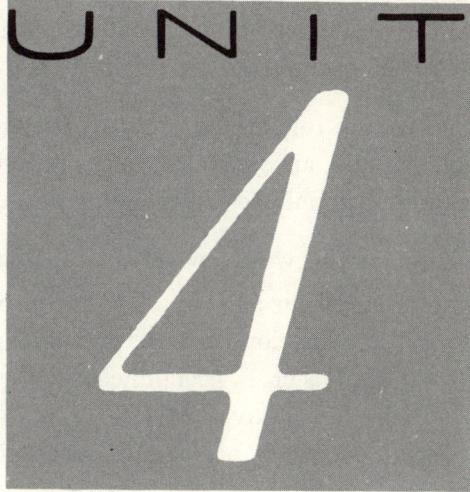

UNIT 4

Which is it?

occu<u>rr</u>ed ✓	trave<u>ll</u>ed	kidna<u>pp</u>ed ✓
occu<u>r</u>ed	trave<u>l</u>ed ✓	kidna<u>p</u>ed

Do you get unsettled, rattled, or confused when you have to choose? You do? If it's any comfort to you, you have plenty of company. But it's the kind of company you don't have to keep. You can easily learn to recognize the correct spelling:

occu<u>rr</u>ed   trave<u>l</u>ed   kidna<u>p</u>ed

Fortunately, there is a rule that will help you with hundreds of words like the ones you've just met. As we pointed out in the preface, we shall cover only those rules that are extremely useful. The rule for doubling the final consonant is such a rule. In fact, it is one of the most useful spelling rules we have. With it you can solve hundreds of spelling problems that you will face every day. More important, it is one of those rare and beautiful rules with few exceptions.

35

Here is the rule. Take it slowly, and you will master it quickly.

> When adding a suffix (word-ending) that begins with a *vowel,* double the final consonant if:
>
> **A.** The word ends in a *single* consonant (except **x**), and
>
> **B.** This consonant is preceded by a *single* vowel, and
>
> **C.** The word is pronounced with the accent on the *last* syllable.

Do *not* double the final consonant unless all three conditions (A, B, and C) are met. This rule may seem complicated—but it's really easy if you take it step by step. Be sure you understand each step before you go on to the next.

Note at once that the rule applies only when you are adding a word-ending that begins with a *vowel,* such as: **able, ance, ary, ed, ence, er, est, ish, ing, ion, ize, ism, ory.** So keep in mind that this rules applies only to word-endings that begin with *vowels* (**a, e, i, o, u**).

Let's work through the word **occur** as an example.

A. **Occur** ends in a single consonant (**r**), and

B. This consonant is preceded by a single vowel (**u**), and

C. **Occur** is pronounced with the accent on the last syllable (you say, **oc-CUR**).

Therefore: **occur, occurred, occurrence, occurring.**

Let's use the word **bid** as a second example.

A. **Bid** ends in a single consonant (**d**), and

B. This consonant (**d**) is preceded by a single vowel (**i**), and

C. **Bid** is accented. (Since **bid** has only one syllable, it must be accented. When using this rule with one-syllable words, you can ignore the accent requirement. *All* one-syllable words meet this requirement automatically.)

Therefore: **bid, bidder, bidding**

Now you work through the next example. Take the word **regret.**

A. Does it end in a single consonant? Yes, **t.**

B. Is this consonant preceded by a single vowel? Yes, **e.**

C. Do we pronounce **regret** with the accent on the final syllable? Yes, we say **re-GRET.**

Since all three conditions are met, we double the final consonant when we add a word-ending beginning with a vowel.

Therefore: **regret, regrettable, regretted, regretting.**

Simple, isn't it? And it works!

Try another one. Take the word **stir.**

        A. Does **stir** end in a single consonant? Yes, **r.**

        B. Is this consonant preceded by a single vowel? Yes, **i.**

        C. Is **stir** accented? Yes, it is *automatically* accented since it consists of only one syllable.

Therefore: **stir, stirred, stirring.**

As a final problem, try the word **benefit.**

        A. Does **benefit** end in a single consonant? Yes, **t.**

        B. Is this consonant preceded by a single vowel? Yes, **i.**

        C. Is **benefit** pronounced with the accent on the last syllable? NO! We say, **BEN**-e-fit. Therefore, *since all three* conditions have not been satisfied, we do NOT double the final consonant.

        benefit, benefited, benefiting.

Remember, **benefited** is *not* an exception to our rule. It *follows* the rule which tells us not to double the final consonant if a word does not satisfy all three conditions: A, B, and C. When **qu** precedes a vowel, as in the word **acquit,** the **u** is not considered a vowel because it has the sound of **w.** Since **acquit** ends in a single consonant (**t**), is preceded by a single vowel (**i**), and is pronounced with the accent on the last syllable, the rule for doubling the final consonant applies.

Therefore: **acquit, acquitted, acquittal.**

Now, analyze each of the following words to see why the final consonant is doubled. Take each word slowly. Write it out on a separate sheet of paper. And as you do so, note how the rule applies at each step.

admit	admitted	admitting	admittance
allot	allotted	allotting	allotment
begin	beginner	beginning	
blot	blotted	blotter	blotting
can	canner	canning	canned

commit	committed	committing	commitment
compel	compelled	compelling	
control	controlled	controlling	controller
cut	cutter	cutting	
deter*	deterred	deterring	deterrent
dispel*	dispelled	dispelling	
drug	drugged	drugging	druggist
equip	equipped	equipping	equipment
excel	excelled	excelling	excellent †
forget	forgettable	forgetting	forgetful
hot	hotter	hottest	
occur	occurred	occurring	occurrence
omit	omitted	omitting	
plan	planned	planning	
propel*	propelled	propelling	propeller
regret	regretted	regretting	regrettable
remit*	remittance	remitting	
rob	robbed	robbing	robber
stab	stabbed	stabbing	
stop	stopped	stopping	stoppage
submit	submitted	submitting	
war	warred	warring	

† *Exception to rule*

Analyze each of the following words to see why the final consonant is *not* doubled. Again, these words are not exceptions to our rule. They just don't satisfy all three conditions (A, B, and C). Why not?

act	acted	acting	actor
appeal	appealed	appealing	
band	banded	banding	bandage
benefit	benefited	benefiting	
board	boarded	boarding	boarder
boom	boomed	booming	
calm	calmed	calmness	calmly
cheer	cheered	cheerfulness	cheery
climb	climbed	climbing	climber
concoct*	concocted	concocting	concoction
condemn	condemned	condemning	condemnation
correspond	corresponded	corresponding	correspondence
curb	curbed	curbing	curbstone
debt	debtor	indebted	
defend	defended	defending	defendant
despair	despaired	despairing	
differ	differed	differing	difference
disappear	disappeared	disappearing	disappearance
fear	feared	fearing	fearless
gain	gained	gaining	gainful

4

grant	granted	granting	grantor
green	greener	greenest	
greet	greeter	greeting	
guard	guarded	guarding	guardian
instill*	instilled	instilling	
kind	kindest	kindness	kindly
parallel*	paralleled	paralleling	parallelogram
pertain*	pertained	pertaining	
point	pointed	pointing	pointer
post	posted	posting	postage
print	printed	printing	printer
prompt	promptly	prompting	promptness
revolt	revolted	revolting	
short	shortly	shortness	shortsighted
strain	strained	straining	strainer
strict	strictly	strictness	strictest
suit	suited	suiting	suitor
sweet	sweeter	sweetly	sweetness
talk	talked	talking	talkative
tax	taxed	taxing	taxable
travel	traveled	traveling	traveler
visit	visited	visiting	visitor

wish	wished	wishing	
worship	worshiped	worshiping	worshiper
wreck	wrecked	wrecking	wreckage

Now look at these words:

confer	conferred	conferring	conference
defer*	deferred	deferring	deference
infer*	inferred	inferring	inference
prefer	preferred	preferring	preference
refer	referred	referring	reference

At first glance **conference, deference, inference, preference,** and **reference** would seem to be exceptions—but they are not! Pronounce **reference** aloud. Where is the accent? That's right, it has shifted to the first syllable. You say:

CON-fer-ence

DEF-er-ence

IN-fer-ence

PREF-er-ence

REF-er-ence

Since the accent is no longer on the last syllable, our rule tells us *not* to double the final consonant. Thus, **conference, deference, inference, preference, reference** are not exceptions to our rule.

SPECIAL NOTE

Overstep is really two words joined together—**over** + **step.** We concentrate on the word **step** and follow the rule for one-syllable words.

The following words are governed by the same principle:

eavesdrop	eavesdropped	eavesdropping	eavesdropper
handicap	handicapped	handicapping	handicapper
horsewhip	horsewhipped	horsewhipping	
outfit	outfitted	outfitting	outfitter
undersign	undersigned	undersigning	
understand	understanding	understandable	understandably
countersign*	countersigned	countersigning	countersignature

EXCEPTIONS

We promised that there are few exceptions to the doubling principle—and here are the important ones. Do you see why these are considered exceptions?

cancel′lation	excel′lent	transfer′able
crys′tallize	gas′eous	transfer′ence

4 | Homonyms

cite—sight—site

cite—to quote as an authority: *Economists cite statistics to prove their theories;* mention as an example: *Let me cite Johnson's experience as a guide.*

sight—one of the five senses; something seen.

site—the seat or scene of any specific thing; the location of a building, the land where a building stands or is to stand: *The school board purchased a site for the new high school.*

coarse—course

coarse—rough, crude, not fine: *coarse language, a coarse towel.*

course—a way, path, or channel taken: *course of action; golf course;* direction taken: *The ship's course was due north;* regular mode of action or development; meal: *a dessert course;* a series of studies in school: *academic course, engineering course.*

colonel—kernel

colonel—(KER-nel) a high army officer.

kernel—a grain or seed: *a corn kernel.*

Know definitions of these two.

complement—compliment

complement—that which completes or brings to perfection: *This green scarf will complement your dress perfectly;* the amount needed to complete or fill: *With the arrival of this new shipment, we have filled our complement of fall-wear.*

compliment—(noun) praise, commendation: *to receive compliments on a job well done;* (verb) to praise, to commend: *We complimented Jones on the way he keeps his books.*

core—corps

core—the central or most important part: *The fate of the refugees was the core of the discussion. The core of an apple contains the seeds.*

corps—a body of people associated under common direction; a branch of the armed forces having some specialized function: *Medical Corps, Signal Corps, Marine Corps.*

creak—creek

creak—to move with a harsh, squeaky, grating noise: *a creaking door.*

creek—a small stream, somewhat larger than a brook.

currant—current

currant—a berry.

current—now in progress: *Read the current issue of the Times;* a body of water flowing in a definite direction: *The Gulf Stream is a warm current;* the flow of electric force: *direct or alternating current.*

dear—deer

dear—beloved: *Children are dear to their parents;* costly, expensive: *These days even everyday staples seem too dear for some people;* a polite form of address: *Dear Sir.*

deer—an animal.

desert—dessert

desert—(de ZERT) to abandon, run away from: *to desert a sinking ship.*

dessert—(di-ZERT) a sweet course served at the end of a meal.

die—dye

die—to stop living; a tool or device for stamping, cutting, molding, or shaping: *A rectangular die is used to stamp out license plates;* singular of *dice.*

dye—(verb) to change the color of anything by saturating it with a coloring substance: *to dye your hair;* (noun) any substance used to color fabric, hair, etc.: *a color-fast dye.*

discreet—discrete

discreet—showing good judgment: *The attorney was always discreet in handling delicate matters.*

discrete—separate and distinct: *Separate the files into eight discrete units.*

dual—duel

dual—having or composed of two parts: *Cars for learners have dual controls.*

duel—a contest fought between two persons: *Alexander Hamilton fought a duel with Aaron Burr.*

faint—feint

faint—(adjective) not clear: *a faint light, a faint image;* feeble, without strength: *faint of heart; faint with hunger;* (verb) to lose consciousness temporarily: *Did she faint from the shock?*

feint—a movement intended to deceive, a pretended blow: *The boxer's feint drew down his opponent's guard.*

fair—fare

fair—impartial: *a fair trial;* reasonable: *a fair price;* light, clear, beautiful: *fair weather;* a festival at which goods are sold: *a country fair.*

fare—sum of money paid for travel: *plane fare;* anything that sustains or nourishes: *bill of fare, good fare.*

fate—fete

fate—destiny: *It was his fate to lose the election.*

fete—a festival, especially one held out-of-doors: *The Mardi Gras is an annual fete held before Lent in New Orleans;* (verb) to celebrate an honor with festivities: *The Colonel was feted by his friends.*

feet—feat

feet—plural of *foot.*

feat—an act or accomplishment showing great daring, skill, ingenuity: *Climbing Mt. Everest was a feat requiring the greatest courage.*

4 | Assignments

A Mentally add the suffix **ed** to each of the following words; then write the complete word in the space provided.

1. rob	*robbed*		16. disturb	*disturbed*
2. occur	*occurred*		17. develop	*developed*
✓3. benefit	*benefitted*		18. stab	*stabbed*
4. control	*controlled*		19. concoct	*concocted*
5. propel	*propelled*		20. dispel	*dispelled*
6. travel	*traveled*		21. deter	*deterred*
7. compel	*compelled*		22. submit	*submitted*
8. admit	*admitted*		23. transfer	*transferred*
9. prefer	*preferred*		24. render	*rendered*
10. regret	*regretted*		25. strap	*strapped*
11. bat	*batted*		26. indent	*indented*
12. cancel	*canceled*		27. spar	*sparred*
13. infer	*inferred*		28. spark	*sparked*
14. demur	*demurred*		29. span	*spanned*
15. defect	*defected*		30. conduct	*conducted*

B Each column contains a word and a **suffix**. Mentally add the **suffix** to the word; then write the complete word in the space provided—like this:

admit + ed   *admitted*

1. transmit + al   *Transmittal*
2. permit + ed   *permitted*
3. propel + er   *propeller*
4. prohibit + ed   *prohibited*
5. profit + ing   *profiting*
6. refer + ence   *reference*
7. visit + or   *visitor*
8. fit + ed   *fitted*
9. fit + ing   *fitting*
10. benefit + ing   *benefiting*
11. regret + able   *regrettable*
12. regret + ing   *regretting*
13. merit + ed   *meritt merited*
14. omit + ed   *omitted*
15. subsist + ing   *subsisting*
16. regret + ful   *regretful*
17. acquit + al   *acquittal*
18. commit + ed   *committed*
19. commit + ment   *commitment*
20. forget + ing   *forgetting*

21. allot + ed   *allotted*
22. blur + ed   *blurred*
23. run + er   *runner*
24. thin + er   *thinner*
25. quiz + ed   *quizzed*
26. tax + ed   *taxed*
27. drum + ed   *drummed*
28. skin + ing   *skinning*
29. lap + ing   *lapping*
30. lap + ed   *lapped*
31. transfer + ence   *transference*
32. cancel + ing   *canceling*
33. equal + ity   *equality*
34. prefer + able   *preferable*
35. appoint + ment   *appointment*
36. descend + ant   *descendant*
37. job + er   *jobber*
38. interrupt + ion   *interruption*
39. equip + ment   *equipment*
40. propel + ant   *propellant*

46

4 | Assignments
(continued)

C Mentally add the suffix **er** to each of the following words; then write the complete word in the space provided.

1. begin — *beginner*
2. worship — *worshiper*
3. control — *controller*
4. travel — *traveler*
5. can — *canner*

6. ship — *shipper*
7. drum — *drummer*
8. transmit — *transmitter*
9. cut — *cutter*
10. rivet — *riveter*

D Each column contains a word and a **suffix.** Mentally add the **suffix** to the word; then write the complete word in the space provided—like this:

admit + ed   *admitted*

1. meter + ed — *metered*
2. parallel + ing — *paralleling*
3. crystal + ize — *crystalize* / *crystallize*
4. begin + ing — *beginning*
5. quiz + ed — *quizzed*
6. confer + ence — *conference*
7. critic + ism — *criticism*

8. stir + ed — *stirred*
9. falter + ed — *faltered*
10. gas + eous — *gaseous*
11. entrap + ed — *entrapped*
12. recur + ing — *recurring*
13. exceed + ing — *exceeding*
14. exist + ence — *existence*

15. refer + ed — *referred*
16. forbid + en — *forbidden*
17. telegram + ed — *telegramed*
18. mix + ed — *mixed*
19. excel + ent — *excellent*
20. shrug + ed — *shrugged*
21. outrun + ing — *outrunning*
22. abhor + ence — *abhorrence*
23. vacation + ing — *vacationing*
24. inhabit + able — *inhabitable*
25. god + ess — *goddess*
26. cancel + ation — *cancellation*
27. man + ish — *mannish*

28. sad + ly — *sadly*
29. shut + er — *shutter*
30. ton + age — *tonnage*
31. wit + y — *witty*
32. bag + age — *baggage*
33. blot + s — *blots*
34. can + ery — *cannery*
35. cut + lery — *cutlery*
36. flat + ness — *flatness*
37. knit + ed — *knitted*
38. net + work — *network*
39. slip + ery — *slippery*
40. knot + y — *knotty*

Score_____

Homonym

4 | Assignments

A Select from the following words the one that correctly fits into the blank in each of the sentences below. Then write it in the space provided.

cite	complement	coarse	dessert	deer
site	compliment	course	desert	dear
sight				

1. The _deer_ is a fleet-footed animal. ....   deer

2. When these last three styles are completed, we shall have our full _complement_ of spring fashions. ....   complement

3. Many business deals are transacted on the golf _course_.   course

4. On this _site_ the city plans to build a new hospital.   site

5. We can _cite_ at least ten instances where Jones was guilty of shady practices. ....   cite

6. It is remarkable to see how modern irrigation methods have made the _desert_ bloom. ....   desert

7. Good supervisors know that one _compliment_ is worth a thousand criticisms. ....   compliment

8. The souvenirs which I have collected through the years are very _dear_ to me. ....   dear

9. Mother made a wonderful peach pie for _dessert_. ....   dessert

10. Coffee used for percolating is usually a _coarse_ grind. ..   coarse

B In the following sentences underline the word in parentheses that makes the sentence correct. Then write it in the space provided.

1. The new sales manager was delighted to find such a competent (core—<u>corps</u>) of salesmen. .... *corps*

2. This is the (cite—sight—<u>site</u>) on which the city will erect the new courthouse. .... *site*

3. We divided the responsibility into (discreet—<u>discrete</u>) parts. *discrete*

4. The principles expressed in the Constitution are (deer—<u>dear</u>) to the American people. .... *dear*

5. The (kernel—<u>colonel</u>) believed that high morale among servicemen is a most important factor in victory. .... *colonel*

6. Always wear accessories that (compliment—<u>complement</u>) your outfit. .... *complement*

7. We have a (<u>dual</u>—duel) purpose for holding this sale. ..... *dual*

8. The swollen stream has a very swift (<u>current</u>—currant). .... *current*

9. Have your exact (<u>fare</u>—fair) ready when you board the bus. *fare*

10. Fabrics colored with permanent (dies—<u>dyes</u>) should resist fading. .... *dyes*

C In some of the following sentences an incorrect word is used; cross it out and write the correct word in the space provided. Where there is no error write **C** in the space.

1. Can I trust you to be ~~discrete~~ about the handling of this problem? .... *discreet*

2. The winds had thrown the ship off ~~coarse.~~ .... *course*

3. The ~~faint~~ in boxing is a very useful maneuver. .... *feint*

4. It was his sad ~~fete~~ never to be a winner. .... *fate*

5. Alexander Hamilton died in a ~~dual~~. .... *duel*

6. The Marine ~~Core~~ believes in rigorous training of new recruits. *Corps*

7. He accomplished the feat of endurance with little difficulty. *C*

8. An unfaithful friend is sometimes referred to as a ~~fare-~~ weather friend. .... *fair-weather*

9. He was ~~sited~~ by the President for his bravery above and beyond the call of duty. .... *cited*

10. The ~~creeking~~ door set our nerves on edge. .... *creaking*

Score _____

4 | Vocabulary Enrichment
Exercise

Below is a list of words with which you should be fully familiar. In the space provided, fill in the word that best completes the meaning of the sentence.

barbarous	compelled	infer
disastrous	environment	allotted
prejudice	postpone	acquit
temperament	deference	candidate

1. The famous soprano was known for her fiery _temperament_. ...... _Temperament_

2. _Prejudice_ leads to bitterness, misunderstanding, and unhappiness; it is better to have an open mind. .... _prejudice_

3. In the Middle Ages, before forks were invented, people resorted to the _____ custom of eating with their fingers. _barbarous_

4. The hurricane was known to have hit the city with _____ results. .... _disastrous_

5. A _____ for public office must possess qualities of leadership, honesty, integrity and must command the confidence of the voters. .... _candidate_

6. It is an indication of laziness to _____ to a later date any work you can do today. .... _pos postpone_

7. A person's early _____ has a great deal to do with shaping his personality. .... _environment_

8. It was the general opinion that Mary would _____ herself well in the business world. .... _acquit_

9. Funds were _____ to the Board of Education so that they could build new schools. .... _allotted_

10. Although Mr. Kennedy did not state it directly, he did _____ that the town's citizens were lacking in civic pride. .... _infer_

There are misspelled words in some of the following sentences. Cross out each misspelled word and write the correct spelling in the space provided. If there are no misspelled words, write **C** in the space next to the sentence.

1. There are many helpful suggestions for those who are ~~beginers~~. _beginners_

2. You establish your credit standing, too, when you do business with the National Bank. _C_

3. A new furnace was ~~instaled~~ a year ago. _installed_

4. Would you be willing to consider an offer on this ~~equippment~~? _equipment_

5. The purchase of savings bonds has ~~benefitted~~ you as well as your Government. _benefited_

6. You will have an ~~excelent~~ chance for success if you choose one of these fields. _excellent_

7. Efficiency is influenced by the use of ~~modren~~ machines. _modern_

8. This listing, of course, is strictly confidential. _C_

9. ~~Prefered~~ stocks may be better suited to your needs. _preferred_

10. The cardboard boxes were held together with gummed tape. _C_

11. We shall ship your order ~~promply~~. _promptly_

12. The shop is equipped with up-to-date machinery. _C_

13. These safety features ~~pretain~~ to all departments. _pertain_

14. Page 10 describes the comfort you will experience when traveling in one of our planes. _C_

15. Thank you for your letter in ~~referrence~~ to our plastic products. _reference_

16. In 1950 the company ~~transfered~~ their main office to New York. _Transfered_

17. When I left the publishing ~~comany,~~ I found a similar position with a merchandising firm. _company_

18. You are to be ~~congradulated~~ on undertaking the job. _congratulated_

19. If you will follow these simple rules, you will never experience ~~dissappointment~~ that comes from losing money. _disappointment_

20. In case you are not ~~familar~~ with our magazine, we are sending you a copy. _familiar_

Dropping the Silent E

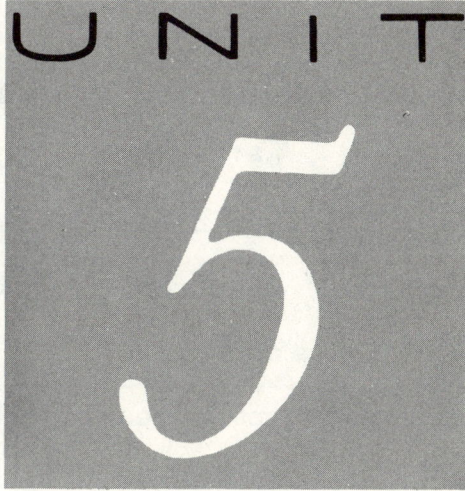

Very few of us ever misspell words like **write, love, please, move, hope, give.** We do not pronounce the final **e** in these words—and yet we almost invariably spell those words correctly. What, then, causes so many people to commit errors like these:

WRONG:	writeing	loveing	pleaseing
WRONG:	hopeing	moveing	giveing

People who make these errors just have not learned the simple rule governing words ending in silent **e.** (Of course, the *perfect* speller has no trouble with these—or with any other words. But the rest of us need a little help occasionally.) The rule is:

> Drop the final **e** when adding a suffix beginning with a vowel: **ing, able, er, ed, or,** etc.

accommodate*	accommodated	accommodating	accommodation
accumulate	accumulated	accumulating	accumulation
achieve	achieved	achieving	

THE RULE: Drop the final **e** when adding a suffix beginning with a vowel.

advise	advisable	advising	advisory
allocate*	allocated	allocating	allocation
aggravate	aggravated	aggravating	aggravation
arrange	arranged	arranging	
assure	assured	assuring	assurance
balance	balanced	balancing	
believe	believed	believing	believable
care	cared	caring	
censure*	censured	censuring	censurable
choose	choosing		
communicate	communicating	communication	
commence*	commenced	commencing	
compensate*	compensated	compensating	compensation
compete	competing	competitor	
complete	completed	completing	completion
concede*	conceded	conceding	
concentrate	concentrated	concentrating	concentration
congratulate	congratulated	congratulating	congratulations
continue	continued	continuing	continuance
contribute	contributed	contributing	contribution
criticize	criticized	criticizing	
debate	debating	debatable	
define	defined	defining	definable

THE RULE: Drop the final **e** when adding a suffix beginning with a vowel.

depreciate*	depreciated	depreciating	depreciation
derive	derived	deriving	derivation
desire	desiring	desirable	desirous
disburse*	disbursed	disbursing	
discipline	disciplined	disciplining	
dissipate*	dissipated	dissipating	dissipation
distribute	distributed	distributing	distribution
divide	divided	dividing	dividend
eliminate	eliminated	eliminating	elimination
emerge	emerged	emerging	emergency
enclose	enclosed	enclosing	enclosure
encourage	encouraged	encouraging	
endure	endured	enduring	endurance
enlarge	enlarged	enlarging	
entitle	entitled	entitling	
enumerate*	enumerated	enumerating	enumeration
exaggerate	exaggerated	exaggerating	exaggeration
exercise	exercised	exercising	
excite	excited	exciting	excitable
excuse	excused	excusing	excusable
exonerate*	exonerated	exonerating	exoneration
facilitate*	facilitated	facilitating	facilitation
fascinate	fascinated	fascinating	fascination

THE RULE: Drop the final **e** when adding a suffix beginning with a vowel.

fluctuate*	fluctuated	fluctuating	fluctuation
force	forced	forcing	forcible
foreclose	foreclosed	foreclosing	foreclosure
forgive	forgiving	forgivable	
give	giving		
guide	guided	guiding	guidance
hope	hoped	hoping	
illuminate	illuminated	illuminating	illumination
imagine	imagined	imagining	imagination
imitate	imitated	imitating	imitation
improve	improved	improving	
infringe*	infringed	infringing	
insinuate*	insinuated	insinuating	insinuation
interfere	interfered	interfering	
italicize*	italicized	italicizing	
license	licensed	licensing	
like	liked	liking	likable
liquidate*	liquidated	liquidating	liquidation
live	lived	living	livable
lose	losing		
love	loved	loving	lovable
measure	measured	measuring	measurable

THE RULE: Drop the final **e** when adding a suffix beginning with a vowel.

merchandise	merchandising	merchandiser	
move	moved	moving	movable
note	noting	notable	notation
participate	participated	participating	participation
persevere*	persevering	perseverance	
practice	practiced	practicing	
prepare	prepared	preparing	preparation
preserve	preserved	preserving	preservation
pursue	pursued	pursuing	pursuant
realize	realized	realizing	realization
receive	received	receiving	receivable
recognize	recognized	recognizing	recognizable
reconcile*	reconciled	reconciling	
reimburse*	reimbursed	reimbursing	
reiterate*	reiterated	reiterating	reiteration
require	required	requiring	
response	responsive	responsible	responsibility
reverse	reversed	reversing	reversible
sale	~~salable~~ *saleable*		
separate	separated	separating	separation
scarce	scarcity		
scene	scenic		

5

THE RULE: Drop the final **e** when adding a suffix beginning with a vowel.

schedule	scheduled	scheduling	
seize	seized	seizing	seizure
supervise	supervised	supervising	supervisor
surprise	surprised	surprising	
survive	survived	surviving	survival
use	used	using	usage
value	valued	valuing	valuable
waste	wasted	wasting	
write	writing		

There are three groups of exceptions to the rule.

A. Words ending in **ce** or **ge** do *not* drop the **e** before **able** and **ous.** We do this to keep the **c** and **g** *soft*—like **s** and **j.** This is the way they sound in words like serviceable, marriageable, courageous.

advantage	advantageous
change	changeable
courage	courageous
damage	damageable
disadvantage	disadvantageous
exchange	exchangeable
manage	manageable
marriage	marriageable

outrage	outrageous
peace	peaceable
pronounce	pronounceable
service	serviceable
trace	traceable

B. A few words do not drop the final **e** because to do so would lead to possible mispronunciation or confusion.

dye	dyeing	singe	singeing

Here is what would happen if we did not retain the **e**:
Hair **singing** is a difficult art. (Difficult? Hair that *sings*? Practically impossible, we'd say!)
Hair **dying** is our specialty. (Here's a beauty parlor that won't get anybody's business!)

hinge	hingeing
shoe	shoeing
toe	toeing

C. Other exceptions: **mileage**   **acreage**

> Retain the final **e** when you add a suffix beginning with a consonant.

achieve	achievement
arrange	arrangement
commence*	commencement
complete	completely

definite	definitely
encourage	encouragement
enlarge	enlargement
excite	excitement
forgive	forgiveness
hope	hopeful
improve	improvement
induce*	inducement
like	likely
live	lively
measure	measurement
move	movement
noise	noiseless
require	requirement
safe	safety

Exceptions:

abridge*	abridgment	judge	judgment
acknowledge	acknowledgment	lodge	lodgment
argue	argument	nine	ninth
awe	awful	true	truly
due	duly	whole	wholly

5 | Homonyms

fir—fur

fir—a type of evergreen tree.

fur—the skin and hair of an animal; garment made of such skins.

fisher—fissure

fisher—a fisherman.

fissure—crack in a wall or rock: *Moss grew in the fissure in the wall.*

flea—flee

flea—a small parasitic jumping insect: *Fleas annoy dogs.*

flee—to run away: *The natives decided to flee to the hills.*

flew—flu—flue

flew—past tense of *fly*: *The plane flew at 10,000 feet.*

flu—short for influenza, a virus disease.

flue—a pipe for conveying smoke: *You should clean the flue in your chimney at least once a year.*

flour—flower

flour—ground grain used in baking.

flower—the bloom of a plant.

for—fore—four

for—as a *preposition*, *for* is used in various ways: *left for dead, a message for the president, left for home, looking for a house,* etc.; as a *conjunction, for* means *because: I believe he will win, for he is sparing no effort in his preparations.*

fore—the front, toward the beginning: *Early in the meeting, the main issues were brought to the fore;* interjection in golf, to warn those ahead that one is about to drive the ball: *Fore!*

four—the number (4).

fort—forte

fort—a fortified building for military defense.

forte—that in which one excels: *Figure skating is his forte.*

forth—fourth

forth—forward, onward: *Ralston went forth to try his fortune.*

fourth—preceded by three others in a series: *first, second, third, fourth.*

foul—fowl

foul—disgusting: *foul odor, foul language;* stormy: *foul weather;* unfair: *foul play;* out of bounds in baseball: *a foul ball.*

fowl—a bird used for food: *Turkey and chicken are fowl.*

gait—gate

gait—the manner of walking or running: *Jameson walked with an unsteady gait;* the various movements of a horse: *This horse has four gaits—walk, trot, canter, and gallop.*

gate—a movable structure across an entrance or exit: *a gate in a fence;* the total admission money paid by spectators to a performance: *The gate for the Sharkey-Mills fight was $1,000,000.*

gilt—guilt

gilt—a thin layer of gold: *His name was put on the office door in gilt letters.*

guilt—state of having committed a wrong: *There was no doubt about the criminal's guilt.*

grate—great

grate—to have an unpleasant effect upon: *Loud noises grate on my nerves;* to grind into small pieces: *to grate an onion;* a framework of iron bars to hold firelogs: *a fireplace grate.*

great—large, important: *a great man.*

guessed—guest

guessed—formed a judgment or estimate of something without actual knowledge: *We guessed what Martinson had in mind.*

guest—a person entertained at the home of another, a visitor.

hail—hale

hail—frozen rain: *a hailstorm;* call loudly to: *to hail a cab;* to greet: *to hail a man as a leader.*

hale—strong, healthy: *hale and hearty;* to compel to come: *to hale into court.*

hair—hare

hair—*The barber cut his hair.*

hare—a rabbit-like animal: *The hounds chased the hare.*

5 | Assignments

A   Mentally add the suffix **ing** to each of the following words; then write the complete word in the space provided.

1. love   *loving*
2. please   *pleasing*
3. move   *moving*
4. hope   *hoping*
5. give   *giving*
6. encourage   *encouraging*
7. shave   *shaving*
8. argue   *argu*
9. taste   *tasting*
10. shoe   *shoeing*
11. waste   *wasting*
12. toe   *toeing*
13. singe   *singeing*
14. judge   *judging*
15. change   *changing*

16. force   *forcing* *forceing*
17. eliminate   *eliminating*
18. illuminate   *illuminating*
19. lose   *losing*
20. prepare   *preparing*
21. commence   *commenceing*
22. schedule   *scheduling*
23. aggravate   *aggravating*
24. exaggerate   *exaggerating*
25. believe   *believing*
26. exercise   *exercising*
27. arrange   *arranging* *arrangeing*
28. compete   *competing*
29. size   *sizing*
30. fascinate   *fasinating*

B Mentally add the suffix **able** to each of the following words; then write the complete word in the space provided.

1. dispose   _disposable_
2. argue   _arguable_
3. move   _movable_
4. desire   _desirable_
5. like   _likable_
6. sale   _salable_
7. change   _changeable_
8. charge   _chargeable_
9. embrace   _embraceable_
10. possess   _possessable_

11. value   _valuable_
12. notice   _noticeable_
13. marriage   _marriageable_
14. pleasure   _pleasurable_
15. wash   _washable_
16. manage   _manageable_
17. advise   _advisable_
18. excuse   _excusable_
19. believe   _believable_
20. receive   _receivable_

C Mentally add the suffix **ous** to each of the following words; then write the complete word in the space provided.

1. courage   _courageous_
2. advantage   _advantageous_
3. outrage   _outrageous_
4. desire   _desirous_
5. murder   _murderous_

6. synonym   _synonymous_
7. adventure   _adventurous_
8. glamour   _glamorous_
9. prosper   _prosperous_
10. nerve   _nervous_

5 | Assignments
(continued)

D Cross out the misspelled word or words in each of the following groups of words and spell them correctly in the space at the right. If there are no errors, mark **C** in the space.

1.	milage	lively	safety	
2.	~~sincerly~~	noiseless	hopeful	*sincerely*
3.	completely	~~acrage~~	argument	*acreage*
4.	bluish	hingeing	disable	*C*
5.	discouragement	~~aweful~~	engagement	*C awful*
6.	manageable	~~duly~~	ninth	*~~duely~~ C*
7.	wisdom	marketable	enforceable	*C*
8.	knowledgeable	wholly	capable	*C*
9.	wasteful	shoeless	truly	*C*
10.	believable	irreplaceable	~~peacable~~	*peaceable*
11.	accommodation	~~chargable~~	advisory	*chargeable*
12.	~~loseing~~	interfered	desirous	*losing*
13.	pursuant	sizeable	perserverance	*C*
14.	~~forgivness~~	achievement	participation	*forgiveness*
15.	competitor	criticized	approval	*C*

65

16. commencment	preservation	~~disciplining~~	*disciplining* C
17. emergency	~~requirment~~	contributor	*requirement*
18. radiator	exercising	fascination	C
19. dividing	realization	~~entitleing~~	*entitling*
20. exaggeration	~~scarcly~~	imitation	*scarcely*
21. surely	enclosure	scenic	C
22. practicing	exonerating	receiveable	~~practicing~~ C
23. survival	separation	reimbursing	C
24. ~~inducement~~	allocation	balancing	*inducement*
25. concentration	~~changable~~	definitely	*changeable*
26. communicative	italicized	liquidation	C
27. fluctuation	exhilaration	~~arrangment~~	*arrangement*
28. acknowledge	owed	surprised	C
29. ~~liklihood~~	observance	accumulation	*likelihood*
30. typewriting	~~livliness~~	preparatory	*liveliness*
31. scenery	~~vyeing~~	elimination	*vying*
32. reconciliation	~~couragous~~	continually	*courageous*
33. completion	congratulate	excusing	C
34. supervision	~~useage~~	survival	*usage*
35. standardization	superseding	reversible	C

5 | Homonym
Assignments

A Select from the following words the one that correctly fits into the blank in each of the sentences below. Then write it in the space provided.

flue	flea	fir	fourth	hare
flu	flee	fur	forth	hair
flew				

1. A good beaver _____ coat is quite expensive. . . . .   *fur*

2. Under the cloak of darkness, the party managed to _____ from the city. . . . .   *flee*

3. In 1958, the Asiatic _____ affected millions of Americans. . . . .   *flu*

4. The _____ is an elusive insect. . . . .   *flea*

5. I assumed that Jim was _____ in line because he followed Bob, who was third. . . . .   *fourth*

6. In the Middle Ages, every knight went _____ to conquer evil for his lady-love. . . . .   *forth*

7. The _____ tree is in the evergreen family. . . . .   *fir*

8. It is difficult to maintain a clean home with a dirty _____ in your chimney. . . . .   *flue*

9. The swallows _____ back to Capistrano. . . . .   *flew*

10. Hasn't Jane a beautiful head of _____! . . . .   *hair*

B In the following sentences underline the word in parentheses that makes the sentence correct. Then write it in the space provided.

1. Lindbergh was the first to perform the almost incredible (feat—feet) of flying alone across the Atlantic Ocean. . . . .   *feat*

2. In the economics race, electronic equipment is leaping to the (for—four—fore). . . . .   *fore*

3. Johnson's green orchid was awarded first prize at the (flower—flour) show. . . . .   *flower*

4. The horses kept an even (gate—gait) for the entire journey. —   *gait*

5. Chicken and other forms of (fowl—foul) are distasteful to some people. . . . .   *fowl*

6. (Fore—Four—For) men were interviewed for the job. . . . . . .   *Four*

7. Although his face looked youthful, his (hare—hair) was snow white. . . . .   *hair*

8. The child who (guest—guessed) the answer won a prize. . . .   *guessed*

9. There was a (great—grate) deal of activity at the bargain counter. . . . .   *great*

10. Despite his severe ordeal, the mountain climber appeared (hail—hale) and hearty. . . . .   *hale*

C In some of the following sentences an incorrect word is used; cross it out and write the correct word in the space provided. Where there is no error write **C** in the space.

1. The jury was soon convinced of the defendant's ~~gilt~~. . . . . . .   *guilt*

2. The person who ~~guest~~ the right answer won first prize. . . . . .   *guessed*

3. ~~Hale~~ storms are not uncommon in July. . . . .   *Hail*

4. Gilt jewelry will not retain its luster long. . . . .   *C*

5. Horseback riding was his ~~fort~~. . . . .   *forte*

6. I caught my heel in a ~~fisher~~ in the rock. . . . .   *fissure*

7. When he arrived home, his wife was waiting at the ~~gait~~. . . . .   *gate*

8. Martin hit three ~~fowl~~ balls in succession. . . . .   *foul*

9. We will print your name in ~~guilt~~ letters. . . . .   *gilt*

10. Many people had to ~~flea~~ from their homes when the hurricane hit the seacoast. . . . .   *flee*

5

Vocabulary Enrichment
Exercise

From the list below, select the word that best fits in the blanks in the following sentences; then write each in the space provided. If you are not sure of the meaning of a word, look it up in your dictionary.

discouragement	outrageous
manageable	desirable
advantageous	courageous
enforceable	argument
replaceable	acknowledgment

1. We believe that the new tax laws will not be _____ by the police. .... _enforceable_

2. Our new automatic washing machine is made so that it has many _____ parts. .... _replaceable_

3. Despite great _____, Banting persisted in his research. _discouragement_

4. Never before have we encountered such an example of _____ dishonesty. .... _outrageous_

5. The horse was so well trained that he was quite _____ even by a child. .... _manageable_

6. Our new credit plan has a number of features which we are sure you will find most _____. .... _desirable_

7. Owing to efficient management, our firm found itself in a highly _____ position at the end of the year. .... _advantageous_

8. We sent you an _____ of your recent order for books on February 15. .... _acknowledgment_

9. I cannot agree with your _____ against the graduated income tax. .... _argument_

10. Corporal Jones was awarded a medal for _____ conduct under fire. .... _courageous_

A In some of the following sentences, the possessive form is incorrectly written. Cross out each error and write it correctly in the space provided. If the sentence has no error, write **C** in the space.

1. A refund will be made as soon as ~~you're~~ account is corrected. *your*
2. The company has been advised to prepare some kind of handbook for ~~it's~~ employees. . . . . *its*
3. They're not interested in our new scheme. . . . . *C*
4. It gives us great pleasure to answer your letter of inquiry. . . *C*
5. ~~Whose~~ going to attend the meeting? . . . . *Who's*
6. This machine has more than repaid you for ~~it's~~ original cost. *its*
7. I hear that ~~your~~ planning a new program. . . . . *you're*
8. I to should like to participate in ~~you're~~ work. . . . . *your*
9. ~~Its~~ easy to open a checking account. . . . . *It's*
10. I shall appreciate your seeing him when he calls. . . . . *C*

B Mentally add the suffix **ing** to each of the following words; then write the complete word in the space provided.

1. surprise — *surprising*
2. owe — *owing*
3. congratulate — *congratulating*
4. facilitate — *facilitating*
5. grieve — *grieving*

6. balance — *balancing* ~~*balanceing*~~ *balancing* ~~*balanceing*~~
7. practice — *practicing* ~~*practiceing*~~
8. enclose — *enclosing*
9. encourage — *encouraging* ~~*encourageing*~~
10. merchandise — *merchandising*

Ei–ie Words

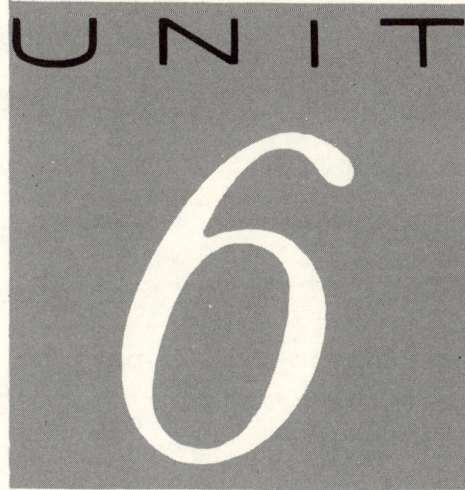

Ever since the **ei—ie** words appeared in our language, they have been a source of difficulty. They resemble each other so closely that, at one time or another, they trip up even the best spellers.

Challenged by the chameleon-like quality of the **ei—ie** words, scholars, teachers, and students have developed the following famous poem to help all of us who are troubled by **ei-ie** words:

> **I** before **E**
> Except after **C**
> Or when sounded like **A**
> As in **neighbor** or **weigh**.

There are about one hundred **ei—ie** words. All but a handful are covered by this rule. Let's analyze this poem line by line:

> a) **I** before **E** . . . . . This is the general rule.

achieve	friend	priest
adieu	frontier	quotient*
alien*	grievous*	rabies

71

6

anc<u>ie</u>nt	handkerch<u>ie</u>f	rec<u>ipie</u>nt*
aud<u>ie</u>nce	h<u>ie</u>rarchy*	rel<u>ie</u>ve
bel<u>ie</u>f	h<u>ie</u>roglyphics*	repr<u>ie</u>ve*
bel<u>ie</u>ve	len<u>ie</u>nt	retr<u>ie</u>ve
b<u>ie</u>r	l<u>ie</u>utenant	rev<u>ie</u>w
br<u>ie</u>f	misch<u>ie</u>f	sh<u>ie</u>ld
cash<u>ie</u>r	misch<u>ie</u>vous*	shr<u>ie</u>k
chandel<u>ie</u>r	n<u>ie</u>ce	s<u>ie</u>ge
ch<u>ie</u>f	pat<u>ie</u>nce	s<u>ie</u>ve
conven<u>ie</u>nt	pat<u>ie</u>nt	th<u>ie</u>f
f<u>ie</u>ld	p<u>ie</u>ce	trans<u>ie</u>nt*
f<u>ie</u>nd	p<u>ie</u>r	unw<u>ie</u>ldy*
f<u>ie</u>ry	p<u>ie</u>rce	y<u>ie</u>ld

b) Except after C . . . . . After C we use ei.

c<u>ei</u>ling	conc<u>ei</u>ve	dec<u>ei</u>ve	rec<u>ei</u>pt
conc<u>ei</u>t	dec<u>ei</u>t	perc<u>ei</u>ve*	rec<u>ei</u>ve

Exceptions:

consc<u>ie</u>nce	effic<u>ie</u>nt	profic<u>ie</u>nt*	suffic<u>ie</u>nt
defic<u>ie</u>nt	financ<u>ie</u>r	sc<u>ie</u>nce	*ancient*

c) Or when sounded like A
As in neighbor or weigh. Then use ei.

There are no exceptions to this part of the rule. It holds true in all instances.

d<u>ei</u>gn	n<u>ei</u>gh	r<u>ei</u>n	v<u>ei</u>l
<u>ei</u>ght	r<u>ei</u>gn	sk<u>ei</u>n	v<u>ei</u>n
f<u>ei</u>gn		sl<u>ei</u>gh	

Now to the exceptions to the general rule. Master these few exceptions and you have mastered *all* **ei** and **ie** words. Any word that is not an exception follows the rule.

caff<u>ei</u>ne*	for<u>ei</u>gn	n<u>ei</u>ther	sl<u>ei</u>ght
cod<u>ei</u>ne*	for<u>ei</u>gner	prot<u>ei</u>n*	sover<u>ei</u>gn
counterf<u>ei</u>t	forf<u>ei</u>t	s<u>ei</u>smograph	sover<u>ei</u>gnty
<u>ei</u>ther	h<u>ei</u>ght	s<u>ei</u>ze	surf<u>ei</u>t*
Fahrenh<u>ei</u>t*	l<u>ei</u>sure	s<u>ei</u>zure	w<u>ei</u>rd

6 | Homonyms

hall—haul

hall—passageway or corridor: *a narrow hall;* a large room for gatherings: *Independence Hall.*

haul—to move by wagon, truck, etc.: *to haul a heavy load;* the distance over which something is transported: *a long haul;* the amount gained at one time: *a good haul of fish.*

heal—heel

heal—to bring back to health: *to heal a wound.*

heel—part of the foot: *his Achilles' heel;* part of a shoe: *a leather heel.*

hear—here

hear—to perceive by ear: *I can't hear what you are saying.*

here—in this place: *Sit down here.*

heard—herd

heard—past tense of *hear*: *We heard from him quite often.*

herd—a flock of animals: *a herd of cows.*

hew—hue

hew—to cut with an ax or knife: *The men proceeded to hew down the trees.*

hue—a particular color: *Her coat was of a reddish hue.*

him—hymn

him—objective case of *he*: *Take him to school.*

hymn—song in praise or honor of God: *The choir sang a beautiful hymn.*

hoard—horde

hoard—to save greedily, store away: *to hoard money, hoard supplies.*

horde—an overwhelming number of things: *A horde of people rushed to the gate.*

hoarse—horse

hoarse—sounding rough and deep: *Nellie's voice is hoarse today.*

horse—a four-legged animal.

hole—whole

hole—an open, hollow, place.

whole—having all its parts, complete: *The baby ate a whole apple.*

holy—wholly

holy—set apart or devoted to the services of God; sacred: *the Holy Bible.*

wholly—entirely: *This plan is wholly right.*

hour—our

hour—60 minutes.

our—belonging to us: *our house, our business.*

idle—idol

idle—doing nothing, not busy, lazy: *The steel plant was idle for two months.*

idol—any object worshipped as a god: *The natives knelt before the golden idol and prayed.*

incite—insight

incite (in-CITE)—to urge to action, to arouse: *The speaker will incite a riot if he continues in this fiery tone.*

insight—(IN-sight) ability to see and understand clearly the nature of things: *A philosopher should have a deep insight into the good that is in others.*

jam—jamb

jam—jelly-like preserves: *peach jam, grape jam;* to press into a tight space; *jam together;* to render unable to perform: *to jam a machine.*

jamb—a side post of a doorway or window frame: *The door slammed against the jamb.*

key—quay

key—an instrument to open locks: *a door key;* that which reveals the inner essence of something: *Truth is the key to a good life.*

quay—a wharf, usually of concrete or stone: *The ship is tied to the quay.*

6 | Assignments

A Insert **ei** or **ie** (whichever is correct) in the spaces in the following words. Then rewrite the complete word on the line to the right.

1. c__ei__ling   _ceiling_

2. n__ei__gh   _neigh_

3. sl__ei__gh   _sleigh_

4. ach__ie__ve   _achieve_

5. bel__ie__ve   _believe_

6. p__ie__r   _pier_

√7. d__ei__gn   _deign_

8. w__ei__gh   _weigh_

9. shr__ie__k   _shriek_

10. rel__ie__ve   _relieve_

11. rab__ie__s   _rabies_

12. s__ei__ze   _seize_

13. w__ie__rd   _wierd_

14. n__ei__ther   _neither_

15. r__ei__gn   _reign_

16. sh__ie__ld   _shield_

17. fr__ie__nd   _friend_

18. consc__ie__nce   _conscience_

19. h__ei__ght   _height_

20. sl__ei__ght   _sleight_

21. f__ie__ry   _fiery_

22. h__ie__rarchy   _hierarchy_

23. counterf__ei__t   _counterfeit_

24. forf__ei__t   _forfeit_

25. for__ei__gn   _foreign_

26. sover__ei__gn   _sovereign_

27. s__ie__ve   _sieve_

28. misch__ie__vous   _mischievous_

29. misch__ie__f   _mischief_

30. al__ie__n   _alien_

75

B

Cross out the misspelled word or words in the following groups of three. Spell the word or words correctly in the space at the right. If there are no misspelled words in the group, mark it **C**.

1. pierce ~~feind~~ chief — *friend*
2. chandelier neighbor freight — *C*
3. deceit ceiling vein — *C*
4. siege ~~sieze~~ ~~surfiet~~ — *surfeit* *seize*
5. leisure either protein — *C*
6. neither feign rein — *C*
7. veil ~~skien~~ eight — *skein*
8. handkerchief ~~greif~~ cashier — *grief*
9. field friend ~~neice~~ — *niece*
10. piece priest ~~Fahrenhiet~~ — *Fahrenheit*

C

Insert **ei** or **ie** (whichever is correct) in the spaces in the following words. Then rewrite the complete word on the line to the right.

1. ach_ie_ve — *achieve*
2. financ_ie_r — *financier*
3. y_ie_ld — *yield*
4. shr_ie_k — *shriek*
5. repr_ie_ve — *reprieve*
6. l_ei_sure — *leisure*
7. dec_ei_t — *deceit*
8. front_ie_r — *frontier*
9. forf_ei_t — *~~forfie~~ forfeit*
10. quot_ie_nt — *quotient*

11. surf_ei_t — *surfeit*
12. c_ei_ling — *ceiling*
13. cash_ie_r — *cashier*
14. for_ei_gn — *foreign*
15. rec_ei_pt — *receipt*
16. f_ei_gn — *feign*
17. r_ei_n — *rein*
18. cod_ei_ne — *codeine* *codeine*
19. n_ei_ghbor — *neighbor*
20. sk_ei_n — *skein skein*

76

6 | Homonym
Assignments

A Select from the following words the one that correctly fits into the blank in each of the sentences below. Then write it in the space provided.

| hews | hear | hymn | heal | hoard |
| hues | here | him | heel | horde |

1. A _____ of ruffians attacked the travelers. ....   *horde*

2. "The Battle _____ of the Republic" is one of America's great songs. ....   *Hymn*

3. The poor acoustics made it impossible to _____ the speaker. ....   *hear*

4. The miser often counted his _____ of money. ....   *hoard*

5. The wound will _____ without a scar. ....   *heal*

6. Our friend doesn't live _____ any more. ....   *here*

7. I have apprised _____ of the change in our plans. ....   *him*

8. Green, brown, gold, and orange are autumn _____. ...   *hues*

9. She caught her _____ in a grate. ....   *heel*

10. A lumberjack _____ down thousands of trees in his life time. ....   *hews*

B In the following sentences underline the word in parentheses that makes the sentence correct. Then write it in the space provided.

1. Farmer Burton owns a large (<u>herd</u>—heard) of cattle. .... *herd*
2. This shoe has the new kind of unbreakable (<u>heel</u>—heal). .... *heel*
3. Have you (<u>heard</u>—herd) the latest news? .... *heard*
4. Alex admitted that the fault was (holy—<u>wholly</u>) his. ... *wholly*
5. Babe Ruth was the (idle—<u>idol</u>) of American youth. .... *idol*
6. Filling that (whole—<u>hole</u>) will prevent an accident. .... *hole*
7. When the fire alarm rang, the (<u>whole</u>—hole) theater was quickly emptied. .... *whole*
8. It has been an (our—<u>hour</u>) since he left. .... *hour*
9. The boat was loaded with cargo at the (<u>quay</u>—key). ...... *quay*
10. Well-chosen words can (insight—<u>incite</u>) a riot. .... *incite*

C In some of the following sentences an incorrect word is used; cross it out and write the correct word in the space provided. Where there is no error write **C** in the space.

1. He had been ~~holy~~ correct in his assumptions. .... *wholly*
2. The ABC Van Line ~~halled~~ our furniture to the new house. *hauled*
3. She was a person of deep insight and was loved by all. .... *C*
4. The agitator was accused of ~~insighting~~ a riot. .... *inciting*
5. After James recovered from his cold he was ~~horse~~ for a week. *hoarse*
6. Have you ~~herd~~ the latest news? .... *heard*
7. The door ~~jam~~ was loosened by too much slamming. ...... *jamb*
8. A ~~hoard~~ of people gathered around the scene of the accident. *horde*
9. In the temple, the natives bowed down to their golden ~~idle~~. *idol*
10. Everyone admired her autumn-hued dress. .... *C*

6 | Review Exercise

A secretary must learn to proofread letters for spelling errors. In this exercise you will be called upon to locate and correct errors. Cross out the misspelled words in the following sentences and spell them correctly in the space provided. If there are no misspelled words in the sentence, write **C** in the space.

1. ~~Their~~ are ~~to~~ many people who are careless about spelling. . . . .   *There   too*

2. A good ~~secetary~~ probably has a ~~libary~~ of ~~modren~~ reference books. . . . .   *secretary, library, modern*

3. When he is ~~planing~~ a trip, a traveler should write down all the places he expects to visit. . . . .   *planning*

4. ~~Modren~~ methods of hair ~~dying~~ are safer and more pleasant than old techniques. . . . .   *Modern, dyeing*

5. It is not ~~to~~ easy to relax at home when one's neighbors have noisy, ~~mischievious~~ children. . . . . . .   *too, mischievous*

6. ~~Febuary~~ is a month of gray skies and freezing ~~tempertures.~~ . . . .   *February, temperatures*

7. I sincerely hope you will be ~~wholely~~ successful in your new job. . . . .   *wholly*

8. It was hard to believe that such a ~~likable~~ young man could have planned this ~~aweful~~ crime. . . . . .   ✓*likable* / *likeable, awful*

9. A friend in need is a friend indeed. . . . .   *C*

10. Please send a written ~~receit~~ as soon as you receive the two dozen books. . . . .   *receipt*

11. Government agents were at the ~~peir~~ waiting to ~~sieze~~ the illegal articles. .... _pier, seize_

12. The Secretary of State has tremendous responsibilities. .... _C_

13. The contest-winning letter was remarkable for its ~~completness.~~ .... _completeness_

14. ~~Giveing~~ is often better than receiving. .... _Giving_

15. Shortages occurring at the ~~heighth~~ of the season can be a ~~tradegy~~ to a manufacturer. .... _height, tragedy_

16. An ~~expidition~~ to the Arctic must be fully ~~equiped.~~ _expedition, equipped._

17. Department stores find that their umbrella sales rise on cloudy days. .... _C_

18. A pleasing personality and ~~temperment~~ is an asset. _temperament_

19. A ~~couragous~~ man is never ~~detered~~ by danger. ..... _courageous, deterred_

20. At the end of the day, the ~~casheir~~ found that his receipts ~~totalled~~ two hundred dollars. .... _a cashier, totaled_

21. Shipping goods by ~~frieght~~ is less expensive than parcel post. .... _freight_

22. Much light industry is ~~moveing~~ to suburban areas, where ~~acerage~~ is less costly. .... _moving, acreage_

23. Their engagement was ended by mutual consent... _C_

24. The winning athlete received a ~~camra~~ as a prize... _a camera_

25. You will find that the successful ~~financeir~~ is neither ~~to~~ timid nor ~~to~~ rash. .... _financier too, too_

26. Employers are ~~compeled~~ by law to pay a share of social security taxes. .... _compelled_

27. A ~~legal~~ secretary must learn to type a brief. ...... _~~bought~~ C_

28. Welders wear special ~~sheilds~~ to protect ~~there~~ eyes. ... _shields, their_

29. An efficient stenographer is speedy and accurate... _C_

30. The hotel offers rooms for both transient and permanent guests. .... _C_

Words Ending in sede, cede, ceed
Adding K After Words Ending in C

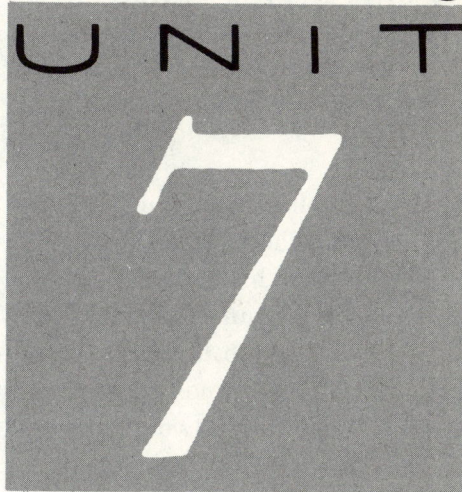

Words Ending in sede, cede, ceed

Life would be beautiful—and simple—if all your spelling problems could be solved as easily as this one. Which of these words is spelled correctly?

    1. supercede   2. proceed   3. intersede

The correct spellings are:

    1. supersede*   2. proceed   3. intercede*

Did you get these three right? Did you guess, or were you positive you were right? Here's the rule that covers all the words that end in the sound "seed":

> **1.** Only *one* word in the entire English language ends in **sede**—super**sede**.
> **2.** Only *three* words end in **ceed**—ex**ceed**, pro**ceed**, suc**ceed**.
> **3.** The rest of the commonly-used words—only *six* of them—end in **cede**—
>   ac**cede**   se**cede**   inter**cede**   pre**cede**   con**cede**   re**cede**

Antecede (meaning: **to go before**) is rarely used nowadays. It has practically dropped out of the language. You will, however, find ante**cede**nt (derived from ante**cede**) in grammar books. An ante**cede**nt is a word that *goes before* a pronoun, or is *referred to* by the pronoun.

Adding K after words ending in C

There aren't too many of these words—and the rule that applies to them is quite simple. Let's look at the one you know best:

picnic

Very few people misspell **picnic.** But many people do begin to have trouble when they add the suffixes **ing, er, ed.** The natural tendency is simply to add these suffixes to **picnic.** When you do this, here is what happens:

1) The final **c** in **picnic** is *hard*. It sounds like **k.**

2) If you merely added **ing** to **picnic,** you would soften the **c** so that it would sound like **s.** (A vowel after **c** (**i** in **ing**) almost always softens the **c** sound to **s.**)

So—if you wrote **picnicing**—you would pronounce it **PIK-niss-ing.**

The problem then becomes: how to retain the hard (**k**) sound of **c** when you add suffixes **ing, er, ed.** The answer is simple: Put a **k** after **c** (**ck**) and then add the suffix. That's all there is to it. Now you'll always spell these words correctly. Just keep that **ck** in your mind's eye—and remember why the **k** is there. Here's how to deal with the words in this group:

colic			colicky
frolic	frolicked		frolicking
mimic	mimicked		mimicking
panic	panicked	panicky	panicking
picnic	picnicked	picnicker	picnicking
shellac	shellacked		shellacking
traffic	trafficked		trafficking

Note that there is no **k** in **mimicry, frolicsome,** etc., because the suffix begins with a consonant, not a softening vowel.

7 Homonyms

kill—kiln

kill—to cause the death of.

kiln—an oven for drying or baking bricks and pottery: *Enamel on copper jewelry can be thoroughly fired in a kiln in five minutes.*

knead—need

knead (pronounced *need*)—to mix by pressing and squeezing: *to knead bread dough, to knead clay.*

need—(noun) a necessity: *Their immediate need was food.*

need—(verb) to require: *to need money.*

knew—new

knew—past tense of *know: I knew him when he was a child.*

new—having been in existence only a short time, opposite of old: *a new invention, a new style.*

knight—night

knight—a nobleman: *a knight in shining armor.*

night—the period of darkness between sunset and sunrise: *the dark of night.*

knot—not

knot—a fastening made by tying together pieces of rope or cord: *a slipknot;* a measure of speed at sea slightly greater than one mile per hour: *The top speed of the the liner United States is over 30 knots.*

not—a negative: *This is not true.*

know—no

know—to have knowledge or information about: *What do you know about astronomy?*

no—a negative: *No, you may not go to the movies.*

lead—led

lead—(rhymes with *bed*) a heavy metallic element: *a lead pipe.*

led—past tense of verb *to lead: Wellington led his troops to victory.*

lean—lien

lean—to rest at an angle on something: *to lean against a fence;* to depend or rely upon: *to lean on someone's advice;* with little or no fat: *lean meat.*

lien—a legal claim on the property of another for the payment of a debt: *The finance company held a lien on Mark's car until he made his last payment.*

lessen—lesson

lessen—to make less, decrease: *Better care of children will lessen the infant death rate.*

lesson—something learned or studied: *a music lesson, a driving lesson;* an instructive experience: *This will teach you a lesson.*

lie—lye

lie—recline: *Lie down on the bed;* an untruth, to tell an untruth: *Did you lie to the old man?*

lye—a strong alkaline solution used in making soap: *Lye is used to clear clogged pipes.*

load—lode

load—a burden: *to carry a load:* to place on or in something: *to load grain onto a truck.*

lode—a major vein of metal ore: *The miners came upon a valuable lode of iron ore.*

loan—lone

loan—something lent: *If your credit is good, you can easily obtain a loan from a bank.*

lone—by itself, solitary: *Salton was the lone survivor of the battle.*

made—maid

made—past tense of *make: Have you made many mistakes?*

maid—a girl or young, unmarried woman; a female servant: *a housemaid.*

mail—male

mail—correspondence transported by the postal system: *The mail must go through;* to send by postal system: *to mail a letter;* armor worn by a knight: *a vest of shining mail.*

male—the masculine sex: *The male robin is more colorful than the female.*

main—mane

main—chief in importance: *Write to our main office;* a large pipe: *a water main, gas main.*

mane—the long hair on the neck of a horse, lion, etc.: *The horse's mane flew in the wind.*

7 | Assignments

A In the following list, some words are misspelled. Cross out each incorrectly spelled word and write the correct word in the space. If the printed word is correctly spelled, write **C** in the space.

1. **acceed**	*accede*	6. **recede**	*C*
2. **exceed**	*C*	7. **succeed**	*C*
3. **procede**	*proceed*	8. **interceed**	*intercede*
4. **supercede**	*supersede*	9. **preceed**	*precede*
5. **concede**	*C*	10. **antecede**	*C*

B Add **ceed, sede,** or **cede** (whichever is correct) to each of the following prefixes; then write the entire word in the space provided.

1. **super**_____	*supersede*	6. **ac**_____	*accede*
2. **ex**_____	*exceed*	7. **con**_____	*concede*
3. **re**_____	*recede*	8. **se**_____	*secede*
4. **pre**_____	*precede*	9. **suc**_____	*succeed*
5. **pro**_____	*proceed*	10. **inter**_____	*intercede*

C In the space provided, write the proper form of the word in parenthesis.

1. The painters have finished (shellac) the parlor floor. .... *shellacking*
2. The entire office squad (picnic) all day yesterday at the beach. *picnicked*
3. The Treasury men knew that Lucas had (traffic) in narcotics. *trafficked*
4. Donald, the new-born baby, was (colic) all evening. .... *colicky*
5. The elephants (panic) when the horses appeared. .... *panicked*
6. All day long, the lone (picnic) ate sandwiches and read..... *picnicker*
7. Although they have gone, the painters have not yet (shellac) the floors. .... *shellacked*
8. At the last May Festival, the children (frolic) around the pole. *frolicked*
9. (Picnic) becomes popular again each year as spring progresses. .... *Picnicking*
10. Marcel is especially skillful at (mimic) the speech and actions of famous comedians. .... *mimicking*
11. Thornfield had long been suspected of (traffic) on the black market. .... *Trafficking*
12. There in the meadow, the lambs and goats were (frolic).... *frolicking*
13. Trainers of animals know that they must prevent their animals from (panic) when the audience applauds. .... *panicking*
14. When Jack got home last evening, he (mimic) the antics of the actor. .... *mimicked*
15. The (panic) woman slipped on the floor where it was still wet. *panicky*
16. (Picnic) are enjoyed by all members of the family. .... *picnics*
17. The art of (mimic) has always been a source of entertainment, especially in the theatre. .... *mimicry*
18. Kittens are (frolic) little creatures. .... *frolicky*
19. Drills were required weekly to prevent (panic) if fires should occur .... *panicking*
20. A clown often (mimic) the antics of others. .... *mimics*

7 | Homonym
Assignments

A Select from the following words the one that correctly fits into the blank in each of the sentences below. Then write it in the space provided.

knead	night	lesson	lone	led	lean
need	Knight	lessen	loan	lead	lien

1. For his services to the king, Selden was made a _____ of the Garter. . . . . _Knight_

2. No machine can _____ dough as effectively as does the human hand. . . . . _knead_

3. This pill will _____ the pain. _lessen_

4. I will _____ a special eraser for this type of paper. . . . . _need_

5. The bank gave him a _____ of $1,000. _loan_

6. The experience served as a _____ to him. . . . . _lesson_

7. The technician was protected from the X-rays by a _____ shield. . . . . _lead_

8. The famous tower in Pisa started to _____ because of the soft foundation. . . . . _lean_

9. The finance company kept a _____ on his car. . . . . _lien_

10. We have been _____ up a "blind alley." . . . . _led_

B   In the following sentences underline the word in parentheses that makes the sentence correct. Then write it in the space provided.

1. Everyone should learn how to tie a square (<u>knot</u>—not). ..... *knot*

2. We have established the (knead—<u>need</u>) for two additional stenographers. .... *need*

3. Some people prefer to drive at (knight—<u>night</u>). .... *night*

4. Man does (knot—<u>not</u>) live by bread alone. .... *not*

5. Thanks to Dr. Salk, we now (<u>know</u>—no) how to prevent polio. ..... *know*

6. The guide (lead—<u>led</u>) the explorers to the mouth of the river. ..... *led*

7. If you want to lose weight, eat (lien—<u>lean</u>) meat. .... *lean*

8. In time, tensions between East and West should (lesson—<u>lessen</u>). .... *lessen*

9. "(Know—<u>No</u>) man is an island entire to himself," wrote John Donne. .... *No*

10. We must obtain a (<u>loan</u>—lone) from the finance company. ..... *loan*

C   In some of the following sentences an incorrect word is used. Cross it out and write the correct word in the space provided. Where there is no error write **C** in the space.

1. The reins became tangled in the horse's ~~main~~. .... *mane*

2. Cardwell's policy of reckless spending ~~lead~~ his company to the verge of bankruptcy. .... *led*

3. When they arrived, the movers proceeded to ~~lode~~ the furniture onto the van. .... *load*

4. The maid served tea at four. .... *C*

5. I paid six per cent interest on my ~~lone~~. .... *loan*

6. We waited for the bowl to be taken out of the ~~kill~~. ...... *kiln*

7. I ~~no~~ that you will agree with me. .... *know*

8. Before starting his model, the artist ~~needed~~ the clay. ..... *kneaded*

9. The ~~mane~~ purpose of our exchange of students with foreign countries is to improve international relations. .... *main*

10. Many young girls envision their true love as a ~~night~~ in shining armor. .... *knight*

Prefixes

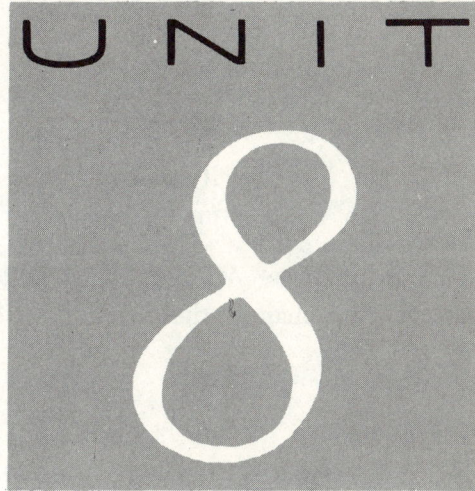

Offhand, you wouldn't think that there is any kind of relationship between spelling and arithmetic. But if you can add **1** and **1** to get **2**, then you can solve a number of spelling problems that trouble many people. If you're a little skeptical, take this test:

A. How many s's in: (Write out each word)

1. di (?) approve   **2.** di (?) appoint   **3.** di (?) satisfy

disapprove   _disappoint_   _dissatisfy_

B. How many l's in: (Write out each word)

4. i (?) legal   **5.** i (?) legible   **6.** i (?) literate

illegal   _illegible_   _illiterate_

C. How many n's in: (Write out each word)

7. u (?) natural   **8.** u (?) necessary   **9.** u (?) able

unnatural   _unnecessary_   _unable_

The Answers

1. disapprove	2. disappoint	3. dissatisfy
4. illegal	5. illegible	6. illiterate
7. unnatural	8. unnecessary	9. unable

Did you get a perfect score? Then your arithmetic is perfect—and your spelling, too. Maybe you weren't aware of it, but you were actually *adding* two things in each of the words you just spelled.

For instance:

$$\text{dis} + \text{approve} = \text{disapprove}$$
$$\text{il} + \text{legal} = \text{illegal}$$
$$\text{un} + \text{necessary} = \text{unnecessary}$$

Dis, il, and **un** are *prefixes*. A *prefix* is a syllable placed before a *root* or *word* like **legal, approve, necessary**—that changes the meaning of the root or word.

$$\textbf{Prefix} + \textbf{Word} = \textbf{New Word}$$
$$\textbf{dis} + \textbf{approve} = \textbf{disapprove}$$

Disapprove is simple enough. But why is a word like **dissatisfy** so often misspelled? Because many people make spelling errors when the prefix *ends* with the same letter with which the root word *begins*. **Dis** ends in **s**, and **satisfy** begins with **s**. When the prefix ends in **s** and the word or root begins with **s**, you have a double **ss**. Be sure you add the *full prefix* to the *word*. *Don't drop any letters.*

$$\textbf{dis} + \textbf{satisfy} = \textbf{dissatisfy}$$

You should be familiar with the following prefixes and the words in which they occur. If you recognize the prefix, you'll have no problems with these words.

Prefix + Word or Root = New Word   **Prefix + Word or Root = New Word**

dis meaning *fail, cease, do the opposite of*

dis + satisfy	= dissatisfy	dis + similar	= dissimilar
dis + sect	= dissect*	dis + sipate	= dissipate
dis + semble	= dissemble*	dis + sociate	= dissociate
dis + seminate	= disseminate*	dis + solve	= dissolve

dis + sent = dissent

dis + sention = dissention

dis + sertation = dissertation*

dis + service = disservice

dis + soluble = dissoluble*

dis + solute = dissolute*

dis + sonance = dissonance*

dis + suade = dissuade*

il meaning *not*

il + legal = illegal

il + legible = illegible

il + legitimate = illegitimate

il + liberal = illiberal

il + licit = illicit*

il + literate = illiterate

il + logical = illogical

il + luminate = illuminate

il + lusion = illusion

im meaning *not*

im + maculate = immaculate

im + material = immaterial

im + mature = immature

im + mediate = immediate

im + merse = immerse

im + migrate = immigrate

im + mobile = immobile

im + moderate = immoderate

im + moral = immoral

im + mortal = immortal

im + movable = immovable

im + mune = immune

mis meaning *wrong, wrongly, bad, badly*

mis + shape = misshape

mis + spell = misspell

mis + state = misstate

mis + step = misstep

over meaning *above, excessive*

over + rate	= overrate	over + ripe	= overripe
over + reach	= overreach	over + rule	= overrule
over + refined	= overrefined	over + run	= overrun
over + ride	= override		

un meaning *not, the opposite of*

un + named	= unnamed	un + negotiable	= unnegotiable*
un + natural	= unnatural	un + neighborly	= unneighborly
un + naturalized	= unnaturalized	un + nerve	= unnerve
un + navigable	= unnavigable	un + noted	= unnoted
un + necessary	= unnecessary	un + noticed	= unnoticed

under meaning *beneath, below standard*

under + rate	= underrate	under + run	= underrun

There are hundreds of other words that may take the prefixes we've just examined. But these words present no special problems. They start with letters different from the letters at the end of the prefix.

dis + entangle	= disentangle	mis + guide	= misguide
dis + taste	= distaste	mis + hap	= mishap*
mis + take	= mistake	mis + lead	= mislead
mis + behave	= misbehave	over + done	= overdone
mis + demeanor	= misdemeanor	under + take	= undertake
mis + fortune	= misfortune	un + easy	= uneasy

8 | Homonyms

mall—maul

mall—a shaded walk or promenade: *They walked down the mall in Central Park.*

maul—to handle roughly: *The mob tried to maul him.*

mantel—mantle

mantel—a shelf above a fireplace: *Two lovely candlesticks stood on the mantel.*

mantle—something that envelops and covers: *The soldiers advanced under the mantle of darkness.*

marshal—martial

marshal—a law officer: *Marshal Matt Dillon;* to arrange in order: *to marshal the facts in the case.*

martial—pertaining to war: *Because of the imminent danger, martial law replaced civil law.*

[Note: Marshall Plan—the plan for aid to Europe named after General George C. Marshall]

meat—meet—mete

meat—the flesh of an animal: *A vegetarian will not eat meat.*

meet—to come together with: *Meet me in St. Louis.*

mete—to allot: *The judge will mete out the sentence to each prisoner. Dividends were meted out to stockholders in proportion to their respective equities.*

medal—meddle

medal—small piece of engraved metal intended to preserve the memory of an event or a person: *She won a gold medal for excellence in creative writing.*

meddle—to concern oneself with other people's affairs without being asked or needed: *It is not wise to meddle in the affairs of others.*

metal—mettle

metal—substance such as iron, lead, gold, silver, etc.

mettle—spirit, courage: *The mettle of a man is tested when he must act under stress.*

miner—minor

miner—one who works in a mine: *a coal miner.*

minor—smaller, less important: *a minor fault, a minor poet;* a person under the legal age of responsibility: *Minors may not vote.*

missed—mist

missed—past tense of *miss: We missed our train.*

mist—a fog or vapor: *The mist enveloped us in a mantle of darkness.*

morning—mourning

morning—the early part of the day, ending at noon.

mourning—sorrow for a person's death: *to go into mourning;* to show such sorrow by observing certain rituals: *Black is often worn when one is mourning the loss of a dear one.*

muscle—mussel

muscle—a bundle of special tissues that function to move a part of the body: *an arm muscle, leg muscle.*

mussel—an edible, clam-like animal: *The French consider steamed mussels a delicacy.*

mustard—mustered

mustard—yellow powder or paste used for seasoning food.

mustered—gathered together, assembled, collected: *The troops were mustered at dawn.*

naval—navel

naval—relating to the navy: *a naval battle, naval vessel.*

navel—small depression in the abdomen.

oar—or—ore

oar—a pole used to row a boat: *The oar fits into an oarlock.*

or—conjunction denoting an alternative: *this or that.*

ore—earth containing some metal: *iron ore, uranium or*

pail—pale

pail— bucket: *a pail of water.*

pale—without much color, whitish: *pale with fright, a pale blue.*

pain—pane

pain—suffering: *pain in the neck.*

pane—a sheet of glass: *a window pane.*

8 | Assignments

A Insert s or ss (whichever is correct) in the spaces in the following words. Then rewrite the complete word on the line to the right.

1. di___approve   *disapprove*

2. mi_____pell   *misspell*

3. mi___tatement   *misstatement*

4. mi_____tep   *misstep*

5. mi_____pent   *misspent*

6. mi___hapen   *mi*

7. di___appear   *disappear*

8. di___ection   *dissection*

9. mi_____hap   *mishap*

10. di___appoint   *disappoint*

11. di_____ent   *dissent*

12. di___avow   *disavow*

13. mi___construe   *misconstrue*

14. di___imilar   *dissimilar*

15. di___ervice   *disservice*

16. di_____olve   *dissolve*

17. di_____olute   *dissolute*

18. di___onance   *dissonance*

19. di_____grace   *disgrace*

20. di___allow   *disallow*

21. di___reputable   *disreputable*

22. di___please   *displease*

23. di___temper   *distemper*

24. di___credit   *discredit*

25. di___comfort   *discomfort*

26. di_____arm   *disarm*

27. di___possess   *dispossess*

28. di___atisfy   *dissatisfy*

29. di___integrate   *disintegrate*

30. di_____like   *dislike*

B Cross out the misspelled word or words in each of the following groups of words and spell them correctly in the space at the right. If there are no errors, mark **C** in the space.

1. discomfort   disconnect   disentangle   *C*
2. dissociate   ~~ilegible~~   unnatural   *illegible*
3. mistake   misfit   mispell   *misspell*
4. impartial   imperfect   illegitimate   *C*
5. impossible   overun   impassive   *C*
6. illogical   ~~imobile~~   improbable   *immobile*
7. ~~misslay~~   immodest   ~~dissable~~   *mislay, disable*
8. ~~imaterial~~   unoccupied   ~~unerve~~   *immaterial, unnerve*
9. immature   uneasy   overripe   *C*
10. uncertain   immigrant   override   *C*
11. underrate   unnoticed   ~~unumbered~~   *unnumbered*
12. impatient   impertinent   impeccable   *C*
13. underscore   undervalue   understate   *C*
14. undermine   imagine   immunity   *C*
15. ~~imoderate~~   distinguished   underplay   *immoderate*
16. illegal   immoral   ~~unecessary~~   *unnecessary*
17. dissuade   ~~disatisfaction~~   disfigure   *dissatisfaction*
18. ~~ilumination~~   immoderate   immensurable   *illumination*
19. ~~disemble~~   dissension   overcharge   *dissemble*
20. illiberal   illicit   ~~misslead~~   *mislead*

Score_____

8 | Homonym

Assignments

A Select from the following words the one that correctly fits into the blank in each of the sentences below. Then write it in the space provided.

mete	marshal	mantle	miner	morning
meet	martial	mantel	minor	mourning
meat				

1. The President's picture hung over the _____ in the Director's room. . . . .   *mantel*
2. Water your garden either in the _____ or at night. . . .   *morning*
3. The sympathetic judge found it difficult to _____ out the harsh sentence which the law required. . . . .   *mete*
4. The widow wore _____ clothes for two years after her husband's death. . . . .   *mourning*
5. The army band played _____ music in the parade. . . . .   *martial*
6. The _____ told his deputies to make sure that the prisoner did not escape. . . . .   *marshal*
7. He proceeded in silence under a _____ of darkness. . .   *mantle*
8. A _____ ailment, if unattended, may become a major one. . . . .   *minor*
9. I'll _____ you under the clock at the Biltmore at 5:00.   *meet*
10. Digging coal is hazardous work for every _____. . . . . .   *miner*

B In the following sentences underline the word in parentheses that makes the sentence correct. Then write it in the space provided.

1. McAuliffe was chosen to be the (marshal—martial) for the Saint Patrick's Day parade. . . . .   *marshal*

2. Mrs. Veitz received a (meddle—medal) for fifteen years of devoted service to the company. . . . .   *medal*

3. All kinds of (metal—mettle) are now being used in costume jewelry. . . . .   *metal*

4. You can maintain proper (muscle—mussle) tone only by daily exercise. . . . .   *muscle*

5. Our child labor laws are designed specifically to protect (miners—minors) against unscrupulous employers. . . . .   *minors*

6. The standards set by the new manager tested the (metal—mettle) of every member of the office staff. . . . .   *mettle*

7. Frankfurters taste good with some (mustered—mustard). . . . .   *mustard*

8. Fragrant flowers are in bloom around the (maul—mall). . . . .   *mall*

9. Uranium is found in an (oar—or—ore) called pitchblende. . .   *ore*

10. The baseball hurtled toward the house and smashed a (pane—pain) of glass. . . . .   *pane*

C In some of the following sentences an incorrect word is used. Cross it out and write the correct word in the space provided. Where there is no error write **C** in the space.

1. No one should suffer undue ~~pane.~~ . . . .   *pain*

2. During the Gold Rush in 1849, nearly every resident of California became a ~~minor.~~ . . . .   *miner*

3. In this company the stockholders' dividends are ~~meated~~ out quarterly. . . . .   *meted*

4. Please put these candlesticks back on the ~~mantle.~~ . . . .   *mantel*

5. What is sometimes needed is less discussion and more ~~mussel.~~   *muscle*

6. During wartime, ~~navel~~ shipping routes are carefully guarded.   *naval*

7. Marie turned ~~pail~~ with fright upon seeing the spider. . . . . .   *pale*

8. These pills will relieve your ~~pane.~~ . . . .   *pain*

9. Don't ~~medal~~ in other people's affairs. . . . .   *meddle*

10. We must ~~martial~~ all the facts before presenting our case. . . .   *marshal*

Suffixes

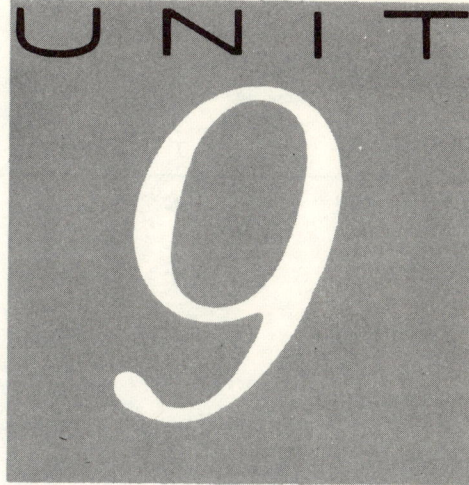

Here we follow the same principle we noted in the preceding section on *Prefixes*. A *suffix* is a syllable that is added to the *end* of a word or root to change its meaning. All we have to remember is the *original word* or *root* and *what we are adding to it*. It's as simple as that. Just watch out for the *double letter* which occurs when the word ends in l and the suffix also begins with l—like this:

$$\text{accidental } + \text{ ly } = \text{ accidentally}$$

In this section, we shall confine ourselves to those suffixes that create the double-letter problem. We shall deal with other suffixes in later sections.

99

9

Root or Word	+	Suffix	=	New Word
accidental	+	ly	=	accidenta<u>lly</u>
actual	+	ly	=	actua<u>lly</u>
annual	+	ly	=	annua<u>lly</u>
beautiful	+	ly	=	beautifu<u>lly</u>
beneficial	+	ly	=	beneficia<u>lly</u>*
biennial	+	ly	=	biennia<u>lly</u>*
careful	+	ly	=	carefu<u>lly</u>
cheerful	+	ly	=	cheerfu<u>lly</u>
classical	+	ly	=	classica<u>lly</u>
confidential	+	ly	=	confidentia<u>lly</u>
continual	+	ly	=	continua<u>lly</u>
cool	+	ly	=	coo<u>lly</u>
doubtful	+	ly	=	doubtfu<u>lly</u>
equal	+	ly	=	equa<u>lly</u>
essential	+	ly	=	essentia<u>lly</u>
ethical	+	ly	=	ethica<u>lly</u>*
eventual	+	ly	=	eventua<u>lly</u>
exceptional	+	ly	=	exceptiona<u>lly</u>
external	+	ly	=	externa<u>lly</u>
financial	+	ly	=	financia<u>lly</u>
formal	+	ly	=	forma<u>lly</u>

Root or Word	+	Suffix	=	New Word
functional	+	ly	=	functiona<u>lly</u>
gainful	+	ly	=	gainfu<u>lly</u>
grateful	+	ly	=	gratefu<u>lly</u>
habitual	+	ly	=	habitua<u>lly</u>
helpful	+	ly	=	helpfu<u>lly</u>
incidental	+	ly	=	incidenta<u>lly</u>
industrial	+	ly	=	industria<u>lly</u>
initial	+	ly	=	initia<u>lly</u>*
internal	+	ly	=	interna<u>lly</u>
international	+	ly	=	internationa<u>lly</u>
legal	+	ly	=	lega<u>lly</u>
local	+	ly	=	loca<u>lly</u>
logical	+	ly	=	logica<u>lly</u>
manual	+	ly	=	manua<u>lly</u>
medial	+	ly	=	media<u>lly</u>
mental	+	ly	=	menta<u>lly</u>
moral	+	ly	=	mora<u>lly</u>
occasional	+	ly	=	occasiona<u>lly</u>
partial	+	ly	=	partia<u>lly</u>
personal	+	ly	=	persona<u>lly</u>

Root or Word	+	Suffix	=	New Word
physical	+	ly	=	physica<u>ll</u>y
practical	+	ly	=	practica<u>ll</u>y
professional	+	ly	=	professiona<u>ll</u>y
psychological	+	ly	=	psychologica<u>ll</u>y*
racial	+	ly	=	racia<u>ll</u>y
real	+	ly	=	rea<u>ll</u>y
respectful	+	ly	=	respectfu<u>ll</u>y
restful	+	ly	=	restfu<u>ll</u>y
skillful	+	ly	=	skillfu<u>ll</u>y
special	+	ly	=	specia<u>ll</u>y
successful	+	ly	=	successfu<u>ll</u>y
total	+	ly	=	tota<u>ll</u>y
universal	+	ly	=	universa<u>ll</u>y
unusual	+	ly	=	unusua<u>ll</u>y
visual	+	ly	=	visua<u>ll</u>y
wistful	+	ly	=	wistfu<u>ll</u>y
woeful	+	ly	=	woefu<u>ll</u>y
wonderful	+	ly	=	wonderfu<u>ll</u>y

Incidentally and **accidentally** are frequently misspelled. Now you can see why. Note the **ll**. That's the tough spot. Once you know how these words are formed, you'll have no trouble spelling them correctly. One variation of this rule: When adding **ly** to words ending in **ll**, we drop one **l**. If we didn't follow this rule, we would find ourselves with words containing three **l**'s—**fully** would be **fullly**, and **dull** + **ly** would be **dullly** instead of **dully**.

Watch out for words ending in silent **e**, like **due**, **true**, **whole**, where you drop the final **e** before adding **ly**.

du~~e~~ + ly = duly   tru~~e~~ + ly = truly

whol~~e~~ + ly = wholly

ally

Adjectives ending in **ic** take the **ally** suffix to form adverbs.

Root or Word + Suffix = New Word

Adjective	Adverb	Adjective	Adverb
academic +ally = academically*		ecstatic +ally = ecstatically	
artistic +ally = artistically		economic +ally = economically	
automatic +ally = automatically		emphatic +ally = emphatically	
basic +ally = basically		erratic +ally = erratically	
chronic +ally = chronically		rhythmic +ally = rhythmically	
critic +ally = critically		romantic +ally = romantically	
eccentric +ally = eccentrically*		specific +ally = specifically	
eclectic +ally = eclectically*		static +ally = statically*	

This rule has *only one notable exception:* publicly

ness

Root or Word   +   Suffix   =   New Word

barren **+** ness = barre<u>nn</u>ess   lean   **+** ness= lea<u>nn</u>ess

common **+** ness = commo<u>nn</u>ess   mean   **+** ness= mea<u>nn</u>ess

drunken **+** ness = drunke<u>nn</u>ess   plain   **+** ness= plai<u>nn</u>ess

even   **+** ness = eve<u>nn</u>ess   thin   **+** ness= thi<u>nn</u>ess

green   **+** ness = gree<u>nn</u>ess   sudden **+** ness= sudde<u>nn</u>ess

keen   **+** ness = kee<u>nn</u>ess   wanton **+** ness= wanto<u>nn</u>ess

less

soul **+** less   =   sou<u>ll</u>ess

9 Homonyms

pair—pare—pear

pair—two of a kind: *a pair of gloves.*

pare—to trim or peel off the outer part: *to pare an apple: The office must pare expenses down to the bone.*

pear—a fruit.

passed—past

passed—past tense of *pass: The time for delay has passed. The judge passed sentence on the defendant.*

past—gone by, ended: *Our troubles are past;* just gone by: *The past year has been a good one;* time gone by: *All of this happened in the dim past.*

patients—patience

patients—persons who are being treated by a doctor or dentist: *Doctor Rogers' patients were satisfied with his treatment.*

patience—willingness to wait or endure: *The successful teacher must have patience with his pupils.*

peace—piece

peace—calm, absence of war: *peace and quiet.*

piece—a part of something: *a piece of cake.*

peak—peek—pique

peak—pointed top of something: *the peak of a roof; a mountain peak.*

peek—to look quickly and furtively: *to peek into a room.*

pique—(pronounced *peek*) (verb) to arouse resentment: *Mrs. Jones was piqued at her daughter's rude behavior;* (noun) resentment: *She showed her pique by refusing to talk to him.*

peal—peel

peal—a loud, long sound: *the peal of church bells, a peal of thunder.*

peel—(noun) the skin of a fruit: *a banana peel;* (verb) to strip the skin from: *to peel an orange.*

pedal—peddle

pedal—(noun) a lever operated by the foot: *a bicycle pedal, an organ pedal;* (verb) to move by pedals: *He pedaled his bicycle up the hill.*

peddle—to go from place to place with wares to sell: *In this city you must have a license to peddle in the streets.*

peer—pier

peer—(verb) to look at closely: *Near-sighted people peer at objects;* to come out slightly: *The sun peered from behind a cloud;* (noun) a person of the same rank, ability, or status: *In every respect, Jorgensen was Smith's peer as a salesman.*

pier—a structure built out over water and supported by pillars: *The Steel Pier at Atlantic City is a famous landmark.*

pray—prey

pray—to speak to God in worship: *Let us pray for peace.*

prey—(noun) an animal hunted by another animal: *Mice are the prey of owls;* a victim: *He was an easy prey for unscrupulous dealers;* (verb)—to seize upon something as a victim: *The lion will prey on other animals.*

presents—presence

presents—(PREZ-ents) gifts: *Christmas presents.*

presence—(PREZ-ence) the condition of being present in a place: *The crime was committed in the presence of the officer;* a commanding appearance: *He was a man of striking presence.*

principal—principle

principal—main, most important: *The principal city is the main city. The principal of a school is the main official at the school;* sum of money on which interest is paid: *He paid 6 per cent interest on the principal.* (Spelling Aid: principAl = mAin)

principle—a fundamental rule or doctrine of behavior or science: *a religious principle, the principle of gravitation.* (Spelling Aid: principLE = ruLE)

plane—plain

plane—short for airplane; a carpenter's tool for smoothing surfaces; level or grade: *The plane of the discussion was quite high;* in geometry, a flat surface.

plain—undecorated: *a plain dress;* easy to understand: *Rourke's language was plain and sincere;* a flat stretch of land: *The Great Plain.*

pole—poll

pole—a long slender piece of wood: *a telephone pole;* either end of the earth's axis: *North Pole and South Pole;* either of two parts where opposite forces are strongest: *a magnetic pole.*

poll—(verb) to take a vote: *Will you poll the Senators on this issue?;* (noun) a place where votes are cast: *You vote at the polls;* a survey of public opinion concerning a particular subject: *The Gallup Public Opinion Poll.*

pore—pour

pore—(noun) an opening in the skin: *a facial pore;* (verb) to study intently: *Every night he would pore over his books in an eager effort to learn.*

pour—to cause to flow in a steady stream: *to pour water.*

rain—reign—rein

rain—water falling in drops from the clouds.

reign—(noun) period during which a ruler holds power: *the reign of Queen Anne;* (verb)—to be prevalent: *Peace will reign over the land;* to rule: *A king reigns over his people.*

rein—part of an animal's bridle: *Pull on the left rein to turn the horse.*

9 | Assignments

A Insert **l** or **ll** or **all** (whichever is correct) in the spaces in the following words. Then rewrite the complete word on the line to the right.

1. actua_____y _____

2. annua_____y _____

3. rea_____y _____

4. du_____y _____

5. artistic_____y _____

6. romantic__y _____

7. public_____y _____

8. emphatic__y _____

9. extreme_____y _____

10. sincere_____y _____

B Insert **n** or **nn** (whichever is correct) in the spaces in the following words. Then rewrite the complete word on the line to the right.

1. drunke____ess _____

2. mea_____ess _____

3. kind_____ess _____

4. wanto_____ess _____

5. happi_____ess _____

6. bitter_____ess _____

7. like_____ess _____

8. delightful ess _____

9. timeless__ess _____

10. tired_____ess _____

Vocabulary Enrichment

Exercise Score____

Below is a list of words with which you should be fully familiar. In the space provided, fill in the word that best completes the meaning of the sentence.

reprieve   intercede   deign
hierarchy   transient   impeccable
retrieve   immobile   emphatic
dissent   immoderate   deference

1. It wasn't easy to _____ the hat after it fell into the lake. _____

2. After many anxious months, the governor finally granted the prisoner a _____. _____

3. Not being a permanent resident, the traffic violator was listed as a _____. _____

4. Editor-in-chief is the highest position you can attain in a newspaper _____. _____

5. Despite circumstantial evidence, the judge was moved to _____ in the prisoner's behalf because he was convinced of his innocence. _____

6. It is not enough to _____; you should give reasons why you disagree. _____

7. He was very conscious of his social status, and would never _____ to notice those who he thought were beneath him. _____

8. It was very unpleasant to be near this young lady because of her _____ use of cheap perfume. _____

9. He doffed his hat in _____ to the venerable old man who commanded the love and respect of the whole community. _____

10. He was as _____ and meticulous in his manner as he was in his dress. _____

9 | Homonym
Assignments

A Select from the following words the one that correctly fits into the blank in each of the sentences below. Then write it in the space provided.

pique	past	poll	pier	presence	plain	principal
peek	passed	pole	peer	presents	plane	principle
peak						

1. Although younger, Smith was Brown's _____ in athletic ability. . . . . _____

2. The _____ of the school spoke to the assembly. . . . . . . _____

3. In an emergency one must try to maintain _____ of mind. . . . . _____

4. The time for discussion has _____; we must act now. _____

5. In a fit of _____, Melinda spoke unkindly to Joan. . . . . _____

6. He has discovered a new _____ for fusion of atomic nuclei. . . . . _____

7. A _____ of customer opinion revealed that a price rise would decrease sales. . . . . _____

8. During the storm, turbulent waters smashed up against the

_____. . . . . _____

9. The discussion was maintained on a very high _____. . . _____

10. I will be glad to repeat this accusation in the _____ of witnesses. . . . . _____

B In the following sentences underline the word in parentheses that makes the sentence correct. Then write it in the space provided.

1. After you have (pealed—peeled) the oranges, put them on the fruit platter. .... _____

2. The (plane—plain) landed safely in the midst of a torrential rainstorm. .... _____

3. This medication will penetrate deep into every (pore—pour). _____

4. It was (plane—plain) to everyone that Hillson was superior to Dougherty. .... _____

5. A foolish customer is (pray—prey) to an unethical storekeeper. .... _____

C In some of the following sentences an incorrect word is used; cross it out and write the correct word in the space provided; where there is no error write **C** in the space.

1. The educated person spends many hours pouring over books. _____

2. The panther pounced on his unfortunate pray. _____

3. For miles and miles all we could see around us was a fertile, grassy plane. .... _____

4. Queen Victoria of England reined for over fifty years. .... _____

5. Patients is a virtue. .... _____

6. If he had followed the correct principal for solving his problem, he would not have made a mistake. .... _____

7. We can learn much about life from our peers. .... _____

8. The Neighborhood Merchants' Association poled its customers to determine how to improve its service. .... _____

9. Admiral Byrd explored the region near the South Poll. ..... _____

10. It was praying on her mind that she had done wrong. ...... _____

Double Letters

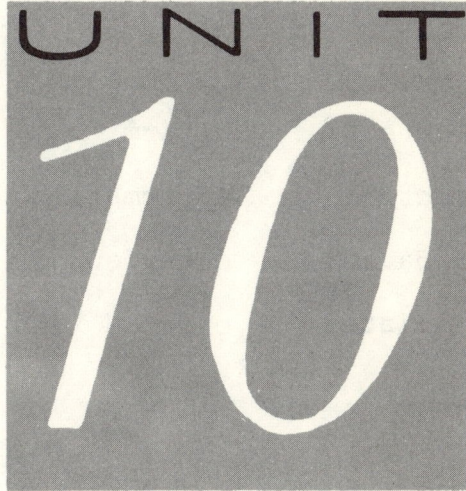

Many words are misspelled because they contain double letters. Some have only one set of double letters, like **accustom.** Others have two sets of double letters, like **accommodate** or **embarrass.** A few have three sets of double letters, like **committee** or **bookkeeper.**

You will find the rule for doubling the final consonant helpful with some of these words. For most of them, however, no single rule applies. The best approach we have found is to group these words according to the double letters they have in common. This will make it easier for you to study the words and concentrate on the difficult "spots."

cc

accede	accomplish	accustom	occupy
accept	accordingly	occur	occur
accident	accordion	occasion	succumb*

acclaim	accumulate	occasional	stucco
accommodate	accurate	occupancy	tobacco
accompany	accuse	occupation	vaccinate

ff

affected	affirm	difference	suffer
affection	affirmative	different	sufficient
affidavit*	chauffeur	difficulty	suffocate
affiliate*	chiffon	sheriff	

gg

aggravate	aggressive	exaggerate	luggage
aggregate*	baggage	haggard*	suggest

ll

allege*	bulletin	college	intelligible*
allergic	bullion*	excellent	millinery
alleviate*	cellophane	fallacy	million
allot	challenge	gallery	parallel
ballast*	collaborate*	illusion	propeller
billion	colleague*	illustrate	rebellion
brilliant	collect	intellect	villain

mm

ammonia	commercial	dilemma*	rummage
ammunition	communicate	immediately	summary
command	communism	immense	summer
commerce	community	recommend	summons

nn

annihilate	annual	centennial*	innovation*
anniversary	annuity*	cinnamon	innumerable*
annotate*	annul*	flannel	questionnaire
announce	beginner	innocent	tyranny

pp

apparatus	appetite	appraisal*	approve
apparel	applause	appreciate	opportunity
appear	apples	approach	oppose
appendicitis	application	approximate	suppose

rr

arrange	errand	irresponsible	surrender
correspond	error	irrigate	surround
corridor	hurricane	irritate	terrestrial
corroborate*	irrelevant*	mirror	territory
currency	irresistible	narrative	warrant*

ss

assail*	assuage*	harass*	necessary
assembly	assumption	losses	profess*
assimilate*	assurance	massacre	professional
assistance	dismissal	massive	professor
associate	excess	messenger	promissory*
assortment	glossary*	molasses	scissors

tt

acquittal*	attitude	flattery	operetta*
attention	attribute*	lettuce	pattern
attire	battalion	mutton	platter

Miscellaneous

accessory	coffee	indiscreet*	stubborn
accommodate	committee	mattress	succeed
balloon	embarrass	possess	success
bookkeeper	grammar	seethe*	suppress
career			vacuum

double u

114

10 | Homonyms

raise—rays—raze

raise—to lift up: *raise your hand, raise your voice;* to gather together: *to raise an army;* to bring up: *to raise dogs, to raise children.*

rays—streams of light: *X-rays.*

raze—tear down and destroy completely: *The Huns razed entire cities, leaving no trace of them.*

rap—wrap

rap—knock sharply: *to rap on the door, a rap on the knuckles.*

wrap—to cover by folding something around: *to wrap a package.*

rapped—rapt—wrapped

rapped—past tense of *rap: He rapped twice on the window.*

rapt—spellbound, engrossed: *The audience gave rapt attention to the play.*

wrapped—past tense of *wrap: The salesgirl wrapped the parcels.*

read—reed

read—(pronounced *reed*) to understand something written or printed: *to read a book.*

reed—a kind of tall grass: *Moses was found among the reeds;* part of a wind instrument: *The reed for the clarinet is made of special bamboo.*

read—red

read—(pronounced *red*) past tense of verb, *to read: Have you read "Exodus"?*

red—a color.

real—reel

real—existing as a fact, true, not made up.

reel—(noun) a spool: *a reel of string;* a roller for film or the film itself: *a movie reel;* (verb) to move with swaying or staggering movements: *to reel with excitement.*

115

reek—wreak

reek—to have a strong, unpleasant smell: *The kitchen reeks of onions.*

wreak—to inflict vengeance or punishment: *Hamlet vowed he would wreak vengeance on the murderer of his father.*

rest—wrest

rest—(verb) to relax: *to rest in bed;* to lie on or against: *Rest it against the wall;* (noun) remainder: *Eat the rest of your food.*

wrest—to tear away by violent twisting: *We shall wrest our freedom from the despots.*

rights—rites—writes

rights—just claims, privileges: *the rights of a citizen.*

rites—solemn ceremonies performed in accordance with prescribed rule: *funeral rites.*

writes—part of the verb, to *write: He writes a good story.*

ring—wring

ring—(verb) to give forth a clear sound: *to ring a bell;* (noun)—a circle of metal or other material generally worn on the finger: *a wedding ring.*

wring—to twist with force: *to wring out wet clothes.*

road—rode

road—street.

rode—past tense of verb, to *ride: The two men rode all night.*

role—roll

role—an actor's part in a play: *the leading role;* a part played in real life: *Harkness played a major role in restoring public confidence.*

roll—to move along by turning over and over: *The ball rolled down the street;* a list of names: *Call the roll;* a small loaf of bread: *a seeded roll.*

sail—sale

sail—(verb) to travel by sea: *to sail the ocean blue;* (noun)—cloth spread to the winds to make a ship move: *a canvas sail.*

sale—exchange of goods for money: *the sale of land;* a selling at lower prices than usual: *Christmas sale.*

scene—seen

scene—the place where any event occurs: *the scene of the crime;* a division of a play: *the second scene of Act I;* a view of people or places: *The scene from Mt. Rainier is beautiful;* a display of strong emotion before others: *making a scene.*

seen—past participle of verb, to *see: I have seen two plays this month.*

seam—seem

seam—a line formed by sewing together two pieces of material; any line marking the joining of edges: *The dress came apart at the seam.*

seem—to appear to be; to be apparently true: *It did seem that he was not ready to go.*

10 Assignments

A Insert **c** or **cc** (whichever is correct) in the spaces in the following words. Then rewrite the complete word on the line to the right.

1. a_cc_omplish — *accomplish*
2. a_cc_umulate — *accumulate*
3. a_cc_urate — *accurate accurate*
4. a_c_tion — *action*
5. a_c_tual — *actual*
6. a_cc_ustomed — *accustomed*
7. o_cc_upy — *occupy*
8. a_cc_ording — *according*
9. o_cc_ur — *occur*
10. o_cc_asion — *occasion*

11. a_cc_ede — *accede*
12. toba_cc_o — *tobacco*
13. stu_cc_o — *stucco*
14. a_ommodate — *accomodate*
15. va____inate — *vaccinate*
16. a____use — *accuse*
17. ba____illus —
18. fa_c_tual — *factual*
19. a_c_orn — *acorn*
20. su_cc_umb — *succumb*

B Insert **f** or **ff** (whichever is correct) in the spaces in the following words. Then rewrite the complete word on the line to the right.

1. a_ff_idavit — *affidavit*
2. a____iliate — *affiliate*
3. a____ter — *after*
4. re____er — *refer*
5. a____ection — *affection*

6. chau____eur — *chauffeur*
7. chi____on — *chiffon*
8. de____er — *defer*
9. su____icient — *sufficient*
10. su____ocate — *suffocate*

C Insert **g** or **gg** (whichever is correct) in the spaces in the following words. Then rewrite the complete word on the line to the right.

1. a____ravate   *aggravate*   6. exa____erate   *exaggerate*
2. lu____age   *luggage*   7. a____ressive   *aggressive*
3. ba____age   *baggage*   8. a____ent   *agent*
4. di____est   *digest*   9. ha____ard   *haggard*
5. a____regate   *aggregate*   10. su____estion   *suggestion*

D Insert **l** or **ll** (whichever is correct) in the spaces in the following words. Then rewrite the complete word on the line to the right.

1. a____ege   *allege*   11. co____ateral   *collateral*
2. a____ergy   *allergy*   12. co____eague   *colleague*
3. a____ot   *allot*   13. co____ect   *collect*
4. a____ternate   *alternate*   14. co____ege   *college*
5. a____most   *almost*   15. fa____acy   *fallacy*
6. a____together   *altogether*   16. fa____ter   *falter*
7. ba____ance   *balance*   17. inte____igent   *intelligent*
8. ba____ast   *ballast*   18. para____el   *parallel*
9. bu____etin   *bulletin*   19. prope____er   *propeller*
10. ce____ophane   *cellophane*   20. rebe____ion   *rebellion*

118

10 | Assignments

(continued)

E Insert **m** or **mm** (whichever is correct) in the spaces in the following words. Then rewrite the complete word on the line to the right.

1. co____petent   *competent*

2. a____onia   *ammonia*

3. co____plete   *complete*

4. co____unity   *community*

5. co____erce   *commerce*

6. dile____a   *dilemma*

7. i____ediately   *immediately*

8. reco____end   *recommend*

9. roo____ate   *roommate*

10. su____er   *summer*

F Insert **n** or **nn** (whichever is correct) in the spaces in the following words. Then rewrite the complete word on the line to the right.

1. a____iversary   *anniversary*

2. a____otation   *annotation*

3. a____uity   *annuity*

4. a____ul   *annual*

5. begi____ing   *beginning*

6. cente____ial   *centennial*

7. i____ocuous

8. i____ovation   *innovation*

9. questio____aire   *questionaire*

10. tyra____y   *Tyranny*

119

G Insert **p** or **pp** (whichever is correct) in the spaces in the following words. Then rewrite the complete word on the line to the right.

1. a_____aratus — *apparatus*
2. pur_____ose — *purpose*
3. su_____ose — *suppose*
4. o_____osite — *opposite*
5. o_____ortunity — *opportunity*
6. a_____roximate — *approximate*
7. a_____ologize — *apologize*
8. a_____reciate — *appreciate*
9. a_____lication — *application*
10. a_____lause — *applause*
11. dis_____osition — *disposition*
12. a_____ear — *appear*
13. a_____arent — *apparent*
14. a_____raisal — *appraisal*
15. disa_____oint — *disappoint*
16. su_____ort — *support*
17. A_____ril — *April*
18. a_____liance — *appliance*
19. a_____alling — *apalling* ✓
20. a_____etite — *appetite*

H Insert **r** or **rr** (whichever is correct) in the spaces in the following words. Then rewrite the complete word on the line to the right.

1. a_____ange — *arrange*
2. te__est__ial — *terrestrial*
3. te_____ito__y — *territory*
✓4. co__oborate — *corrabordte* *corraborate*
5. se_____iously — *seriously*
6. e_____and — *errand*
7. i_____elevant — *irrelevant*
8. i_____esistible — *irresistible*
9. i__esponsible — *irresponsible*
10. i_____igate — *irrigate*
11. i_____itate — *irritate*
12. su_____ender — *surrender*
13. a_____ogance — *arogance* ✓
14. te_____ific — *terrific*
15. hu_____icane — *hurricane*
16. i_____ate — *irritate*
17. fu_____or — *furor*
18. fu_____ier — *furrier*
19. wa_____ant — *warrant*
20. cu_____ent — *current*

120

10 | Assignments
(continued)

I Insert **t** or **tt** (whichever is correct) in the spaces in the following words. Then rewrite the complete word on the line to the right.

1. a_____ire   *attire*
2. a_____ic   *attic*
3. a_____ack   *attack*
4. a__en__ion   *attention*
5. ba_____alion   *battalion*

6. a__ribu__e   *attribute*
7. glu_____on   *glutton*
8. pa_____ient   *patient*
9. pa_____ern   *pattern*
10. fla_____ery   *flattery*

J Insert **s** or **ss** (whichever is correct) in the spaces in the following words. Then rewrite the complete word on the line to the right.

1. sci_____ors   *scissors*
2. po__e__ion   *possesion* ✓
3. mola_____es   *molasses*
4. me_____enger   *messenger*
5. ma_____acre   *massacre*

6. a_____leep   *ass asleep*
7. ma_____culine   *masculine*
8. hara_____   *harass*
9. nece_____ary   *necessary*
10. dismi_____al   *dismissal*

K Cross out the misspelled word or words in each of the following groups of words and spell them correctly in the space at the right. If there are no errors, mark **C** in the space.

1. apparel   ~~afiliate~~   assail   sheriff   *affiliate*
2. assert   assimilate   associate   accuse   *C*
3. appliance   assurance   suffocate   dismissal   *C*
4. excess   ~~aportion~~   scissors   intelligible   *apportion*
5. appraisal   harass   millinery   ~~masacre~~   *massacre*
6. massive   messenger   approve   difference   *C*
7. molasses   profess   receive   ~~supose~~   *suppose*
8. ~~proffessor~~   apply   assumption   deference   *professor*
9. accessory   accommodate   ~~appalling~~   rebellion   *apalling   (c)*
10. balloon   ~~bookeeper~~   coffee   appetite   *bookkeeper*
11. committee   ~~asociate~~   mattress   summary   *associate*
12. possess   suppress   vacuum   ~~tyrrany~~   ~~Tyrany~~ *tyranny*
13. ammonia   dilemma   ~~reccomend~~   promissory   *recommend*
14. roommate   irresistible   irritate   commerce   *C*
15. hurricane   ~~irelevant~~   errand   summons   *irrelevant*
16. brilliant   disappeared   ~~sugest~~   ~~questionaire~~   *suggest, questionnaire*
17. challenge   embarrass   occasional   irregular   *C*
18. (necesarily)   ~~disapointment~~   correspond   territory   *disappointment   ½*
19. ~~comunity~~   commission   ~~imediately~~   opportunity   *community, immediately*
20. intelligent   nineteenth   college   clipping   *C*

10 | Assignments
(continued)

L There are misspelled words in some of the following sentences. Cross out each misspelled word and write the correct spelling in the space provided. If there are no misspelled words, write **C** in the space next to the sentence.

1. The errors in the new ~~curiculum~~ correspond to those in the old. . . . . *curriculum*

2. We can ~~coroborate~~ every statement our employees have made. *corroborate*

3. His behavior is so ~~eratic~~ that we are inclined to think he is ~~totaly~~ irresponsible. . . . . *erratic, totally*

4. The French government is having its usual currency problems. *C*

5. Mr. Sheridan's actions embarassed his employer. . . . . *C*

6. Be sure to ~~interogate~~ every soldier who surrenders. . . . . *interrogate*

7. The newly-acquired ~~teritory~~ will require large-scale irrigation. . . . . *territory*

8. The new ~~opereta~~ follows a pattern set long ago. . . . . *operetta*

9. ~~Glutons~~ usually overeat. . . . . *Gluttons*

10. The ~~sherriff~~ almost suffocated. *sheriff*

11. Mutton and ~~letuce~~ make an attractive dish. . . . . *lettuce*

12. During the attack, the general's attention was diverted from the scene of the battle. . . . . *C*

13. You can read something of a man's or a woman's ~~atitude in~~ the kind of ~~atire~~ he or she chooses. . . . . *attitude, attire*

14. This button will set the ~~batery~~ in motion. . . . . *battery*

15. An ~~agressive~~ selling campaign will bring positive results. . . . *aggressive*

Exercise *Score*_____

Below is a list of words with which you should be fully familiar. In the space provided, fill in the word that best completes the meaning of the sentence.

appalling	assail	indiscreet
assuage	erratic	innocuous
annihilate	irrelevant	connote
accommodate		assumption

1. The damage resulting from the storm was _____ in its proportions. . . . . _____

2. A well-run hotel aims to _____ its guests with every possible comfort. . . . . _____

3. It is _____ to reveal someone else's secrets. . . . . _____

4. The evidence presented was rejected by the judge because it was _____ and had nothing to do with the case. . . . . _____

5. His remarks, far from being offensive, were completely _____. . . . . _____

6. There is no doubt that the atom bomb can _____ hundreds of thousands of people more quickly than any other modern weapon. . . . . _____

7. While the letter seemed friendly in intent, its curt tone seemed to _____ hostility. _____

8. After provoking a bitter quarrel the president of the organization attempted to _____ the ruffled feelings of the members present. . . . . _____

9. It was useless to _____ the policies of the Mayor because the majority of the voters were solidly behind him. . . _____

10. They couldn't follow the compass because the needle jumped in _____ fashion. . . . . _____

Score_____

10 | Homonym

Assignments

A Select from the following words the one that correctly fits into the blank in each of the sentences below. Then write it in the space provided.

raise	rights	rap	reek	role
rays	rites	wrap	wreak	roll
raze	writes			

1. Churchill swore to _____ vengeance upon the enemy.   *wreak*

2. Our Constitution guarantees your _____ as a citizen.   *rights*

3. Sunglasses screen out the harmful _____ of the sun. ..   *rays*

4. Winston Churchill played a leading _____ in securing victory in World War II. . . . .   *role*

5. The wrecking crew was on hand to _____ the old building. . . . .   *raze*

6. Among primitive societies ceremonial _____ are performed at different stages of life. . . . .   *rites*

7. Breakfast consisted of juice, two eggs, a _____, and coffee. . . . .   *roll*

8. Barton _____ with his left hand. . . . .   *writes*

9. In the middle of the night we were awakened by a _____ on the front door. . . . .   *rap*

10. All those who know the answer, please _____ their hands.   *raise*

B In the following sentences underline the word in parentheses that makes the sentence correct. Then write it in the space provided.

1. Be sure to (read—reed) carefully all notices. . . . . _____

2. The (road—rode) to town is full of holes. . . . . _____

3. The front doorbell has a sharp, insistent (ring—wring). . . . . _____

4. Our new washing machine does not (ring—wring) clothes. . . _____

5. After he smoked his cigar for two minutes the room (wreaked
—reeked) of tobacco. . . . . _____

6. They discovered the oil in a pool among the (reads—reeds)
in the swamp. . . . . _____

7. You should have (read—red) Chapter 6. . . . . _____

8. Victory was (rested—wrested) from his grasp at the very last
moment. . . . . _____

9. Upon receipt of the defective (reel—real), we will send you
a replacement. . . . . _____

10. Grandma Moses is known for painting rural (seens— scenes). _____

C In some of the following sentences an incorrect word is used. Cross it out and write the correct word in the space provided. Where there is no error write **C** in the space.

1. The audience's rapped attention was a tribute to the per-
former's great talent. . . . . *rapt*

2. The first ten amendments to the Constitution are called the
Bill of Writes. . . . . *Rights*

3. Tribal rights are an integral part of all primitive societies. . . . *rites*

4. Before you mail the package, be sure that it is rapped securely. *wrapped*

5. We will process your reel of film at half price. . . . . *C*

6. We road in circles looking for the main highway. . . . . *rode*

7. In the last seen of the play the stage was dimly lit. . . . . *scene*

8. If you have read the instructions carefully, you will make no
mistakes. . . . . *C*

9. Although she had the leading roll in the play, the star treated
other cast members as peers. . . . . *role*

10. Many ill-treated employees would like to reek vengeance on
their unfair employers. . . . . *wreak*

Silent Letters

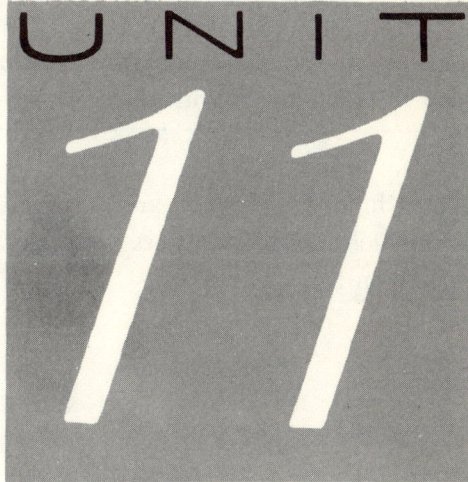

UNIT 11

There are a number of misspelled words in the following sentences. They are all misspelled for the same reason. See how many of them you can find; then cross out each one. Write the misspelled words correctly in the space provided.

1. Sally ~~renched~~ her ~~rist~~ pulling out the file.

    wrenched
    wrist

2. The ~~sychologist~~ and the ~~sychiatrist~~ have much in common.

    psychologist
    psychiatrist

3. The choir sang a ~~solem~~ ~~hym.~~

    solemn
    hymn

4. There is no ~~dout~~ that all his life Jones had to struggle to stay out of ~~det.~~

    doubt, debt

Here are the misspelled words, correctly spelled:

1.	wrenched	wrist	
2.	psychologist	psychiatrist	

3.	solemn	hymn
4.	doubt	debt

Why are these words misspelled? Because they contain silent letters— **w, p, n, b.** Because the letters are not pronounced, they are very often omitted by careless spellers. The cue for you: *You can't trust your ear* with these words. You must *keep a very careful eye* on them.

In the lists that follow, the words are arranged in groups according to the silent letters they contain. In addition, the silent letters are underlined. Look at each group of words carefully— and concentrate on the silent spots.

Silent b

bom<u>b</u>	de<u>b</u>t	lam<u>b</u>	plum<u>b</u>er
clim<u>b</u>	dou<u>b</u>t	lim<u>b</u>	thum<u>b</u>
crum<u>b</u>	dum<u>b</u>	num<u>b</u>	tom<u>b</u>

Silent g

ali<u>g</u>n*	ensi<u>g</u>n	<u>g</u>nat	si<u>g</u>n
ali<u>g</u>nment*	<u>g</u>narled*	<u>g</u>naw	resi<u>g</u>n
beni<u>g</u>n*	<u>g</u>nash	mali<u>g</u>n*	

Silent gh

borou<u>gh</u>	dou<u>gh</u>	si<u>gh</u>	thorou<u>gh</u>
bou<u>gh</u>	hi<u>gh</u>	thi<u>gh</u>	throu<u>gh</u>

gh pronounced f

enou**gh**	lau**gh**	slou**gh** (to throw away)
cou**gh**	rou**gh**	tou**gh**

Silent gh followed by t

bou**gh**t	fli**gh**t	ni**gh**t	strai**gh**t
bri**gh**t	fou**gh**t	nau**gh**t	tau**gh**t
brou**gh**t	frei**gh**t	ou**gh**t	thou**gh**t
cau**gh**t	hau**gh**ty*	ri**gh**t	ti**gh**t
dau**gh**ter	hei**gh**t	si**gh**t	wei**gh**t
ei**gh**t	nau**gh**ty	sli**gh**t	
fi**gh**t		sou**gh**t	

Silent h

g**h**astly	g**h**oul	r**h**eumatism	r**h**yme
g**h**ost	r**h**apsody	r**h**ubarb	r**h**ythm

Silent k

knack	**k**nee	**k**night	**k**now
knapsack	**k**nell	**k**nit	**k**nowledge
knave	**k**nife	**k**nock	**k**nuckle
knead		**k**not	

Silent l

almond	balm	caulk*	stalk
alms	calf	half	talk
balk	calm	palm	walk

Silent n

autumn	column	condemn	hymn	solemn

Silent p

pneumatic*	psalm	psychoanalysis*	psychosis*
pneumonia	psychiatry	psychology	ptomaine*

Silent s

aisle	island	isle

Silent t

fasten	glisten	hasten	listen	often

Silent ue

league	plaque	tongue	vogue
plague	rogue	vague	

Silent w

wrangle	wrench	wring	writhe
wrath	wrestle	wrinkle	wrong
wreath	wretch	wrist	wrote
wreck	wretched	write	playwright

11 Homonyms

seas—sees—seize

seas—large bodies of salt water: *the seven seas.*

sees—part of verb, to *see: God sees all.*

seize—to take hold of suddenly or violently; to take possession by force: *to seize an opportunity.* (Note *ei* construction.)

serge—surge

serge—a kind of cloth with slanting lines on its surface: *a blue serge suit.*

surge—to rise and fall violently, to rush forward in a great wave: *The mob surged up to the walls of the prison.*

sew—so—sow

sew—to fasten with needle and thread: *to sew a seam.*

so—in this manner: *Hold your pen so;* to this degree: *Do not walk so fast;* very: *You are so considerate;* therefore: *The child was cold, so we took him into the house.*

sow—to scatter seed on the ground: *to sow a field with wheat.*

shear—sheer

shear—to cut with shears or scissors: *The farmer shears his sheep.*

sheer—very thin, almost transparent: *sheer stockings;* not mixed with anything else: *sheer nonsense, sheer joy;* straight up and down: *a sheer drop of 1000 feet.*

shone—shown

shone—past tense or past participle of verb *to shine: The moon shone brightly.*

shown—past participle of verb *to show: I have shown you how to solve these problems.*

slay—sleigh

slay—to kill: *The assassins vowed to slay their enemies.* (Note. past tense is *slew: Cain slew Abel.*)

sleigh—a carriage mounted on runners for use on ice or snow, a sled: *a two-horse sleigh.*

sleight—slight

sleight—(pronounced same as *slight*)—dexterity, skill: *The magician used sleight of hand to make the coin disappear.*

slight—(adjective) small, thin, meager: *a slight cold, a slight little girl;* (verb)—to treat discourteously, to treat indifferently: *Did the mayor intentionally slight the visiting dignitary by failing to attend?*

soar—sore

soar—to fly at a great height, fly upward: *Eagles soar to enormous altitudes.*

sore—painful, aching: *a sore throat, sore leg;* a break in the skin: *a festering sore.*

sole—soul

sole—bottom of a shoe or foot: *a leather sole;* one and only: *the sole survivor, the sole purpose.*

soul—inner spirit: *Does man's soul live after death?*

stairs—stares

stairs—series of steps: *a flight of stairs.*

stares—looks long or directly at something with eyes wide open: *He stares blankly into space.*

stake—steak

stake—a wooden post: *a fence stake, to be burned at the stake;* to risk money on a chance happening: *to stake a fortune on the outcome.*

steak—meat from steer: *a beefsteak.*

stationary—stationery

stationary—not moving, standing still: *The price of eggs has been stationary for a year.*

stationery—writing materials: paper, cards, envelopes, etc.: *Please send me a box of white stationery.* (Spelling Aid: stationAry refers to plAce; stationERy refers to papER.)

steal—steel

steal—to rob: *to steal a wallet;* to win by art or charm: *She steals all hearts;* to move secretly: *He steals silently out of the house.*

steel—a metal made from iron: *a steel safe.*

straight—strait

straight—direct, not curved: *a straight line.*

strait—a narrow body of water: *The Bering Strait separates Alaska from Siberia;* a distressing situation: *dire straits.*

suite—sweet

suite—(pronounced *sweet*) a connected series of rooms: *The Bridal Suite;* a set of matching furniture: *a living room suite;* a musical composition: *Grand Canyon Suite.*

sweet—pleasant tasting, opposite of sour: *a sweet drink.*

11 | Assignments

A Each of the following words contains one or more **silent letters.** There is a blank where those silent letters should be. Insert the letters and then rewrite the entire word correctly in the space provided.

1. plum____er   *plumber*
2. num_____   *numb*
3. dou_____t   *doubt*
4. g_____oul   *ghoul*
5. hau____ty   *haughty*
6. strai____t   *straight*
7. r____apsody   *rhapsody*
8. r____ubarb   *rhubarb*
9. r__eumatism   *rheumatism*
10. r_____ythm   *rhythm*
11. _____nee   *knee*
12. _____nell   *knell*
13. a_____mond   *almond*
14. ba_____k   *balk*
15. ba_____m   *balm*

16. colum_____   *column*
17. solem_____   *solemn*
18. beni_____n   *benign*
19. mali_____n   *malign*
20. _____tomaine   *ptomaine*
21. _____salm   *psalm*
22. ai_____le   *aisle*
23. i_____le   *isle*
24. vog_____   *vogue*
25. vag_____   *vague*
26. rog_____   *rogue*
27. leag_____   *league*
28. _____rithe   *writhe*
29. play____right   *playwright*
30. _____rist   *wrist*

31. has_____en	*hasten*	36. r_____yme	*rhyme*
32. glis_____en	*glisten*	37. plag_____	*plaque*
33. of_____en	*often*	38. tong_____	*tongue*
34. _____riggle	*wriggle*	39. plaq_____	*plaque*
35. _____restle	*wrestle*	40. hym_____	*hymn*

B   Insert the letters missing from the words; then rewrite the entire word in the space provided.

1. _____nock	*knock*	16. of_____en	*often*
2. frei_____t	*freight*	17. _____nash	*~~knash~~ gnash*
3. ai_____le	*aisle*	18. hau_____ty	*haughty*
4. play_____right	*playwright*	19. condem_____	*condemn*
5. _____sychosis	*ps psychosis*	20. _____renched	*wrenched*
6. fli_____t	*flight*	21. clim_____	*climb*
7. plum_____er	*plumber*	22. thorou_____	*thorough*
8. colum_____	*column*	23. _____now	*know*
9. de_____t	*debt*	24. wa_____k	*walk*
10. i_____le	*isle*	25. resi_____n	*resign*
11. _____nit	*knit*	26. thou_____t	*thought*
12. _____rath	*wrath*	27. _____rote	*wrote*
13. _____tomaine	*ptomaine*	28. _____nowledge	*knowledge*
14. lis_____en	*listen*	29. throu_____	*through*
15. dou_____	*doubt*	30. enou_____	*enough*

134

11 | Homonym

Assignments

A Select from the following words the one that correctly fits into the blank in each of the sentences below. Then write it in the space provided.

| seas | stationary | sheer | shone | sleight | serge | sew |
| seize | stationery | shear | shown | slight | surge | sow |

1. It takes intelligence to _____ an opportunity at the right moment. . . . . *seize*

2. Although his condition was still critical, the doctor said there had been a _____ improvement. *slight*

3. The cost-of-living index has remained _____ for three months. *stationary*

4. Our new advertising campaign will _____ the seeds of future demand for our product. . . . . *sow*

5. We ordered 5,000 sheets of pink _____ for our office. . . *stationery*

6. We marveled at the magician's mastery of _____ of hand. *sleight*

7. _____ stockings look good, but they do not generally wear well. . . . . *sheer*

8. Before the veterinarian could treat the sheep, he had to _____ off all its wool. . . . . *shear*

9. The new office spirit has _____ in our rising sales. . . . . *shown*

10. He felt a _____ of emotion swell within him as he faced the crowd. . . . . *surge*

In the following sentences underline the word in parentheses that makes the sentence correct. Then write it in the space provided.

1. From where he stood, the captain could see the surf (serge—surge) against the rocks. ....

2. The sun (shown—shone) brightly all day. ....

3. A nail penetrated the (soul—sole) of the soldier's shoe. ......

4. All of us have a great (stake—steak) in our government. .....

5. When you arrive at the airport, you will be (shown—shone) where to check your baggage. ....

6. Oil of wintergreen is often recommended for (sore—soar), aching muscles. ....

7. The store detective saw the young lady (steal—steel) a pair of gloves. ....

8. Your supply of (stationary—stationery) should reach you in a few days. ....

9. The President occupied a four-room (suite—sweet) at the hotel. ....

10. I prefer my (stake—steak) medium rare. ....

C In some of the following sentences an incorrect word is used; cross it out and write the correct word in the space provided. Where there is no error write **C** in the space.

1. Please send two boxes of Crawford stationary to the above address. .... *stationery*

2. The new officer felt he was sleighted by your remark. ...... *slighted*

3. He said it was shear luck that pulled him through the crisis. *sheer*

4. During the steal strike the price of this metal went soaring. *steel*

5. His soul aim in life is to please others. .... *sole*

6. He had steaked a fortune on the outcome of the race. ...... *staked*

7. While you are young, seize every opportunity to increase your knowledge. .... *C*

8. Most people are very uncomfortable when others stair at them. .... *stare stare*

9. Have we shone you our new spring line? .... *shown*

10. This tie will go well with your blue surge suit. .... *C*

136

11 | Review Exercise

There are misspelled words in some of the following sentences. Cross out each misspelled word and write the correct spelling in the space provided. If there are no misspelled words, write **C** in the space next to the sentence.

1. The Civil War began after a number of states decided to ~~seceed~~ from the Union. .... *secede*

2. In order to achieve a good finish, you should be sure that raw wood is ~~shellaced~~ before being painted. .... *shellacked*

3. Jay-walking is now ~~ilegal~~ in New York City. .... *illegal*

4. The auditor could not read the (bookeeper's) illegible handwriting. .... *C* ✓

5. The students were very eager to learn how to ~~disect~~ a frog. *dissect*

6. Modern music is full of ~~disonance~~. .... *dissonance*

7. A landlord may ~~disspossess~~ a tenant who does not pay his rent. .... *dispossess*

8. The pianist played ~~rhythmicaly~~. .... *rhythmically* ✓

9. Large businesses usually pay their ~~employes~~ once a week. *employees*

10. There has been a marked drop in polio because so many people have been ~~vacinated~~ against it. .... *vaccinated*

11. Many summer evening dresses are made of silk or nylon ~~chifon~~. .... *chiffon*

12. Workers in chemical plants must wear masks to avoid suffocation from fumes. .... *C*

13. A ~~beginer~~, if ~~inteligent~~, can soon become efficient at almost any job. .... *beginner, intelligent*

14. Applicants for the position were required to fill out a ~~questionaire~~. .... *questionnaire*

15. Manufacturers of ladies' apparel find it necessary to read the fashion news. .... *C*

16. Modern household appliances are great time-savers. . . . .   *c*

17. Alaska, formerly a ~~teritory~~, is now a state. . . . .   *teritory*

18. Manufacturers of modern textiles ~~reccomend~~ laundering in cool water. . . . .   *recommend*

19. Our sales have risen at an apparently fantastic rate. . . . . . .   *c*

20. It is not necessary to use a ~~vaccum~~ cleaner on foam rubber mattresses. . . . .   *vacuum* ~~vacuum~~

21. Many people are not aware that a considerable amount of ~~tobaco~~ is grown in Connecticut. . . . .   *tobacco*

22. A bank will ~~usualy~~ insist on ~~colateral~~ for a large loan. . . . . . .   *usually, collateral*

23. Many articles that were once sold uncovered are now wrapped in plastic sheets. . . . .   *c*

24. Chicken ~~sallad~~ is a favorite American dish. . . . .   *salad*

25. The fashion model wore a black dress with red ~~accesories~~. . .   *accessories*

26. When the flood waters ~~receeded~~, the people began to clear away the debris. . . . .   *receded*

27. The unsuccessful candidate ~~conceeded~~ the election before all the votes were counted. . . . .   *conceded*

28. ~~Picnicing~~ is one of the joys of summer. . . . .   *Picnicking*

29. Reliable stores cheerfully refund money to customers who are ~~disatisfied~~ with their purchases. . . . .   *dissatisfied*

30. Sugar will ~~disolve~~ more quickly in hot water than in cold.   *dissolve*

31. The attorney objected to the question because it was ~~imaterial~~. . . . .   *immaterial*

32. The Senate voted to ~~overide~~ the President's veto. . . . .   *override*

33. Some of the new detergents make dirt disappear as if by magic. . . . .   *c*

34. The model apartment was ~~beautifuly~~ furnished in the modern style. . . . .   *beautifully*

35. The will was ~~dully~~ signed and witnessed. . . . .   *duly*

36. One of the most powerful groups in the Senate is the Foreign Affairs ~~Comittee~~. . . . .   *Committee*

37. ~~Stuco~~ is a favorite building material in California. . . . .   *Stucco*

38. Hair fashions and ~~milinery~~ styles are closely related. . . . . . .   *millinery*

39. Many college students work part time to help defray their expenses. . . . .   *c*

40. The attorney for the defense started to ~~interogate~~ the witness.   *interrogate*

WORDS Ending in able and ible

The **able-ible** words illustrate the point made earlier—that the pronunciation of a word doesn't *always* help you with its spelling.

Because these words trouble so many people, they have received a great deal of attention from language experts, teachers . . . and victims, too. Out of those studies and analyses has come a series of helpful guides that should solve most of your **able-ible** problems.

These guides are the best we have. But since they aren't absolutely foolproof, we shall have to qualify each one with "generally" or "usually." This means that the guides apply to the vast majority of words you use or come across.

I. Words usually end in **able** when:

> **A.** The *base, root,* or *stem* is a *complete* word. Keep in mind the word *complete.* You'll see its importance in a moment.

adapt<u>able</u>	avail<u>able</u>	lament<u>able</u>*	question<u>able</u>
accept<u>able</u>	depend<u>able</u>	prefer<u>able</u>	tax<u>able</u>
agree<u>able</u>	detest<u>able</u>	profit<u>able</u>	

In each instance, see what happens when you drop the **able:**

adapt	avail	lament	question
accept	depend	prefer	tax
agree	detest	profit	

You have a *full, complete* word left.

B. The *root* is a *full, complete* word from which the **final e** has been dropped.

---

advis<u>able</u>	desir<u>able</u>	imagin<u>able</u>	receiv<u>able</u>
compar<u>able</u>*	excit<u>able</u>	lik<u>able</u>	
debat<u>able</u>	excus<u>able</u>	not<u>able</u>*	

Drop the **able** and we have a *full* word that *lacks* a **final e.**

advis (<u>e</u>)	desir (<u>e</u>)	imagin (<u>e</u>)	receiv (<u>e</u>)
compar (<u>e</u>)	excit (<u>e</u>)	lik (<u>e</u>)	
debat (<u>e</u>)	excus (<u>e</u>)	not (<u>e</u>)	

C. The *base, root,* or *stem* ends in **i** or the original word ends in **y.**
This part of the rule is especially easy to fix in your mind. If we did not
follow this rule with roots ending in **i**, we would soon find ourselves with
such odd-looking words as **reliible** (which is clearly wrong).

So it makes good sense to have **able** follow all roots ending in **i** or when
y is changed to **i.**

applic<u>able</u>	(apply)	piti<u>able</u>	(pity)
envi<u>able</u>	(envy)	pli<u>able</u>*	(ply)
justifi<u>able</u>	(justify)	reli<u>able</u>	(rely)
		undeni<u>able</u>	(deny)

D. The *base, root,* or *stem* is related to other words with a long **a** sound
as in **way:**

communic<u>able</u>	(communicate)	irrit<u>able</u>	(irritate)
dur<u>able</u>	(duration)	toler<u>able</u>	(tolerate)
implac<u>able</u>*	(placate)	vener<u>able</u>	(venerate)

E. The *base, root,* or *stem* ends in hard **c** (as in **cook**) or hard **g** (as in **dig**):

amic<u>able</u>*	indefatig<u>able</u>*	navig<u>able</u>
despic<u>able</u>*	irrevoc<u>able</u>*	practic<u>able</u>

Remember: **a—o—u** are *hardening vowels.* Hence, the **g** and **c** before **a**
(as in the words above) have the hard sound.

141

F. The following words end in **able,** but do not fall into any of the above groups. Look at them carefully. Visualize each one individually. Write each one a few times while you concentrate on the **able** ending.

aff**able***	hospit**able***	manage**able**
amen**able***	indomit**able***	marriage**able**
cap**able**	inevit**able**	memor**able**
chang**eable**	inexor**able***	palp**able***
charg**eable**	inflamm**able**	peace**able**
controll**able**	inscrut**able***	port**able**
enforce**able**	insepar**able**	prob**able**
equit**able***	intoler**able**	unpronounce**able**
exchange**able**	malle**able***	vulner**able***
formid**able***		

Retain the "e" (handwritten note, with changeable and chargeable circled)

II. Words usually end in **ible** when:

A. The *base, root,* or *stem* is *not a full, complete* word. Just a few examples will suffice to illustrate this point:

aud**ible**	imposs**ible**	percept**ible**
cred**ible***	incred**ible**	plaus**ible***
ed**ible**	indel**ible**	poss**ible**
fall**ible***	intellig**ible**	suscept**ible***
feas**ible***	invis**ible**	terr**ible**
horr**ible**	neglig**ible***	vis**ible**

We must distinguish here between what is a *full* word and what is *not* a *full* word. Under I-B above, we discussed roots that lack only a **final e.** These take **able** endings:

    desirable - desir (<u>e</u>)   likable - lik (<u>e</u>)

These roots are *complete* words *except for one letter*. The following **ible** words contain roots that are really not words. They aren't even barely recognizable as anything else but roots:

    horrible - <u>horr</u>   indelible - <u>indel</u>   terrible - <u>terr</u>

> **B.** The *base, root,* or *stem* is a *full, complete* word that can add **ion** without adding any letters in between the end of the word and the **ion.**

    exhaustible

The root is **exhaust**—a *full, complete* word. We can add **ion** to **exhaust** without any intervening letters: exhaust**ion**.

access*	acces<u>sion</u>	acces<u>sible</u>
collect	collec<u>tion</u>	collect<u>ible</u>
connect	connec<u>tion</u>	connect<u>ible</u>
corrupt	corrupt<u>ion</u>	corrupt<u>ible</u>
deduct	deduc<u>tion</u>	deduct<u>ible</u>
destruct	destruc<u>tion</u>	destruct<u>ible</u>
digest	diges<u>tion</u>	digest<u>ible</u>
perfect	perfec<u>tion</u>	perfect<u>ible</u>

Exceptions:

    correct<u>able</u>   predict<u>able</u>

C. The *base, root,* or *stem* ends in **ns** or **ss**.

access**ible**   indefens**ible**   reprehens**ible***

admiss**ible***   insens**ible**   respons**ible**

defens**ible**   irrespons**ible**   sens**ible**

incomprehens**ible***   permiss**ible**

✱*Exception:* indispens**able.** This is covered by the **able** rule: If any form of the word has a long **a,** the word takes the **able** ending. Indispens**able** is related to dispensation.

D. The *base, root,* or *stem* ends in soft **c** (as in **force**) or soft **g** (as in **giant**).

cruc**ible***   illeg**ible***   invinc**ible**

deduc**ible***   incorrig**ible***   leg**ible**

elig**ible**   intang**ible***   neglig**ible***

forc**ible**   intellig**ible**   reduc**ible**

Other **ible** words:

collaps**ible**   discern**ible***   inflex**ible**

contempt**ible**   flex**ible***   irresist**ible**

convert**ible**   gull**ible***   revers**ible**

divis**ible**

12 | Homonyms

tail—tale

tail—the hind part: *a dog's tail, a shirt tail.*

tale—a story: *A Tale of Two Cities.*

taught—taut

taught—past tense of verb *to teach: He taught that lesson yesterday.*

taut—tight, not slack: *Pull the rope taut.*

tear—tier

tear—(rhymes with *here*)—a droplet from the eye: *to shed a tear.*

tier—a row, a layer: *a three-tier layer cake, the upper tier in the grandstands.*

threw—through

threw—past tense of verb *to throw: The new manager threw caution to the winds.*

through—in one side and out the other: *He walked through the room;* in the midst of: *to travel through a state;* finished: *through with his work.*

tide—tied

tide—the daily rise and fall of a body of water: *high tide;* change from one condition to the other: *to turn the tide of battle;* to help along for a time: *This money will tide you over until you get a job.*

tied—past tense of verb *to tie: He tied a knot.*

timber—timbre

timber—lumber: *The timber was cut with saws.*

timbre—distinctive tone or character: *Her voice has a bell-like timbre.*

toe—tow

toe—a digit of the foot: *the large toe.*

tow—to pull along: *to tow a car.*

tracked—tract

tracked—past tense of verb *to track: The criminal was tracked down.*

tract—area or region not specifically bounded: *a tract of land;* a pamphlet or leaflet: *a tract on economics;* a system of living organs having a special function: *the digestive tract.*

troop—troupe

troop—a body of soldiers or scouts: *a Boy Scout troop;* a great number: *a troop of children;* to go in large numbers: *They watched the crowd troop into the yard.*

troupe—a group of actors or singers: *a ballet troupe.*

vain—vane—vein

vain—having too much pride: *Vain men are easily flattered and deceived;* of no use, without success: *All his efforts were in vain.*

vane—an indicator of wind direction: *a weather vane.*

vein—a blood vessel: *the jugular vein;* a large deposit of ore: *a copper vein;* the general disposition running through something: *in a humorous vein.*

vice—vise

vice—(rhymes with *ice*) evil conduct, corruption: *Gambling is a vice.*

vise—(rhymes with *ice*) tool used for holding an object firmly while it is being worked upon: *a carpenter's vise.*

waive—wave

waive—to give up a right or claim to something: *Garson was offered $100,000 to waive his rights to the Burton estate.*

wave—(noun) a moving swell of water or any movement like it: *an ocean wave;* (verb) to move back and forth: *to wave a flag.*

waiver—waver

waiver—relinquishment of a right: *I accept your waiver of claim to the property.*

waver—to be hesitant, indecisive: *to waver between one side and the other.*

ware—wear

ware—a manufactured utensil, usually of metal: *hardware, kitchenware;* (as a plural)—goods for sale: *He sold his wares cheaply.*

wear—to carry on one's person for covering, ornament, defense: *to wear clothes;* to impair by constant use or friction: *to wear away;* to hold up in use: *Those shoes wear well.*

waste—waist

waste—to spend uselessly: *to waste money, to waste time;* useless or worthless material: *garbage is waste;* a desert, a wilderness: *a barren waste.*

waist—the circumference of the body between the ribs and the hips: *a narrow waist.*

way—weigh

way—manner, method, path, means, direction: *This is the best way to invest your money.*

weigh—to find the weight of; to consider: *Weigh all the evidence before you reach your conclusions.*

weather—whether

weather—condition of the atmosphere: *stormy weather.*

whether—indicating a choice or alternative: *I don't know whether to stay or to go.*

weak—week

weak—not strong: *a meek, weak man.*

week—seven successive days: *Sunday is the first day of the week.*

wet—whet

wet—to dampen: *to wet the clothes;* damp: *wet clothes.*

whet—to sharpen by rubbing: *to whet a knife;* stimulate: *Seasoned foods whet the appetite.*

which—witch

which—(pronoun or adjective) *Which is yours? Which way?*

witch—evil woman with magical powers: *Witch-hunting was common in old Salem.*

wrung—rung

wrung—past tense of *wring: The clothes were wrung dry in the machine.*

rung—past tense of *ring: The church bells rung out the call to services;* a cross-rib of a ladder or chair: *He climbed up the ladder one rung at a time.*

yoke—yolk

yoke—a wooden frame used to fasten two animals together: *a yoke for oxen;* servitude, bondage: *to struggle under the yoke of tyranny.*

yolk—the yellow part of an egg.

12 | Assignments

A Insert **able** or **ible** (whichever is correct) in the spaces in the following words. Then rewrite the complete word on the line to the right.

1. agree_____ *agreeable*

2. excit_____ *excitable*

3. envi_____ *enviable*

4. toler_____ *tolerable*

5. neglig_____ *negligible*

6. navig*able* *navigable* ~~navigible~~

7. indigest_____ *indigestible*

8. aff_____ *affable*

9. predict_____ *predictable*

10. respons_____ *responsible*

11. permiss_____ *permissible*

12. prob_____ *probable*

13. indispens_____ *indispensable*

14. flex_____ ~~flexable~~ *flexible*

15. vis_____ *visible*

16. irresist_____ *irresistible*

17. avail_____ *available*

18. lik_____ *likable*

19. indel_____ *indelible*

20. amic_____ ~~amicible~~ *amicable*

B

Insert **able** or **ible** (whichever is correct) in the spaces in the following words. Then rewrite the complete word on the line to the right.

1. avail_____	*available*	11. indomit_____	*indomitable*
2. adapt_____	*adaptable*	12. cred_____	*credible*
3. indel_____	*indelible*	13. vulner_____	*vulnerable*
4. horr_____	*horrible*	14. digest_____	*digestable* ible
5. aud_____	*audible*	15. predict ᵒable	*predictable* predictible
6. aff_____	*affable*	16. detest_____	*detestable*
7. equit_____	*equitable*	17. sens_____	*sensible*
8. neglig_____	*negligible*	18. defens_____	*defensible*
9. suscept_____	*susceptable* ible	19. excus_____	*excusable*
10. formid_____	*formidible (able)*	20. practic_____	*practicable*

C

Cross out the misspelled words. Spell them correctly in the spaces at the right. If the word is correct, mark **C** in the space.

1. adaptable	*C*	11. incomprehensible	*C*
2. lamentable	*C*	12. insensible	*C*
3. gullible	*C*	13. durible	*durable*
4. discernible	*C*	14. audible	*C*
5. indelable	*indelible*	15. forcable	*forcible*
6. agreeable	*C*	16. visible	*C*
7. legible	*C*	17. susceptible	*susceptable* C
8. illegible	*C*	18. excitible	*excitable*
9. desirible	*desirable*	19. amicable	*C*
10. enforceable	*C enforcible* *enforceable*	20. indispensable	*C*

148

Homonym

12 | Assignments

A Select from the following words the one that correctly fits into the blank in each of the sentences below. Then write it in the space provided.

tow	tied	tracked	threw	waist	taught	waive
toe	tide	tract	through	waste	taut	wave

1. The tightrope walker said his wire was too _____; it had to be slackened. . . . .   _taut_

2. The hounds _____ the escaped convict through the snow. . . . .   _tracked_

3. The reinforcements turned the _____ of battle. . . . . . .   _tide_

4. Every woman would like to have a small _____ measurement. . . . .   _waist_

5. Travel _____ space no longer seems impossible. . . . . . .   _through_

6. Will you _____ your rights to the inheritance? . . . .   _waive_

7. The way a subject is _____ partly determines how well it is learned. . . . .   _taught_

8. Careless shoppers may _____ significant sums of money through foolish buying. . . . .   _waste_

9. When the _____ was receding, the swimmers felt a strong undertow. . . . .   _tide_

10. On this _____ of fertile land we plan to raise corn. . . . .   _tract_

B In the following sentences underline the word in parentheses that makes the sentence correct. Then write it in the space provided.

1. What dress are you going to (ware—<u>wear</u>) to the dinner party? _wear_

2. Employment in the steel industry acts as a weather (<u>vane</u>—vein—vain) reflecting employment in the whole economy. _vane_

3. We cannot tell you (<u>whether</u>—weather) they will make any changes in their spring prices. _whether_

4. Even today we hear of (which—<u>witch</u>) hunts. _witch_

5. The ox broke his (yolk—<u>yoke</u>). _yoke_

6. (<u>Tears</u>—Tiers) of unhappiness came cascading from the bride's eyes. _Tears_

7. A (troop—<u>troupe</u>) of U.S.O. singers entertained the soldiers in the field. _troupe_

8. In the circulatory system, (vanes—<u>veins</u>—vains) carry blood to the heart. _veins_

9. Her voice has a pleasant, vibrant (<u>timbre</u>—timber). _timbre_

10. The carpenter put the board in a (<u>vise</u>—vice). _vise_

C In some of the following sentences an incorrect word is used; cross it out and write the correct word in the space provided. Where there is no error write **C** in the space.

1. When checking your diet, always ~~way~~ yourself at the same time of day. _weigh_

2. I came in at the ~~tale~~ end of the meeting. _tail_

3. One of the carpenter's most essential tools is the ~~vice~~. _vise_

4. Among the gifts for the bride, fine ~~kitchenwear~~ was included. _kitchenware_

5. He could not decide whether or not to sign the ~~waver~~ relinquishing his claim to the property. _waiver_

6. In mythology Narcissus was a ~~vane~~ young man. _vain_

7. The sight of a mountain of whipped cream ~~wet~~ his appetite. _whet_

8. Most of the important nutrients of an egg are found in its yolk. _C_

9. Mother made a seven-tier layer cake for Bob's homecoming party. _C_

10. The men struck a ~~vain~~ of gold. _vein_

150

WORDS
Ending in ary-ery
Ending in efy-ify

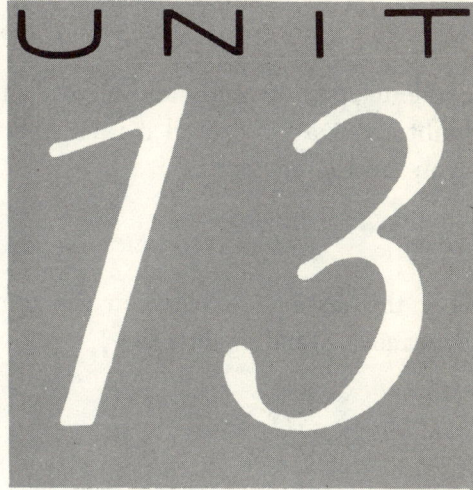

UNIT
13

Words Ending in ary-ery

You can solve your **ary-ery** problems very simply. Just concentrate on these seven words that end in **ery:**

cemet<u>ery</u>   distill<u>ery</u>   millin<u>ery</u>   station<u>ery</u>
                                                                    (writing paper)
confection<u>ery</u>   dysent<u>ery</u>*   monast<u>ery</u>

These are the only ones that are likely to pose any problem whatsoever for you. There are other words that end in **ery**—but hardly anyone ever misspells them:

artill<u>ery</u>   cel<u>ery</u>   flatt<u>ery</u>

bak<u>ery</u>   fin<u>ery</u>   v<u>ery</u>

Once you've fixed these seven in your mind:

cemet<u>ery</u>   distill<u>ery</u>   milli<u>nery</u>   station<u>ery</u>

confection<u>ery</u>   dysent<u>ery</u>   monast<u>ery</u>

you will be able to spell correctly and almost automatically the words that end in **ary.** When you're in doubt about a word (and it's not one of the seven), you'll be right in almost every instance if you use the **ary** ending.

Note carefully the distinction between the word station**ery** (meaning, writing **paper**) and stationary (meaning, standing in place).

arbitr<u>ary</u>*   imagin<u>ary</u>   moment<u>ary</u>   salut<u>ary</u>*

contempor<u>ary</u>   infirm<u>ary</u>   not<u>ary</u>*   solit<u>ary</u>

diet<u>ary</u>   judici<u>ary</u>*   prelimin<u>ary</u>   tempor<u>ary</u>

emiss<u>ary</u>*   liter<u>ary</u>   prim<u>ary</u>   tribut<u>ary</u>

exempl<u>ary</u>*   lumin<u>ary</u>*   propriet<u>ary</u>*   vision<u>ary</u>

honor<u>ary</u>   mission<u>ary</u>   pulmon<u>ary</u>*   volunt<u>ary</u>

Words Ending in efy-ify

Memorize only four words—and you have solved all your problems with words in these two groups. Only four words end in the suffix **efy**.

liqu<u>efy</u>*   putr<u>efy</u>*   rar<u>efy</u>*   stup<u>efy</u>*

Follow the same procedure here as you've done for all other exceptions to spelling rules: *Concentrate on the exceptions*. Study them carefully. Write each one a few times. Try to visualize each in your mind's eye. With these four words safely salted away, your troubles are over. In practically every other instance where you have to choose between **ify** and **efy**, your answer will be **ify**.

class<u>ify</u>	glor<u>ify</u>	pur<u>ify</u>	rect<u>ify</u>*
ed<u>ify</u>*	mod<u>ify</u>	qual<u>ify</u>	spec<u>ify</u>
fort<u>ify</u>	pac<u>ify</u>*	rat<u>ify</u>*	test<u>ify</u>

When the **efy** words add suffixes or change their forms, the **e** is still retained before the **f**.

liqu<u>efy</u>	liqu<u>efy</u>ing	liqu<u>efi</u>ed	liqu<u>ef</u>action
putr<u>efy</u>	putr<u>efy</u>ing	putr<u>efi</u>ed	putr<u>ef</u>action
rar<u>efy</u>	rar<u>efy</u>ing	rar<u>efi</u>ed	rar<u>ef</u>action
stup<u>efy</u>	stup<u>efy</u>ing	stup<u>efi</u>ed	stup<u>ef</u>action

13 | Words Often Confused

Words that sound almost alike—for example, **accept** and **except**—are frequently confused by the untrained secretary. Like homonyms, they are often written with the same shorthand outline and must be transcribed in terms of their context. Accordingly, the successful secretary must know the exact meanings of such words so that she always transcribes the proper word correctly and automatically.

accelerate—exhilarate

accelerate *(ak-SELL-uh-rate)*—to cause to go or to happen faster: *By working this pedal you will accelerate the motor.*

exhilarate *(eg-ZILL-uh-rate)*—stimulate, put into high spirits: *Most people feel exhilarated in cold, snappy weather.*

accept—except

accept *(ak-sept)*—to receive or to take something that is offered: *I accept your apology. The driver will accept all packages after 5 P.M.*

except *(ek-sept)*—other than, to take or leave out: *Send us everything except the mimeograph paper and stencils. Tell no one except me.*

addition—edition

addition *(a as in add)*—the act or process of adding, something added: *Miss Jones will be a valuable addition to our secretarial staff.*

edition *(e as in editor)*—all the copies of a book, newspaper, or magazine issued at the same time:
The first edition of THE JUNGLE *is now a collector's item.*

admission—admittance

admission—the act of allowing a person to enter; the price or fee paid for being allowed to enter; acknowledgment or confession that something is true.
The Immigration Service will act on the admission of aliens into this country.
The admission fee is one dollar.
Jackson's admission of his part in the failure of the company surprised everyone.

admittance—almost always used in the sense of "being allowed to enter."
The familiar NO ADMITTANCE *sign means you are not allowed to enter. A* NO ADMISSION *sign would mean you may enter without paying any fee.*

adapt—adept—adopt

adapt—to adjust, to make fit or suitable, to modify or alter for a different purpose:
We can't take your plan as is. We'll have to adapt it to our own needs.
When you adapt yourself to a new job, you adjust yourself to new conditions and demands.
This adaption will take time.

154

adept—very skilful: *A good carpenter is adept in the use of his tools.*

adopt—to take for one's own, to take (a child of other parents) and bring up as one's own, to accept formally:
Our company will adopt a new payroll plan next January.
Bill and Mary decided to adopt a child.
At its last meeting, the Executive Board adopted the Finance Committee's report.

adverse—averse

adverse—(watch the *d*)—unfriendly (adverse criticism), unfavorable, harmful:
The company managed to survive even under adverse conditions.

averse—opposed, unwilling:
We are averse to making new investments at this time.
We have an aversion to making investments just now.
These two words can be troublesome. But it's easy to master them. Don't try to guess at which one to use. Study the meaning and spelling of each one carefully. Then you will be sure—and you will be correct all the time.

advice—advise

advice (rhymes with *ice*)—an opinion about what should be done: *Most people give advice (very often good advice) quite liberally.*
Unfortunately, those who need this advice do not always take it.

advise (rhymes with *size*)—to tell others what one thinks is good for them to do or say:
The auditor advised the president of the company to take his advice not to cut salaries.

affect—effect

affect—a verb meaning to influence, to stir the emotions or the mind; also, to pretend, to assume the character or the appearance of:
The policies of the Federal Reserve Bank affect our whole economy.
Jazz music does not affect (move or stir) some people at all.
Some really bright people affect (pretend) ignorance. They are said to have an "affectation."

effect—most commonly used as a noun meaning result, outcome, consequence of; accomplishment or fulfillment; impression:
The effect (consequence) of the new taxes was felt in every business.
Every member of the staff must work hard to put the new payroll incentive plan into effect (fulfillment).
The painting produced a startling effect (impression) on the audience.

Note: Effects (plural) also means goods or possessions: *household effects, business effects,* etc.

alley—ally

alley (rhymes with *valley*)—narrow, back street; a place for bowling.

ally—noun (a-LIE) or (A-lie)—person or nation united with another person or nation:
England was our ally in World War II.

ally—verb (a-LIE)—to unite by formal agreement as by a treaty or alliance:
A weak nation will naturally want to ally itself with a stronger nation.

all ready—already

all ready—completely ready:
The filing cabinets are all ready to be shipped.

already—by this time, before the time, even now, by now:
When we called, we found that the weather stations had already been alerted.

Score_____

13 | Assignments

A Insert **ary** or **ery** (whichever is correct) in the spaces in the following words. Then rewrite the complete word on the line to the right.

1. secret*ary* — *secretary*
2. diction*ary* — *dictionary*
3. cemet*ery* — *cemetery*
4. ✓ sedent*ary*
5. actu*ary* — *actuary*
6. millin*ery* — *millinery*
7. diet*ary* — *dietary*
8. comment*ary* — *commentary*
9. liter*ary* — *literary*
10. gran*ary* — *granary*
11. emiss*ary*
12. infirm*ary*
13. monast*ery*
14. vocabul*ary*
15. distill*ery*

16. dispens*ary*
17. cel*ery*
18. bak*ery*
19. flatt*ery*
20. artill*ery*
21. dysent*ery*
22. advers*ary*
23. dignit*ary*
24. station*ary* *(standing still)*
25. station*ery* *(paper)*
26. confection*ery*
27. prelimin*ary*
28. arbitr*ary*
29. contempor*ary*
30. judici*ary*

157

B Insert **ify** or **efy** (whichever is correct) in the spaces in the following words. Then rewrite the complete word on the line to the right.

1. mod_ify_ — _modify_
2. ed_ify_ — _edify_
3. glor_ify_ — _glorify_
4. myst_ify_ — _mystify_
5. liqu_efy_ — _liquefy_
6. qual_ify_ — _qualify_
7. spec_ify_ — _specify_
8. fort_ify_ — _fortify_
9. rect_ify_ — _rectify_
10. pur_ify_ — _purify_

11. rar_efy_ — _rarefy_
12. class_ify_ — _classify_
13. rat_ify_ — _ratify_
14. putr_efy_ — _putrefy_
15. test_ify_ — _testify_
16. stup_efy_ — _stupefy_
17. pac_ify_ — _pacify_
18. cruc_ify_ — _crucify_
19. ampl_ify_ — _amplify_
20. d_____ — _defy_

C Cross out the misspelled words in the following groups of three. Spell the misspelled words correctly in the spaces at the right. If there are no misspelled words in a group, mark it **C**.

1. ~~rarify~~   vilify   codify — _rarefy_
2. mollify   edify   crucify — _C_
3. ~~liquify~~   signify   ~~glorefy~~ — _liquefy, glorify_
4. ~~stupify~~   pacify   ~~classefy~~ — _stupefy, classify_
5. beautify   certify   putrefy — _C_
6. ~~falsefy~~   verify   ~~notefy~~ — _falsify   notify_
7. diversefy   ~~justefy~~   ratify — _justify_
8. exemplify   ~~typefy~~   ~~personefy~~ — _typify, personify_
9. ~~gratefy~~   simplify   indemnify — _gratify_
10. humidify   identify   terrify — _C_

13 | Words Often Confused
Assignments

A Select from the following words the one that correctly fits into the blank in each of the sentences below. Then write it in the space provided.

addition	admission	accept	adopt	accelerate
edition	Admittance	except	adapt	exhilarate

1. Opening the valve will _____ the flow of water. ...... *accelerate*

2. Mr. Axtel tells me that we cannot _____ the terms you are offering. .... *accept*

3. When the _____ to our factory is completed, we shall be able to make more and faster deliveries. .... *addition*

4. Children under fourteen will not have to pay any _____ charge. .... *admission*

5. We can _____ this new blower to fit any old vacuum cleaner you may have. .... *adapt*

6. The mere thought that he might succeed would _____ him for days. .... *ex exhilarate*

7. We do not permit our name brands to be sold to anyone _____ licensed dealers. .... *except*

8. The second _____ of Mooney's "Financial Figures" was published yesterday. .... *edition*

9. An armed guard stood in front of the No _____ sign. .... *admittance*

10. There are thousands of couples eager to _____ children. *adopt*

B   In the following sentences underline the word in parentheses that makes the sentence correct. Then write it in the space provided.

1. Our (advice—advise) to all our customers is to buy from only reputable dealers. ....   *advice*

2. (Averse—Adverse) economic conditions reflect themselves immediately in the falling sales of durable goods such as automobiles. ....

3. Did the recent changes in the Federal Tax laws (effect—affect) your company? ....   *affect*

4. Now that I have all my things, I am (already—all ready) to go. ....   *all ready*

5. This place is so pleasant, we are (adverse—averse) to going home. ....

6. We (advice—advise) you to hold down your production costs.   *advise*

7. Our company is not at all (averse—adverse) to extending you all the credit you will need for the next thirty days. ....

8. The large doses of antibiotics had no (effect—affect) on the patient's condition. ....   *effect*

9. Under present world conditions, we need every (alley—ally) we can get. ....   *ally*

10. When we arrived at the station, we discovered that Fontaine had (already—all ready) left. ....   *already*

C   In some of the following sentences an incorrect word is used; cross it out and write the correct word in the space provided. Where there is no error write **C** in the space.

1. The man at the ~~newsstand~~ said that the evening ~~addition~~ of the Tribune had been sold out. ....   *edition*   *a newsstand*

2. Many people feel they are accelerated by a long, brisk walk on a cold winter's day. ....   *& exhilarated*

3. It takes many years of practice to become ~~adopt~~ at playing the 'cello. ....   *adept*

4. Any unused merchandise will be ~~excepted~~ by us for exchange.   *accepted*

5. Susan was elated when she learned that she had been accepted for fall entrance at college. ....   *C*

Score_____

13 | Vocabulary Enrichment
Exercise

Below is a list of words with which you should be
fully familiar. In the space provided, fill in the word
that best completes the meaning of the sentence.

inevitable	affable	wring
irrevocable	balked	reprehensible
wrangle	susceptible	vulnerable
inexorable	formidable	amicable

1. The election caused a bitter _____ between the two
opposing factions. . . . . _wrangle_

2. The horse _____ at jumping the six-foot fence. . . . . . . _balked_

3. The two partners settled their differences in an _____
manner and resumed running their business with even greater
efficiency. . . . . _affable_ ✓

4. Despite their attempts to change his mind, he stubbornly
maintained that his decision was _____. . . . . _irrevocable_

5. The judge said that he had never seen such disgraceful and
_____ behavior in his court. . . . . _reprehensible_ ✓

6. Due to Mrs. Smith's _____ knowledge of educational
theory, it was difficult to dispute her findings. . . . . _formidable_

7. Constantinople fell to the Turks because its fortified walls
proved _____ to cannon fire. . . . . _susceptible_

8. Since wages went up, it was _____ that prices would
rise too. . . . . _inevitable_

9. The prosecuting attorney was relentless and _____ in
his attempt to convict the defendant. . . . . _inexorable_ ✓

10. Despite many precautions by the Medical Corps, many soldiers proved _____ to malaria during the war. . . . . . . _vulnerable_

There are misspelled words in some of the following sentences. Cross out each misspelled word and write the correct spelling in the space provided. If there are no misspelled words, write **C** in the space next to the sentence.

1. Mr. John McMann bought all of his ~~stationary~~ supplies from us. *stationery*

2. The future looks very bright for your firm. .... *C*

3. Please ~~notefy~~ me as soon as the X rays are ready. .... *notify*

4. Model ~~kiehens~~ are now on display for your inspection. ...... *kitchens*

5. Plastic ~~rappers~~ are used exclusively in packaging these household ~~wears~~. .... *wrappers, wares*

6. We carry a large stock of ~~plumming~~ supplies. .... *plumbing*

7. The man was ~~arrained~~ before Judge Herman. .... *arraign* *arraigned*

8. A survey will be made in the state of Rhode ~~Iland~~ this fall. .... *Island*

9. A series of ~~preliminery~~ hearings will be held in the case of White versus Brandon. .... *preliminary*

10. Your note was due and payable on July 15. .... *C*

11. This settlement is not satisfactory to me because I am convinced that the accident is responsible for my present condition. *C*

12. Let me know ~~weath~~er you will be availible from 10 to 12 a.m. on September 15. .... *whether*

13. This office would be suitable for ~~temporery~~ quarters until the first of the year. .... *temporary*

14. Use the enclosed card to specify the quantity and quality you will need. .... *C*

15. The present volume of business does not ~~justefy~~ an additional expense. .... *justify*

WORDS
Ending in ance-ence

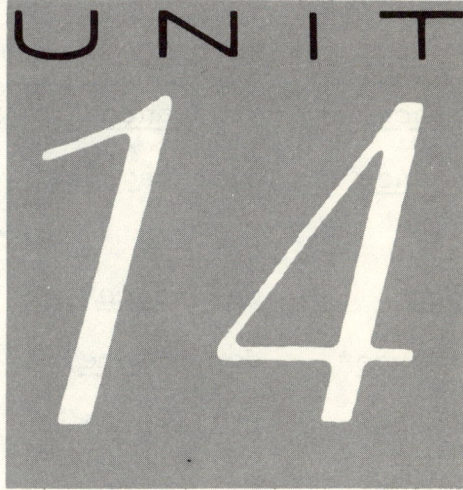

The only way to master these words is to get the "feel" of them. Look at them. Mentally picture them. Write them again and again until you are certain which ending is correct.

ance

abey<u>ance</u>*	assur<u>ance</u>	forbear<u>ance</u>*	relev<u>ance</u>
abund<u>ance</u>	attend<u>ance</u>	fragr<u>ance</u>	reluct<u>ance</u>
accept<u>ance</u>	brilli<u>ance</u>	griev<u>ance</u>	reli<u>ance</u>
accord<u>ance</u>	clear<u>ance</u>	guid<u>ance</u>	repent<u>ance</u>
acquaint<u>ance</u>	compli<u>ance</u>	hindr<u>ance</u>	resist<u>ance</u>
admitt<u>ance</u>	continu<u>ance</u>	ignor<u>ance</u>	remitt<u>ance</u>
allegi<u>ance</u>	contriv<u>ance</u>*	inherit<u>ance</u>	rom<u>ance</u>

alliance	conveyance*	insurance	significance
allowance	defiance	importance	substance
ambulance	deliverance	maintenance	sustenance*
annoyance	distance	nuisance	temperance
appearance	entrance	observance	tolerance
arrogance	endurance	performance	vengeance
assistance	extravagance	perseverance	vigilance

ence

absence	deference*	influence	precedence*
abstinence*	dependence	innocence	preference
adherence*	diligence*	insistence	presence
affluence	eloquence	insolence	prominence
audience	essence*	intelligence	quintessence*
benevolence	excellence	interference	recurrence*
commence	existence	irreverence	reference
competence*	experience	lenience*	reminiscence*
condolence*	impatience	negligence*	residence
conference	impertinence	obedience	reticence*
confidence	impudence	obsolescence*	reverence*
consequence	incompetence	occurrence	sentence
convalescence	independence	penitence	subsistence*
convenience	indulgence	permanence	transference
corpulence*	inference	persistence	violence

14 | Words Often Confused

all together—altogether

all together—gathered in a group:
After a long separation, we were all to-gether at last.

altogether—entirely, completely, all in-cluded:
It is altogether too early in the morning to have breakfast.

allude—elude

allude—to mention casually; to refer to in-directly:
In the course of his talk, Larkins alluded occasionally to his European adventures.

elude—to avoid or escape by cunning or quickness; to escape detection:
The criminal successfully eluded the police dragnet.

allusion—illusion

allusion (from *allude*)—a passing, casual, or indirect reference:
A classical allusion: *He had the strength of a Hercules.*
A Biblical allusion: *He had as many troubles as did Job.*
A Shakespearean allusion: *His character was somewhat like Hamlet's.*
His allusion to our failures was not in the best of taste.

illusion—something that deceives by pro-ducing a false impression:
A mirage (seeing water in the desert where there is no water) is an illusion, an impres-sion that is false.

angel—angle

angel (*g* pronounced like *j* in *jell* because it is followed by a softening *e*)—attendant and messenger of God, a good spirit, a good, lovely or innocent person.

angle (*g* pronounced like *g* in *good*)—the geometric measurement of two intersecting lines; also a point of view, an aspect, a phase of something:
Viewed from this angle, the house looks larger.

appraise—apprise

appraise—to estimate the value or quality of an object; to set or fix the value:
The jeweler appraised the ring at $200. His appraisal was accurate.

apprise—to give notice, to inform, to ad-vise:
We shall apprise you of any change in our prices.

assistants—assistance

assistants—helpers:
Our new manager will have two assistants.

assistance—help:
These two assistants will give him all the assistance he needs.

ballad—ballot—ballet

ballad—a romantic or sentimental song; a song or poem, usually of unknown authorship:
He sang old English ballads before a large audience.

ballot—a ticket or form by which a vote is registered; the act or method of voting.
He cast his vote by putting his ballot into the box.

ballet (BAL ay)—an intricate group dance using pantomime and stylized movements to tell a story:
She danced the ballet with the grace of Pavlova.

beside—besides

beside—at the side of:
Sit down beside the desk.

besides—in addition to:
There will be others at the convention besides our representative.

bet—beat

bet (rhymes with *set*)—to wager:
Harcourt bet Jackson a hundred dollars that the stock market would remain steady.

beat (rhymes with *seat*)—to defeat, to conquer:
Our new product is sure to beat anything our competitors can offer.

breath—breathe—breadth

breath (rhymes with *death*)—air taken in and given out in breathing: *a single breath.*

breathe (rhymes with *seethe*)—the act of taking breaths, to inhale and exhale:
Breathe deeply before you dive into the water.

breadth (pronounced *bredth*)—distance from side to side. (Spelling Aid: **dth** as in *wi***dth**.)
This street has a breadth of 35 feet.

14 Assignments

A Insert **ance** or **ence** (whichever is correct) in the spaces in the following words. Then rewrite the complete word on the line to the right.

1. abhorr*ence* _____

2. defer*ence* _____

3. abund*ance* _____

4. refer*ence* _____

5. accept*ance* _____

6. concurr*ance* _____

7. admitt*ance* _____

8. confer*ence* _____

9. prefer*ence* _____

10. occurr*ence* _____

11. brilli*ance* _____

12. allegi*ance* _____

13. allow*ance* _____

14. abs*ence* _____

15. assist*ance* _____

16. clear*ance* _____

17. compet*ence* _____

18. confid*ence* _____

19. diffid*ence* _____

20. preval*ance* *ence* _____

21. repent*ence* _____

22. deliver*ance* _____

23. persist*ence* _____

24. toler*ance* _____

25. transfer*ence* _____

26. extravag*ance* _____

27. subsist*ance* _____

28. exist*ance* _____

29. mainten*ence* *ance* _____

30. promin*ence* _____

B Cross out the misspelled word or words in each of the following groups of words and spell them correctly in the space at the right. If there are no errors, mark **C** in the space.

1. compliance ~~excellance~~ defiance — *excellence*
2. ~~fragrance~~ hindrance irrelevance — *fragrance* C
3. ~~insurence~~ audience benevolence — *insurance*
4. diligence eloquence experience — C
5. remittance substance ~~temperence~~ — *temperance*
6. conveyance interference innocence — C
7. irreverence transference reticence — C
8. annoyance abeyance prominence — C
9. ~~entrence~~ repentance romance — *entrance*
10. diligence adherence condolence — C
11. reference abhorrence concurrence — C
12. ~~recurrance~~ reverence acceptance — *recurrence*
13. residence admittence ~~assurence~~ — *assurance*
14. ~~violence~~ alliance allegiance — *violence* C
15. ~~hindrence~~ ignorance maintenance — *hindrance*
16. resistance arrogance vigilance —
17. importance affluance consequence —
18. absence innocence reluctance —
19. abstinence eloquence precedence —
20. reliance dependence existance —

168

14 | Words Often Confused
Assignments

A Select from the following words the one that correctly fits into each blank in the sentences below. Then write it in the space provided.

all together	allusions	assistants	apprise	angle
altogether	illusions	assistance	appraise	angel

1. Our family is _____ at last. . . . . *all together*

2. Did you understand Mr. Farrell's _____ to last year's figures? . . . . *allusions*

3. The religious book was illustrated with the picture of an _____. . . . . *angel*

4. Drop in whenever you can and we'll be happy to _____ your jewels and furs. . . . . *appraise*

5. When Mr. Manlius became office manager, he added two _____ to his staff. . . . . *assistants*

6. Our accountants think that the clerical staff is making _____ too many errors. . . . . *altogether*

7. Magicians fool their audiences by creating optical _____. *illusions*

8. The beam juts out from the building at an _____ of 20 degrees. . . . . *angle*

9. We feel it our duty to _____ you of the dangers you must expect. . . . . *apprise*

10. We now are doing so well that we shall be able to get along with very little _____. . . . . *assistance*

B In the following sentences underline the word in parentheses that makes the sentence correct. Then write it in the space provided.

1. We did not recognize the person who was sitting (<u>beside</u>—besides) you at the last convention. . . . . *beside*

2. No matter how long the odds, Markson was willing to (beat—<u>bet</u>). . . . . *bet*

3. The doctor detected the odor of liquor on the man's (breathe—<u>breath</u>). . . . . *breath*

4. Who is expected at the party (<u>besides</u>—beside) you and your immediate family? . . . . *besides*

5. Before he mixed the ingredients, he (<u>beat</u>—bet) the eggs thoroughly. . . . . *beat*

6. Mary was dressed as an (angle—<u>angel</u>) for the school play. . . *angel*

7. His (<u>allusion</u>—illusion) to the fact that our integrity in the matter might be questioned greatly disturbed the president of the company. . . . . *allusion*

8. The Police Commissioner was convinced that there had been (all together—<u>altogether</u>) too many juvenile crimes. . . . . *altogether*

9. It is rewarding to offer your (assistants—<u>assistance</u>) as a volunteer worker in the children's ward of a hospital. . . . . *assistance*

10. The value of my sapphire ring was (apprised—<u>appraised</u>) at $500. . . . . *appraised*

C In some of the following sentences an incorrect word is used; cross it out and write the correct word in the space provided. Where there is no error write **C** in the space.

1. The same object can look entirely different when viewed from different angles. . . . . *C*

2. Although he tried to avoid it, Mr. Johnson could not help ~~eluding~~ to the fact that our bill was overdue. . . . . *at alluding*

3. After much consideration, the Board unanimously cast their ~~ballads~~ for Mr. Jackson as president. . . . . *ballots*

4. ~~Beside~~ being a world-renowned poet, he excelled in playwriting, too. . . . . *Besides*

5. The reunion group was ~~altogether~~ when Mr. Blake arrived. . . *all together*

WORDS
Ending in ant–ent

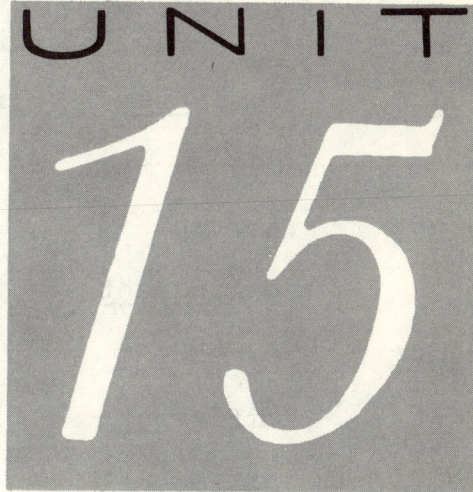

UNIT 15

The story is the same here as for the **ance-ence** words. Here are some of the most commonly misspelled **ant-ent** words.

ant

abund<u>ant</u>	def<u>iant</u>	import<u>ant</u>	reluct<u>ant</u>
account<u>ant</u>	descend<u>ant</u>	inhabit<u>ant</u>	remn<u>ant</u>
applic<u>ant</u>	disinfect<u>ant</u>	irrelev<u>ant</u>*	repent<u>ant</u>*
arrog<u>ant</u>	dist<u>ant</u>	insignific<u>ant</u>	repugn<u>ant</u>*
assail<u>ant</u>	domin<u>ant</u>	lieuten<u>ant</u>	resist<u>ant</u>
assist<u>ant</u>	dorm<u>ant</u>	malign<u>ant</u>*	reson<u>ant</u>*
attend<u>ant</u>	eleg<u>ant</u>	observ<u>ant</u>	restaur<u>ant</u>

brilli<u>ant</u>   exorbit<u>ant</u>*   occup<u>ant</u>   signific<u>ant</u>

buo<u>yant</u>   extravag<u>ant</u>   page<u>ant</u>   stimul<u>ant</u>

compli<u>ant</u>   exuber<u>ant</u>*   penn<u>ant</u>   ten<u>ant</u>

convers<u>ant</u>   frag<u>rant</u>   petul<u>ant</u>*   vag<u>rant</u>*

coven<u>ant</u>*   gall<u>ant</u>   pleas<u>ant</u>   vigil<u>ant</u>*

defend<u>ant</u>   igno<u>rant</u>   relev<u>ant</u>*   war<u>rant</u>*

ent

abhor<u>rent</u>*   current   impat<u>ient</u>   irreve<u>rent</u>*

abs<u>ent</u>   delinqu<u>ent</u>   impertin<u>ent</u>   magnific<u>ent</u>

adja<u>cent</u>*   depend<u>ent</u>   impud<u>ent</u>*   obedi<u>ent</u>

afflu<u>ent</u>*   differ<u>ent</u>   incandes<u>cent</u>*   oppon<u>ent</u>

anci<u>ent</u>   diffid<u>ent</u>*   incohe<u>rent</u>*   perman<u>ent</u>

bellige<u>rent</u>*   dili<u>gent</u>   incompet<u>ent</u>*   persist<u>ent</u>*

benevo<u>lent</u>*   effici<u>ent</u>   inconsistent   pertin<u>ent</u>*

cli<u>ent</u>   eloqu<u>ent</u>*   incumb<u>ent</u>*   pres<u>ent</u>

compet<u>ent</u>*   emin<u>ent</u>*   independ<u>ent</u>   preval<u>ent</u>*

compon<u>ent</u>   evid<u>ent</u>   inno<u>cent</u>   promin<u>ent</u>

concur<u>rent</u>   excell<u>ent</u>   inso<u>lent</u>*   prud<u>ent</u>*

confid<u>ent</u>   expedi<u>ent</u>*   insol<u>vent</u>*   quoti<u>ent</u>*

constitu<u>ent</u>*   expon<u>ent</u>*   insuffici<u>ent</u>   recur<u>rent</u>

convales<u>cent</u>   fraudu<u>lent</u>*   insur<u>gent</u>*   resid<u>ent</u>

conveni<u>ent</u>   frequ<u>ent</u>   intelli<u>gent</u>   superintend<u>ent</u>

correspond<u>ent</u>   immin<u>ent</u>*   intermitt<u>ent</u>*   viol<u>ent</u>

Words Often Confused

bibliography—biography

bibliography—a list of books or articles about a subject or person, or by an author:
He compiled an extensive bibliography of articles on automation.

biography—story of a person's life written by someone else:
Carl Van Doren has written what is probably the finest biography of Benjamin Franklin.

carton—cartoon

carton (*CAR-ton*)—box generally made of cardboard.

cartoon (*car-TOON*)—an exaggerated, amusing, or humorous sketch or line drawing, generally poking fun at people or events.

causal—casual

causal—implying a cause:
There is a causal connection between rising prices and rising profits and wages.

casual (three syllables)—happening by chance: *a casual meeting;* offhand, unpremeditated: *a casual remark;* careless, negligent: *casual air or casual dress;* occasional, irregular: *a casual worker or visitor.*

cease—seize

cease (rhymes with *geese*)—to stop:
The President called upon all nations to cease arming.

seize (rhymes with *sneeze*)—to take hold of suddenly or violently; to take possession by force:
The cargo was seized on the high seas by a band of pirates.

censor—censure

censor—to examine things like motion pictures, mail, etc., and to prohibit anything considered unsuitable; a person whose task it is to perform such functions:
In wartime, the censors read the mail of suspected persons.

censure (*SEN-shur*)—to blame, to condemn as wrong:
The principal censured the entire school for the disorder.

clothes—cloths

clothes (rhymes with *loathes*)—wearing apparel such as suits, dresses, and skirts:
Civilized people wear clothes.

cloths (rhymes with *moths*)—fabrics:
The yardgoods section at the department store is showing its new line of cloths.

collision—collusion

collision—coming into violent contact; a crash:
Ten people died in the collision of a bus with a passenger car.

collusion—a secret understanding between two or more persons to cheat or defraud or damage the interest of a third person:
The king was overthrown as a result of collusion among members of his own cabinet.

coma—comma

coma *(KO-ma)*—a state of prolonged unconsciousness from which it is difficult or impossible to arouse a person:
Sergeant Filmore fell into a coma shortly after he was injured in an automobile accident.

comma *(KOM-ma)*—a mark of punctuation (,):
Have you mastered the uses of the comma?

command—commend—comment

command—to direct, to order, to be in control of:
General Wingate will command the First Army.

command—an order, a directive, authority, power, control:
A soldier must learn to obey every command.

commend—to mention favorably, to praise:
The wise employer will commend his employees when their work merits recognition. They appreciate this commendation.

comment—a casual remark:
The speaker made a brief comment about the proceedings.

compromise—comprise

compromise *(KOM-pra-mize)*—a settlement in which each side makes concessions, or the result of such settlement; exposure of one's reputation to danger, suspicion, or disrepute:
The strike was settled by a compromise of the demands of labor and the position of management.
To reverse my stand on civil liberties would compromise my reputation with the voting public.

comprise *(kom-PRIZE)*—to include, to consist of:
The set comprises ten volumes bound in leather.

15 | Assignments

A Add **ant** or **ent** (whichever is correct) to the following roots; then write the complete word in the space provided.

1. **account** ant	*accountant*	16. **intellig** ent — *intelligent*
2. **benevol** ent	*benevolent*	17. **innoc** ent — *innocent*
3. **abund** ant	*abundant*	18. **assist** ant — *assistant*
4. **resid** ent	*resident*	19. **reluct** ant — *reluctant*
5. **dilig** ent	*diligent*	20. **brilli** ant — *brilliant*
6. **eloqu** ent	*eloquent*	21. **exuber** ~~ent~~ ant — *exuberant*
7. **descend** ant	*descendant*	22. **observ** ant — *observant*
8. **defend** ant	*defendant*	23. **inhabit** ant — *inhabitant*
9. **independ** ~~ant~~ ent	*independent*	24. **afflu** ent — *affluent*
10. **depend** ent	*dependent*	25. **incompet** ~~ent~~ ~~ant~~ — *incompetent*
11. **pres** ent	*present*	26. **insol** ent — *insolent*
12. **excell** ent	*excellent*	27. **applic** ant — *applicant*
13. **ignor** ant	*ignorant*	28. **assail** ant — *assailant*
14. **occup** ant	*occupant*	29. **perman** ent — *permanent*
15. **vigil** ant	*vigilant*	30. **incumb** ent — *incumbent*

175

B Cross out the misspelled word or words in each of the following groups of words and spell them correctly in the space at the right. If there are no errors, mark **C** in the space.

1. ~~irreverant~~ compliant disinfectant — *irreverent*
2. restaurant ~~existant~~ impatient — *existent*
3. ~~attendent~~ insignificant observant — *attendant*
4. pleasant obedient persistent — *C*
5. prevalent impudent ~~impatiant~~ — *impatient*
6. distant important ~~irrelevent~~ — *irrelevant*
7. deficient extravagant (repentent) — *C   repentant*
8. observant prevalent ~~arrogant~~ — *arrogant C*
9. abundant ambulant ~~convalescant~~ — *convalescent*
10. brilliant attendant ~~complient~~ — *compliant*
11. abhorrent distant ~~entrant~~ — *entrent C*
12. extravagant fragrant ~~ignorent~~ — *ignorant*
13. ~~irrelevent~~ important diligent — *irrelevant*
14. reluctant reliant ~~resistent~~ — *resistant*
15. significant petulant vigilant — *C*
16. ~~excellant~~ absent ~~independant~~ — *excellent, independent*
17. competent ~~confident~~ eloquent — *confidant C*
18. impatient permanent innocent — *C*
19. ~~obediant~~ insolent persistent — *obedient, persistant*
20. present pertinent reticent — *C*

15 | Words Often Confused
Assignments

A Select from the following words the one that correctly fits into the blank in each of the sentences below. Then write it in the space provided.

| compromise | censor | ceased | casual | cartoon | bibliography |
| comprised | censure | seized | causal | carton | biography |

1. Before you proceed, you will have to compile a _____ of books on the subject. ....   *bibliography*

2. These bottles come packed one hundred in each _____.   *carton*

3. I never got to know Herbert too well. He was just a _____ acquaintance. ....   *casual*

4. The advertising agency _____ making exaggerated claims for its products after being cited by the F.C.C. ......   *ceased*

5. Have you read the most recent _____ of George Washington? ....   *biography*

6. The political _____ helps in molding public opinion...   *cartoon*

7. Economists are not sure about the _____ relationship between depressions and business policies. ....   *causal*

8. The harbor police _____ a boatload of contraband whiskey. ....   *a seized*

9. The city of New York is _____ of five boroughs. ......   *comprised*

10. Do not _____ your pupils without just cause. ....   *censure*

B In the following sentences underline the word in parentheses that makes the sentence correct. Then write it in the space provided.

1. When rain (~~seizes~~—ceases) the air smells fresh and clean. .... _____

2. The teacher (~~censored~~—censured) the pupil for talking out of turn. .... _____

3. After weeks of deliberation, the workers (~~comprised~~—compromised) on a new schedule. .... _____

4. Many people look at nothing but the (cartoons—~~cartons~~) in the newspaper. .... _____

5. The teacher (~~commanded~~—~~commented~~—commended) Bill for the fine work he had done. .... _____

6. One can find great enjoyment in reading (~~bibliographies~~—biographies) of famous persons. .... _____

7. Always be sure that you are using the (comma-~~coma~~) correctly. .... _____

8. The impact of the cars was so great that the noise of the (~~collusion~~—collision) could be heard blocks away. .... _____

9. A good secretary should always be dressed in neat (clothes—~~cloths~~). .... _____

10. Alan felt that Bob's (casual—~~causal~~) remark about his poor work was unnecessary. .... _____

C In some of the following sentences an incorrect word is used; cross it out and write the correct word in the space provided. Where there is no error, write **C** in the space.

1. Often your ~~causal~~ acquaintances become lifelong friends. .. *casual*

2. The doctors feared that the patient might never come out of the ~~comma~~. .... *coma*

3. When writing college term-papers, students may compile extensive ~~biographies~~. .... *bibliographies*

4. The actors were ~~commanded~~ by the director for their fine work. .... _____

5. Synthetic fibers can be woven into a variety of cloths. ...... *C*

15 | Review Exercise

There are misspelled words in some of the following sentences. Cross out each misspelled word and write the correct spelling in the space provided. If there are no misspelled words, write **C** in the space next to the sentence.

1. We owe a ~~det~~ of gratitude to all those who have sacrificed so much for our defense. . . . . *debt*

2. ~~Rythm~~ and ~~ryme~~ are two characteristics of poetry. . . . . *Rhythm, Rhyme*

3. Gershwin's "~~Rapsody~~" is known the world over. . . . . *"Rhapsody"*

4. The heir to the Warden millions made it a point of honor to be an hour late for every appointment. . . . . *C*

5. The couple brought back many ~~gastly~~ statues from Europe. . . *ghastly*

6. The choir sang a solem ~~hym~~. . . . . *hymn* — ½ *hymn*

7. The calf developed a fondness for ~~amonds~~. . . . . *almonds*

8. Eugene O'Neill is one of our great ~~playrights~~. . . . . *playwrights*

9. Bob ~~renched~~ his ~~rist~~ ~~restling~~ with friends. . . . . *wrenched, wrist wrestling*

10. The terrible ordeal he experienced left an ~~indelable~~ impression on the young boy. . . . . *indelible*

11. People with ~~affible~~ manners are likable. . . . . *affable*

12. The radio tower was visible for ten miles around. . . . . *C*

13. We are ~~reluctent~~ to recommend this man to you. We have serious doubts about his competence. . . . . *reluctant*

14. If you encounter any resistance or interference, call the main office immediately. . . . . *C*

15. There is a growing feeling that society must find some permanent protection against the ~~incorrigable~~ criminal. . . . . *incorrigible*

16. We are still trying to discover who is ~~responsable~~ for the reprehensible practices that have been allowed to go on unchecked. . . . . *responsible*

17. Since we have trained all our employees to write ~~legably~~, the number of complaints we now receive is negligible. . . . . *legibly*

18. The ~~cemetary~~ is just one mile from the millinery store. . . . *cemetery*

19. Please send two boxes of ~~stationary~~ to the Walker ~~Distillary~~. *stationery, Distillery*

20. You'll find the dictionary very valuable in your vocabulary study. . . . . *C*

21. The secretary posted the new dietary regulations in the infirmary and the ~~dispensery~~. . . . . *dispensary*

22. At the trial tomorrow, the chemists will testify that the gas under consideration will ~~liquify~~ at 0° centigrade. . . . . *liquefy*

23. The Council is sure to modify its stand and ~~ratefy~~ the treaty. *ratify*

24. Please let us know what has gone wrong with our shipment of hose. We are eager to rectify any errors. . . . . *C*

25. We understand that you have a ~~preferance~~ for an early conference this fall. . . . . *preference*

26. We hope there will be no recurrence of last week's unhappy occurrence. . . . . *C*

27. You have our ~~assurence~~ that our accountant will give you intelligent assistance. . . . . *assurance*

28. Present your grievances and annoyances to the proper authorities. . . . . *C*

29. The observant restaurant ~~attendent~~ put in his appearance at the employees' entrance. . . . . *attendant*

30. It is important that you recognize the need for more maintenance and inheritance ~~insurence~~. . . . . *insurance*

31. Baldwin was an ~~arrogent,~~ violent, ignorant man. . . . . *arrogant*

32. Mr. Bentley has our complete confidence. We can vouch for his competence, brilliance, and general excellence. . . . . *C*

33. Our experience has taught us that impudence and impatience are qualities that hamper a man on the job. . . . . *C*

34. ~~Persistance~~ and ~~independance~~ are likely to lead people to success in their chosen careers. . . . . *Persistence, independence*

35. A benevolent Providence watched over the Pilgrims when they landed on our shores. . . . . *C*

WORDS
Ending in ar–or–er

UNIT 16

There is really no simple rule or memory aid that will help you with words that end in **ar, or, er.** These words can be mastered, however, if you give them your full attention. You will find that most of the words on the following lists are familiar to you. So all you need do is concentrate on those few you aren't sure of.

The following are words you will frequently use:

ar

begg<u>ar</u>	coll<u>ar</u>	peculi<u>ar</u>	(schol<u>ar</u>)
burs<u>ar</u>*	doll<u>ar</u>	pol<u>ar</u>	simil<u>ar</u>
calend<u>ar</u>	famili<u>ar</u>	registr<u>ar</u>	singul<u>ar</u>
circul<u>ar</u>	(gramm<u>ar</u>)	regul<u>ar</u>	vic<u>ar</u>

er

adjuster	comptroller*	laborer	purchaser
advertiser	consumer	lawyer	receiver
adviser	designer	ledger	shipper
amplifier*	employer	manager	stenographer
appraiser	eraser	manufacturer	subscriber
beginner	farmer	merger	teacher
bookkeeper	foreigner	officer	teller
caterer	interpreter	passenger	treasurer
character	jeweler	prisoner	writer

or

accelerator	counselor	governor	solicitor
actor	creditor	incinerator*	spectator
administrator	debtor	indicator	sponsor
auditor*	depositor	inferior	successor
author	dictator	inventor	superior
aviator	distributor	investigator	supervisor
bachelor	doctor	janitor	surveyor
calculator	duplicator	operator	survivor
collector	editor	proprietor*	tabulator
commentator	educator	protector	tailor
competitor	elevator	radiator	tractor
conductor	emperor	realtor	traitor
contractor	escalator	refrigerator	vigor

16 | Words Often Confused

conscience—conscious

conscience—"The still, small voice" within us that helps us choose between right and wrong:
Her conscience bothered her because she had not done her homework.

conscious—to be aware of; able to feel:
The good secretary is conscious of her speech, dress, and manners. This consciousness makes her a better secretary.

consul—council—counsel

consul (*KON-sul*)—an official appointed by a government to live in a foreign city and look after his country's business interests and citizens living or visiting there:
Most foreign countries send a consul to New York. They reside in consulates.

council (*KOWN-sil*)—a group of people selected, appointed, or elected to make laws, settle questions, give advice, etc.:
The town council reported its findings and recommendations to the mayor.

counsel (*KOWN-sil*)—to advise:
We counsel you not to make any further investments in this company.

costume—custom

costume (*KOS-tume* or *KOST-yume*)—style of dress peculiar to a nation, class, or historical period; style of dress appropriate to a particular time or occasion; garments worn on the stage:
Elizabeth Taylor wears a most unusual costume in her latest motion picture.

custom (*KUSS-tim*)—the usual way of acting in given circumstances: *It is the custom in late December to give Christmas gifts.*

credible—creditable

credible—believable, reliable, trustworthy.
The jurors agreed that Tawney's testimony was credible.

creditable—worthy of credit, honorable, respectable:
Even when Marlin did not win the race, his car always turned in a creditable performance.

deceased—diseased

deceased (*de-SEEST*)-dead; a dead person:
The deceased had been known in his youth for his musical talent.

diseased (*dih-ZEEZD*)—sick, unhealthy, in a disordered condition:
One diseased chicken can infect a whole brood.

desert—dessert

desert *(DEZ-ert)*—a dry, barren, sandy, treeless region:
The caravan wound its way slowly over the desert.

desert *(dih-ZERT)*—to abandon, leave behind:
Do rats really desert a sinking ship?

dessert *(dih-ZERT)*—course served at the end of a meal:
If you must keep your weight down, stay away from rich desserts.

device—devise

device *(dih-VICE)*—machine; piece of mechanical apparatus; plan, scheme or trick:
We are sending you our latest defrosting device.

devise *(dih-VIZE)*—to plan, invent, think out:
Our engineers tell us that they will shortly be able to devise a manned rocket to the moon.

decent—descent

decent *(DEE-sint)*—proper, right, respectable, in good taste:
What we want for everyone in America are decent living conditions.

descent *(dee-SENT)*—coming down from a higher to a lower place:
The hiking party found the descent into the valley quite difficult.

diary—dairy

diary (three syllables)—periodic (daily, weekly, etc.) written account of what one has felt, thought, or experienced. The book in which this account is written is also called a diary:
Many executives find it most useful to keep a full and accurate diary of their business day.

dairy (two syllables)—farm, building, store, or business establishment where milk, cream, and milk products are kept, stored, produced, or sold:
The Ralston Dairy driver leaves milk at our door.

disapprove—disprove

disapprove (three syllables)—not to approve:
Mr. Blandings is sure to disapprove of your expense budget.

disprove (two syllables)—to prove that something is false or incorrect:
Bohr's research disproved earlier theories about the inside of the atom.

disburse—disperse

disburse—to pay out, to expend:
The paymaster disburses the funds of the company.

disperse—to break up and scatter in all directions; distribute widely:
When the tanks appeared, the enemy soldiers dispersed into the woods.

empire—umpire

empire—a group of countries or states under one ruler:
The capital of the British Empire is London. An empire is ruled by an emperor.

umpire—one who rules on the plays in a game; one who is chosen to settle a dispute:
The umpire at third base called the man out.

16 | Assignments

A   Cross out all misspelled words. Spell them correctly in the spaces provided. If the word is correctly spelled, write **C** in the space.

1. beggar	_C_	16. grammer	_grammar_
✓2. adjustor	_~~C~~ adjuster_	17. familiar	_C_
3. advertiser	_C ~~advertisor~~_	18. appraisor	_appraiser_
4. aviator	_C_	19. beginner	_C_
5. accelerater	_accelerator_	20. consumor	_consumer_
6. bursar	_C_	21. bookkeeper	_~~bo~~ C_
7. calender	_calendar_	22. tailer	_tailor_
8. cedar	_C_	23. tractor	_C_
9. circuler	_circular_	24. purchasor	_purchaser_
10. similar	_C_	25. registrer	_registrar_
11. coller	_collar_	26. peculiar	_C_
12. amplifior	_amplifier_	27. ~~polor~~	_polar_
13. author	_C_	28. ~~subscribor~~	_subscriber_
14. auditer	_auditor_	29. collector	_C_
15. singuler	_singular_	30. distributer	_distributor_

185

B Insert **ar**, **er**, or **or** (whichever is correct) in the spaces in the following words. Then rewrite the complete word on the line to the right.

1. tabul*ator* — *Tabular*
2. design*er* — *designer*
3. employ*er* — *employer*
4. deposit*or* — *depositor*
5. doct*or* — *doctor*
6. duplicat*or* — *duplicator*
7. eras*er* — *eraser*
8. interpret*er* — *interpreter*
9. lodg*er* — *lodger*
10. generat*or* — *generator*
11. invent*or* — *inventor*
12. indicat*or* — *indicator*
13. investigat*or* — *investigator*
14. lawy*er* — *lawyer*
15. manufactur*er* — *manufacturer*
16. merg*er* — *merger*
17. passeng*er* — *passenger*
18. incinerat*or* — *incinerator*
19. refrigerat*or* — *refrigerator*
20. peddl*er* — *peddler*

21. petition*er* — *petitioner*
22. janit*or* — *janitor*
23. operat*or* — *operator*
24. radiat*or* — *radiator*
25. plaster*er* — *plasterer*
26. offic*er* — *officer*
27. receiv*er* — *receiver*
28. shipp*er* — *shipper*
29. visit*or* — *visitor*
30. protect*or* — *protector*
31. spectat*or* — *spectator*
32. senat*or* — *senator*
33. slipp*er* — *slipper*
34. stenograph*er* — *stenographer*
35. subscrib*er* — *subscriber*
36. spons*or* — *sponsor*
37. govern*or* — *governor*
38. counsel*or* — *counselor*
39. teach*er* — *teacher*
40. tell*er* — *teller*

Score_____

16 | Words Often Confused
Assignments

A Select from the following words the one that correctly fits into the blank in each of the sentences below. Then write it in the space provided.

council	devise	conscience	custom	creditable
counsel	device	conscious	costume	credible
consul				

1. Hitler was a man without a _____. . . . .   *conscience*
2. The American _____ at Beirut checked my passport. . .   *consul*
3. Next Saturday there will be a _____ ball at the New Yorker Hotel. . . . .   *costume*
4. On the witness stand, Martens told a very _____ story.   *credible*
5. With the new type of anesthetics, it is possible for patients to remain _____ throughout lengthy operations. . . . . . .   *conscious*
6. The attorney will _____ you concerning your rights under the law. . . . .   *counsel* ~~*consel*~~
7. It has long been our _____ to have special orientation meetings with all our salesmen. . . . .   *custom*
8. The _____ for the defense has arrived. . . . .   *counsel*
9. Can you _____ a good rudder for my boat? . . . .   *devise*
10. Although he did not win, his performance was highly _____.   *creditable*

187

B In the following sentences underline the word in parentheses that makes the sentence correct. Then write it in the space provided.

1. Samuel Pepy's (diary—~~dairy~~) gives us a fascinating picture of life in the 17th century. . . . . *diary*

2. We (disapprove—~~disprove~~) of any practices that might cast discredit upon our products or policies. *disapprove*

3. The British (Empire—~~Umpire~~) has shrunk in size and influence. . . . . *Empire*

4. A new (~~diary~~—dairy) is being constructed in the town of Baltsville. . . . . *dairy*

5. Every day new things are discovered that (~~disapprove~~—disprove) what people once regarded as true. . . . . *disprove*

6. Every baseball (~~empire~~—umpire) is carefully trained for his job. . . . . *umpire*

7. The A.S.P.C.A. hospital tries to cure all (~~deceased~~—diseased) animals. . . . . *diseased*

8. This new (device—~~devise~~) will enable you to use your old machine for many more years. . . . . *device*

9. The explorers fainted from the heat of the (desert—~~dessert~~). . . *desert*

10. It is not our (custom—~~costume~~) to give credit to new customers. . . . . *custom*

C In some of the following sentences an incorrect word is used; cross it out and write the correct word in the space provided. Where there is no error write **C** in the space.

1. Grime's former employers attested to his ~~credible~~ work. . . . . *creditable*

2. One might question whether society makes customs or customs make society. . . . . *C*

3. The Trusteeship ~~Consul~~ is an integral part of the United Nations. . . . . *Council*

4. When the ambulance arrived, the patient was no longer ~~conscience.~~ . . . . *conscious*

5. It is interesting to study how plants ~~disburse~~ their seeds. . . . . *disperse*

WORDS
Ending in ize-ise-yze

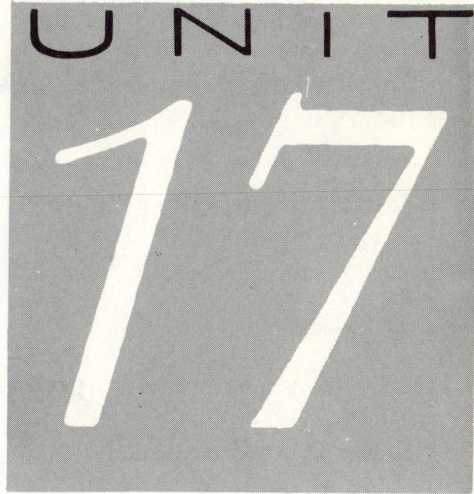

There are over 400 words that end in either **ize, ise,** or **yze.** To make matters more difficult, the endings of all these words sound the same. You couldn't possibly tell whether the ending should be **ize** or **ise** or **yze** simply by pronouncing the word correctly.

Can you or anyone else master all these words? Yes—and very simply, too. First, realize that your ear won't help you. Second, concentrate on *seeing* these endings so that you will automatically write the right ending when you merely hear the word. Third, don't get panicky. You don't have to memorize these hundreds of words. All you need is an approach. And here's that approach.

A. Only *two* words end in **yze.**

ana<u>lyze</u>   para<u>lyze</u>

189

B. There are just a *few* words that end in **ise.**

  1. Words ending in **wise:**

like<u>wise</u>   length<u>wise</u> other<u>wise</u> side<u>wise</u>

  2. Words ending in **vise:**

ad<u>vise</u> de<u>vise</u>* impro<u>vise</u>* re<u>vise</u> super<u>vise</u>

  3. Words ending in **rise:**

        sun<u>rise</u>

  4. Words ending in **prise:**

enter<u>prise</u> sur<u>prise</u> com<u>prise</u>* ap<u>prise</u>*

    Exception : <u>prize</u>

  5 Words ending in **guise:**

        dis<u>guise</u>

  6. Words ending in **cise:**

exer<u>cise</u> in<u>cise</u>* ex<u>cise</u>* exor<u>cise</u>*

   Note: **All other words which sound like these four,**
     end in cize: criticize, ostracize, etc.

7. Words ending in **mise:** There are only three of these—

surm<u>ise</u>* dem<u>ise</u>* compromise

8. The following words do not fall into any group. Study them very carefully.

advert<u>ise</u> chast<u>ise</u>* franch<u>ise</u>*

desp<u>ise</u> merchand<u>ise</u>

What we have left now are approximately 400 words that end in **ize.** So actually, about 90 per cent of these **ize—ise—yse** words end in **ize.** We don't advocate guessing. But if, when you are in doubt, you were to put down an **ize** ending, you would probably be right most of the time. Don't, however, push your luck too far. It's better—and easier—to be sure. Here is a list of frequently-used **ize** words:

agon<u>ize</u>	genera<u>ize</u>	patron<u>ize</u>
alka<u>ize</u>*	harmon<u>ize</u>	pena<u>ize</u>
alphabet<u>ize</u>	hypnot<u>ize</u>	plagiar<u>ize</u>*
amort<u>ize</u>*	idol<u>ize</u>	pulver<u>ize</u>
antagon<u>ize</u>	immun<u>ize</u>	rationa<u>ize</u>*
apolog<u>ize</u>	individua<u>ize</u>	rea<u>ize</u>
atom<u>ize</u>	italic<u>ize</u>	recogn<u>ize</u>
author<u>ize</u>	item<u>ize</u>	scrutin<u>ize</u>*
capita<u>ize</u>	jeopard<u>ize</u>*	specia<u>ize</u>

character<u>ize</u>	lega<u>lize</u>	standard<u>ize</u>
circular<u>ize</u>	loca<u>lize</u>	steri<u>lize</u>
civi<u>lize</u>	magnet<u>ize</u>	subsid<u>ize</u>*
critic<u>ize</u>	mechan<u>ize</u>	synchron<u>ize</u>*
crystall<u>ize</u>	minim<u>ize</u>	synthes<u>ize</u>*
demora<u>lize</u>	mobi<u>lize</u>	systemat<u>ize</u>
dramat<u>ize</u>	modern<u>ize</u>	tanta<u>lize</u>*
econom<u>ize</u>	monopo<u>lize</u>*	terror<u>ize</u>
emphas<u>ize</u>	mora<u>lize</u>	uti<u>lize</u>*
epitom<u>ize</u>*	nationa<u>lize</u>	verba<u>lize</u>*
equa<u>lize</u>	natura<u>lize</u>*	visua<u>lize</u>
familiar<u>ize</u>	neutra<u>lize</u>*	vita<u>lize</u>
ferti<u>lize</u>	organ<u>ize</u>	voca<u>lize</u>
fratern<u>ize</u>*	ostrac<u>ize</u>*	vulcan<u>ize</u>*
galvan<u>ize</u>*	pasteur<u>ize</u>	

17 Words Often Confused

elicit—illicit

elicit—to draw forth: *elicit a reply, elicit applause, elicit an opinion.*

illicit—forbidden by law, improper: *Ponzi was imprisoned for his illicit stock-market transactions.*

eminent—emanate—imminent

eminent—distinguished, important, exalted, noteworthy:
Buckley was an eminent scholar and historian.

emanate—to flow forth from a source:
The Mississippi emanates from the Great Divide.

imminent—likely or about to happen:
Economists predict that a depression is not imminent.

envelope—envelop

envelope *(EN-vuh-lope)*—wrapper or covering; a folded paper container for letters, etc.:
The letter was placed in an envelope and mailed.

envelop *(en-VEL-op)*—to wrap up or to cover; to surround completely:
The fog envelops the harbor every morning.

era—error

era *(EE-ruh)*—a historical period distinguished by certain important or unusual happenings; a period of time starting from some significant happening or date; one of five extensive periods in the development of the earth:
The launching of the first earth satellite ushered in the new space era.

error (rhymes with *terror*)—a mistake:
You had better check your inventory again to find the error.

executor—executioner

executor *(eg-ZEK-u-ter)*—person named in a will to carry out the provisions of the will:
John Mason named his friend, Sidney Hobson, as the executor of his estate.

executioner—one who carries out a death sentence:
Anne Boleyn died at the hands of the executioner.

expansive—expensive

expansive—sympathetic, demonstrative:
A man has an expansive personality when he understands people and gets along well with them.

expensive—high-priced, costly:
The star of the show wore an expensive fur coat.

extant—extent

(handwritten: meaning)

extant *(EKS-tant)*—still in existence:
There are still extant some original copies of Shakespeare's works.

extent *(eks-TENT)*—area, scope, range, size, space, length, amount:
No one knew the real extent of Marlow's financial holdings and influence.

facet—faucet

facet (rhymes with *basset*)—one of the small, polished surfaces of a cut gem: *facet of a diamond;* a phase or aspect:
The guided missile is a new facet of our technical program.

faucet *(FAW-sit)*—a device controlling the flow of water from a pipe:
The plumber fixed the leaky faucet.

facilitate—felicitate

(handwritten: meaning)

facilitate—to make something easy or easier, to lessen the labor of:
This new computer will facilitate the clerical work your staff will have to do at the end of the month.

felicitate—to express good wishes formally, to congratulate:
Our president felicitates you on your fifteenth year with our company.

finale—finally

finale *(fee-NAH-lay)*—the last part of a piece of music or a play:
The finale of Beethoven's SIXTH SYMPHONY is unforgettably moving.

finally *(FIE-nuh-lee)*—at last:
Finally, Burckhardt agreed to install the new heating system.

flagrant—fragrant

flagrant—outrageous, scandalous, notorious, glaring:
Benson's flagrant mismanagement of his company's funds landed him in jail.

fragrant—having a pleasing odor, sweet-smelling:
Roses are fragrant flowers.

formally—formerly

formally—in accordance with certain rules, forms, procedures, regulations:
At the last meeting of the stockholders, Mr. Harris was formally presented as the next Director of Publicity.

formerly—in the past, some time ago:
Harry Truman was formerly President of the United States of America.

Score_____

17 | Assignments

A Insert **ize**, **ise**, or **yze** (whichever is correct) in the spaces in the following words. Then rewrite the complete word on the line to the right.

1. merchand_ise_   *merchandise*   16. surpr_ise_ _____
2. chast_ize ise_   *chastise*   17. equal_ize_ _____
3. desp_ise_   *despise*   18. econom_ize_ _____
4. likew_ise_   *likewise*   19. modern_ize_ _____
5. dev_ise_   *devise*   20. surm_ise_ _____
6. anal_yze_   *analyze*   21. harmon_ize_ _____
7. adv_ise_   *advise*   22. emphas_ize_ _____
8. superv_ise_   *supervise*   23. otherw_ise_ _____
9. civil_ize_   *civilize*   24. ar_ise_ _____
10. sunr_ise_ _____   25. mechan_ize_ _____
11. enterpr_ise_ _____   26. improv_ise_ _____
12. comprom_ise_ _____   27. compr_ise_ _____
13. exerc_ise_ _____   28. disgu_ise_ _____
14. critic_ize_ _____   29. exc_ise_ _____
15. paral_yze_ _____   30. advert_ise_ _____

Cross out the misspelled word or words in each of the following groups of words and spell them correctly in the space at the right. If there are no errors, mark **C** in the space.

1. **comprise**   surmise   economize — *C*

2. **excise**   despise   ~~paralize~~ — *paralyze*

3. **surmise**   ~~emphasise~~   localize — *emphasize*

4. **minimize**   franchise   ~~generalise~~ — *generalize*

5. **legalize**   minimize   moralize — *C*

6. **harmonize**   sidewise   verbalize — *C*

7. ~~crystallise~~   vocalize   mechanize — *crystallize*

8. **circularize**   ~~analize~~   terrorize — *analyze*

9. ~~hypnotise~~   nationalize   rationalize — ~~*hypnotiz*~~ *hypnotize*

10. **visualize**   synchronize   ~~vitalise~~ — *vitalize*

11. **magnetize**   ~~civilise~~   naturalize — *civilize*

12 **stigmatize**   ~~amortise~~   alphabetize — *amortize*

13. **immunize**   recognize   sterilize — *C*

14. ~~ostracyze~~   plagiarize   arise — ~~*ostracise*~~ *ostracize*

15. **tantalize**   ~~sensitise~~   disguise — *sensitize*

16. **pasteurize**   realize   ~~excize~~ — *excise*

17. **legalize**   serialize   ~~incize~~ — *incise*

18. **equalize**   penalize   ~~compromize~~ — *compromise*

19. **summarize**   modernize   lengthwise — *C*

20. ~~atomyze~~   ~~specialise~~   otherwise — *atomize, specialize*

17 | Words Often Confused
Assignments

A Select from the following words the one that correctly fits into the blank in each of the sentences below. Then write it in the space provided.

faucets	executioner	extant	eminent	edition	error	illicit
facets	executor	extent	imminent	addition	era	elicit

1. The country was shocked to learn that the _____ judge had died so suddenly. .... *eminent*

2. We are entering a new _____ in our relationship with the rest of the world. .... *era*

3. Mr. Hotchkiss was named _____ of the estate. .... *executor*

4. The District Attorney finally succeeded in exposing the _____ dealings in which Harrison was involved. .... *illicit*

5. Our museum owns the only copy of the first _____ of this book still _____. .... *edition*

6. There are many different _____ to our employee training program. .... *extant*

7. You will lose fifteen points from your score for each _____ in transcription. .... *facets*

8. To what _____ have you been affected by recent changes in your neighborhood? .... *extent*

9. The newest _____ for kitchen sinks are made of stainless steel. .... *faucets*

10. No one could _____ a response from the sullen child. .. *elicit*

B In some of the following sentences an incorrect word is used; cross it out and write the correct word in the space provided. Where there is no error, write **C** in the space.

1. The Federal Government exercises great care in preventing the smuggling of ~~elicit~~ drugs. . . . . *illicit*

2. We are living in an ~~error~~ of intensive scientific investigations. *era*

3. Dr. Van Tyne was an ~~imminent~~ surgeon. . . . . *eminent*

4. The Post Office requests that all ~~envelops~~ bear postal zone numbers. . . . . *envelopes*

5. The quality of an item is not always determined by how ~~expansive~~ it is. . . . . *expensive*

6. ~~Formally~~ we employed four people to do this job that now requires only three. . . . . *Formerly*

7. In his will, Luther Adams named John Freel as the ~~executioner~~ of his estate. . . . . *executor*

8. Automation in our shipping department will ~~felicitate~~ the handling of your orders. . . . . *facilitate*

9. The secretary should pay attention to every facet of her duties. . . . . *c*

10. The audience in the theatre was alive with comments after the ~~finally~~. . . . . *finale*

C In the following sentences underline the word in parentheses that makes the sentence correct. Then write it in the space provided.

1. New electronic devices (facilitate—~~felicitate~~) bookkeeping transactions. . . . . *facilitate*

2. After the (finale—~~finally~~), the audience applauded the performers for five minutes. . . . . *finale*

3. We have never seen such an example of (flagrant—~~fragrant~~) disregard of the law. . . . . *flagrant*

4. At the next meeting, you will be (formally—~~formerly~~) inducted as secretary. . . . . *formally*

5. His co-workers (~~facilitated~~—felicitated) Morrison on the successful sales campaign he had led. . . . . *felicitated*

17 | Vocabulary Enrichment
Exercise

Below is a list of words with which you should be fully familiar. In the space provided, fill in the word that best completes the meaning of the sentence.

benevolent	compliant	prevalent
reluctant	eloquent	improvise
diligent	petitioner	exuberant
chastise	reticent	impudent

1. If you are industrious and _____ in your pursuit of learning, you are bound to succeed. . . . . *dill diligent*

2. No one in the audience could resist such an _____ plea for help. . . . . *eloquent*

3. We, in this country, are fortunate in not having to cope with the poor economic conditions _____ in other parts of the world. . . . . *prevalent*

4. _____ behavior is a sign of bad breeding. . . . . *impudent*

5. It is sensible to be _____ with any logical request. . . . . *compliant*

6. He gained a reputation for shyness because of his _____ manner. . . . . *reticent*

7. His fine portrayal of Hamlet brought forth an _____ ovation from the audience. . . . . *exuberant*

8. Instead of seeking revenge after World War II, the Allies adopted a _____ policy toward their former enemies. . . . *benevolent*

9. Parents must often _____ children for misbehaving. . . . . *chastise*

10. Expediency often forces people to _____ new methods to solve problems. . . . . *improvise*

17 | Review Exercise

Score_____

There are misspelled words in some of the following sentences. Cross out each misspelled word and write the correct spelling in the space provided. If there are no misspelled words, write **C** in the space next to the sentence.

1. Are you familiar with a similar ~~circuler~~ sent by the burser of the college? .... *circular, bursar*

2. The lawyer tried to arbitrate the differences between the ~~laborers~~ and the managers. .... ~~laborors~~ *C*

3. The aide to our advertiser needs a bookkeeper. .... *C*

4. We count among our subscribers many ~~aviaters,~~ actors, stenographers, doctors, and ~~editers~~. .... *aviators, editors*

5. Please let me have a list of our debtors and creditors. .... *C*

6. Our ~~depositars~~ may use either the elevators or the escalators. *depositors*

7. The local ~~distributer~~ will deliver to your house the latest model ~~incinerater~~ and refrigerator. .... *distributor incinerator*

8. The indicator showed that both the ~~generater~~ and the ~~accelerater~~ were defective. .... *generator, accelerator*

9. The senator joined the rest of the spectators at the ball game. *C*

10. The proprietor of the camp was very careful in hiring ~~counsellars~~. .... *counselors* ~~counsellors~~

11. Our new ~~superviser~~ is an inferior kind of man. .... *supervisor*

12. The Board of Directors is looking for a ~~successer~~ to our old solicitor. .... *successor*

13. We refuse to ~~compromize~~ with our principles. .... *compromise*

14. You will shortly receive a franchise which will permit you to sell our ~~merchandize~~ in your area. .... *merchandise*

15. The Department of Health will ~~analyse~~ samples of the food consumed by the sick family. .... *analyze*

200

PLURALS–1

Do you know how to spell the plural of **attorney?** of **solo?** of **brother-in-law?** It's really quite easy . . . if you learn a few simple rules.

A. Most nouns form their plurals by adding s to the singular, as in this group.

SINGULAR	PLURAL	SINGULAR	PLURAL
barrack	barrack<u>s</u>	relationship	relationship<u>s</u>
camera	camera<u>s</u>	screen	screen<u>s</u>
development	development<u>s</u>	stenographer	stenographer<u>s</u>
herd	herd<u>s</u>	typewriter	typewriter<u>s</u>
office	office<u>s</u>	umbrella	umbrella<u>s</u>

B. Most nouns ending in **ch** (as in **itch**), s, sh, ss, x, and z add **es** to the singular to form their plural, as in this group.

SINGULAR	PLURAL	SINGULAR	PLURAL
box	box<u>es</u>	catch	catch<u>es</u>
brush	brush<u>es</u>	kiss	kiss<u>es</u>
bush	bush<u>es</u>	mass	mass<u>es</u>
business	business<u>es</u>	patch	patch<u>es</u>
buzz	buzz<u>es</u>	waltz	waltz<u>es</u>

C. A few nouns add **en** to the singular to form the plural, or make changes within the word.

SINGULAR	PLURAL	SINGULAR	PLURAL
child	child<u>ren</u>	man	m<u>en</u>
foot	f<u>ee</u>t	mouse	m<u>ice</u>
gentleman	gentlem<u>en</u>	ox	ox<u>en</u>
goose	g<u>ee</u>se	woman	wom<u>en</u>
louse	l<u>ice</u>		

D. Nouns ending in **y:**
(1) When the **y** is preceded by a *consonant*, change the **y** to **i** and add **es.**

Singular: **lady**—consonant **d** before **y.**
Plural: **lad** + **i** (**y** changes to **i**) + **es** = **ladies.**

SINGULAR	PLURAL	SINGULAR	PLURAL
company	compan<u>ies</u>	patty	patt<u>ies</u>
courtesy	courtes<u>ies</u>	quality	qualit<u>ies</u>
fifty	fift<u>ies</u>	sky	sk<u>ies</u>
fly	fl<u>ies</u>	study	stud<u>ies</u>

(2) When the **y** is preceded by a *vowel*, add **s** to the singular to form the plural.

Singular: **bay**—vowel **a** before **y.**
Plural: **bay** + s = **bays.**

SINGULAR	PLURAL	SINGULAR	PLURAL
alley	alle<u>ys</u>	monkey	monke<u>ys</u>
attorney	attorne<u>ys</u>	play	pla<u>ys</u>
boy	boy<u>s</u>	ray	ra<u>ys</u>
chimney	chimne<u>ys</u>	trolley	trolle<u>ys</u>
day	da<u>ys</u>	turkey	turke<u>ys</u>
delay	dela<u>ys</u>	valley	valle<u>ys</u>
journey	journe<u>ys</u>	volley	volle<u>ys</u>
joy	joy<u>s</u>	way	wa<u>ys</u>
key	key<u>s</u>	whiskey or	whiske<u>ys</u> or
		whisky	whisk<u>ies</u>

Special Note: Proper names ending in **y** add **s** to form the plural.

Mary – Mary<u>s</u>   Henry – Henry<u>s</u>

Words Often Confused

hangar—hanger

hangar—a shed for airplanes:
The plane stood outside the hangar.

hanger—one who hangs something: *a paper hanger;* a thing on which something is hung: *a coat hanger.*

healthful—healthy

healthful—good for the health, producing or contributing to good health:
Florida has a healthful climate.

healthy—having or showing good health:
Jim looks healthy. If you eat healthful foods, you'll stay healthy.

historical—hysterical

historical—providing evidence for a fact of history: *a historical document;* based on people or events of the past: *an historical novel.*

hysterical—wildly excited, subject to uncontrollable fits of laughter or crying:
The shock of seeing the accident caused the woman to become hysterical.

hospital—hospitable

hospital—place where sick or injured people or animals are cared for:
The sick man was taken to Roosevelt Hospital.

hospitable *(HOS-pi-tabl)*—to give welcome, food, or shelter to guests or strangers; also, favorable, receptive:
His business grew and prospered because he was hospitable to new ideas.

human—humane

human *(HEW-min)*—having the form, and qualities natural to or characteristic of man:
To err is human.
Selfishness is a human weakness.

humane *(hew-MANE)*—kind, merciful, compassionate:
People will always remember Dr. Schweitzer for his many humane acts.

humility—humidity

humility *(hew-MIL-i-ty)*—humbleness, having a modest sense of one's own importance:
Though he was a great scientist, Albert Einstein always accepted praise with deep humility.

humidity *(hew-MID-i-ty)*—dampness; the amount of moisture in the air:
Summer days are sometimes hard to bear because of the high humidity.

illegible—ineligible

illegible—very hard or impossible to read: *Careless handwriting is usually illegible.*

ineligible—not suitable, not qualified: *The committee on admissions found Jones ineligible for membership.*

immigrate—emigrate

immigrate—to come into a country of which one is not a native: *In the past many Europeans have had to immigrate to America.*

emigrate—to leave a country for residence in another: *During the French Revolution many aristocrats emigrated from France to England.*

ingenious—ingenuous *— meaning?*

ingenious (*in-JEAN-yus*)—clever, skillful at inventing, resourceful, cleverly made and planned: *The phonograph is an ingenious invention. Edison had an ingenious mind.*

ingenuous (*in-JEN-you-us*)—frank, sincere, open, honest, simple, natural, innocent; often meaning unsophisticated, unworldly, innocent in a childlike way: *For one who had seen as much of life as he had, Frank's outlook was quite ingenuous.*

intelligent—intelligible

intelligent—able to learn quickly, alert, wise: *Some of the lower animals, like the chimpanzee, are fairly intelligent.*

intelligible—capable of being understood: *If you wish your speech to be intelligible, speak clearly, distinctly, and slowly.*

interstate—intrastate *know difference*

interstate—between states: *The Interstate Commerce Act covers all transactions taking place from state to state.*

intrastate—within a single state: *Each state has exclusive control over its intrastate affairs.*

later—latter

later (rhymes with *cater*)—at a future time, after an occurrence: *I'll meet you later in the day.*

latter—the second of two: *Our executive staff is comprised of a president, vice-president, secretary, and treasurer. The latter two posts are currently held by one man.*

18 | Assignments

A For each word shown, write the plural in the space provided.

1. office	_offices_	16. waltz	_waltzes_
2. goose	_geese_	17. foot	_feet_
3. tooth	_teeth_	18. ox	_oxen_
4. child	_children_	19. box	_boxes_
5. man	_men_	20. stock	_stocks_
6. woman	_women_	21. barrel	_barrels_
7. baby	_babies_	22. pass	_passes_
8. enemy	_enemies_	23. push	_pushes_
9. valley	_valleys_	24. playwright	_playwrights_
10. ally	_allies_	25. daisy	_daisies_
11. catch	_catches_	26. buzz	_buzzes_
12. stitch	_stitches_	27. business	_businesses_
13. mass	_masses_	28. tax	_taxes_
14. attorney	_attorneys_	29. Betty	_Bettys_
15. thirty	_thirties_	30. scratch	_scratches_

B For each word shown, write the plural in the space provided.

1. trolley	*trolleys*	21. stenographer	*stenographers*
2. tally	*tallies*	22. glass	*glasses*
3. party	*parties*	23. duty	*duties*
4. overtone	*overtones*	24. company	*companies*
5. receipt	*receipts*	25. piece	*pieces*
6. typist	*typists*	26. ax	*axes*
7. secretary	*secretaries*	27. lunch	*lunches*
8. screen	*screens*	28. group	*groups*
9. mouse	*mice*	29. debt	*debts*
10. cigarette	*cigarettes*	30. doily	*doilies*
11. cotton	*cottons*	31. act	*acts*
12. machine	*machines*	32. heir	*heirs*
13. buzz	*buzzes*	33. forty	*forties*
14. crutch	*crutches*	34. desk	*desks*
15. crush	*crushes*	35. economy	*economies*
16. house	*houses*	36. hope	*hopes*
17. hose	*hoses*	37. neighbor	*neighbors*
18. fly	*flies*	38. lady	*ladies*
19. flea	*fleas*	39. desire	*desires*
20. gas	*gases*	40. color	*colors*

18 | Words Often Confused
Assignments

A Select from the following words the one that correctly fits into the blank in each of the sentences below. Then write the word in the space provided.

humidity	hangers	healthful	hospitable	humane
humility	hangars	healthy	hospital	human

1. The _____ at Bennet Air Base are too small for modern jets. .... *hangars*

2. Florida's climate is _____, making Florida a favorite winter resort. .... *healthful*

3. We are sending you our new catalog of _____ supplies for the operating room. .... *hospital*

4. Man is a _____ being. .... *human*

5. The truly great man approaches his work in a spirit of _____. *humility*

6. We can let you have these wooden coat _____ at a discount of 30 per cent. .... *hangers*

7. Exercise regularly and eat sensibly if you wish to stay _____ *healthy*

8. The people of Salem were not noted for their _____ treatment of strangers. .... *humane* ✓

9. Many laws have been enacted to enforce _____ treatment of children. .... *humane*

10. In the summer the _____ is often oppressive. .... *humidity*

B In the following sentences underline the word in parentheses that makes the sentence correct. Then write it in the space provided.

1. According to the rules governing the club, you are (illegible—ineligible) for membership. .... *ineligible*

2. The Wright brothers had an (ingenious—ingenuous) idea when they invented the airplane. .... *ingenious*

3. Because he spoke so fast, he was often not (intelligent—intelligible). .... *intelligible*

4. All trading between states is controlled by the (Interstate—Intrastate) Commerce Commission. .... *Interstate*

5. Many people (immigrated—emigrated) from Ireland to America in the 1880's. .... *emigrated*

6. Though his manner was (ingenuous—ingenious), he was actually a very sophisticated and worldly man. .... *ingenuous*

7. Each state has exclusive control over its (intrastate—interstate) affairs. .... *intrastate*

8. The bolero jacket, chemise, and trapeze are all recent innovations in women's fashion. The (latter—later) two, however, are no longer fashionable. .... *latter*

9. Monkeys are considered to be highly (intelligent—intelligible) animals. .... *intelligent*

10. It was hard to determine his name because his handwriting was so (ineligible—illegible). .... *illegible*

C In some of the following sentences an incorrect word is used; cross it out and write the correct word in the space provided. Where there is no error write **C** in the space.

1. The Boston Tea Party was an important hysterical event. ... *historical*

2. The checkroom attendant will place your coat on a hangar. *hanger*

3. The Carlsons were well liked because of the hospital atmosphere they created for visitors. .... *hospitable*

4. Many of the Founding Fathers immigrated to America because of religious oppression. .... *C*

5. Certain foods may be healthful for some and harmful to others. *C*

Plurals 2: Nouns Ending In F, FE, O

UNIT 19

A. Some nouns ending in **f** or **fe** form their plurals by changing **f** or **fe** to **ves**.

SINGULAR	PLURAL	SINGULAR	PLURAL
calf	cal_ves_	self	sel_ves_
half	hal_ves_	shelf	shel_ves_
knife	kni_ves_	thief	thie_ves_
leaf	lea_ves_	wharf	whar_ves_
life	li_ves_	wife	wi_ves_
loaf	loa_ves_	wolf	wol_ves_

B. Some nouns ending in **f** or **fe** simply add **s** to the singular to form the plural.

SINGULAR	PLURAL	SINGULAR	PLURAL
belief	beliefs	kerchief	kerchiefs
chef	chefs	proof	proofs
chief	chiefs	reef	reefs
cliff	cliffs	roof	roofs
cuff	cuffs	safe	safes
grief	griefs	serf	serfs

C. Most nouns ending in **o** add **es** to the singular to form the plural.

SINGULAR	PLURAL	SINGULAR	PLURAL
buffalo	buffaloes	mosquito	mosquitoes
calico	calicoes	motto	mottoes
cargo	cargoes	Negro	Negroes
domino	dominoes	potato	potatoes
echo	echoes	tomato	tomatoes
embargo	embargoes	tornado	tornadoes
grotto	grottoes	torpedo	torpedoes
hero	heroes	veto	vetoes
innuendo	innuendoes	volcano	volcanoes

D. Most musical terms that end in **o** add **s** to the singular to form the plural.

SINGULAR	PLURAL	SINGULAR	PLURAL
alto*	altos	contralto*	contraltos
banjo	banjos	piano	pianos
basso	bassos	piccolo	piccolos
concerto	concertos	solo	solos

E. The following nouns ending in **o** add **s** to form the plural.

SINGULAR	PLURAL	SINGULAR	PLURAL
albino*	albinos	halo	halos
auto	autos	kimono	kimonos
cameo	cameos	memento	mementos
casino	casinos	radio	radios
curio*	curios	ratio	ratios
Eskimo	Eskimos	zero	zeros
folio	folios		

19 Words Often Confused

legislator—legislature

legislator—lawmaker or member of a law-making body:
Senators, representatives, and city council-men are legislators.

legislature—body of people charged with responsibility, duty, or power to make laws for a country, state, or city:
The Kansas Legislature convenes next week for its annual session.

liable—libel

liable (*LIE-uh-ble*)—responsible, bound to make good a loss; likely to have or suffer from, or subject to:
We are liable for all expenses incurred by our employees.
He is liable to have a heart attack.

libel (*LIE-ble*)—the publication of any written or printed statement which may injure a person's reputation:
It is a libel to accuse an innocent person of being a thief.
The magazine printed an article about dishonesty in government that libeled an innocent statesman.

lightning—lightening

lightning (*LIGHT-ning*)—discharge or flash of electricity in the sky:
Lightning struck a tree.

lightening (*LIGHT-en-ing*)—making lighter or brighter; reducing the load:
The Legislature is now considering laws for lightening our tax burden.

local—locale

local (*LO-kl*)—having to do with a certain place: *the local doctor, local news, of local interest;* making all, or almost all stops: *a local train.*

locale (*lo-KAL*)—a place where something specific occurred or will occur; a locality:
The locale of the new motion picture is the Pyrenees Mountains.

lose—loose

lose (rhymes with *choose*)—to mislay or be deprived of:
When did you lose your pocketbook?
It looked as if the fireman would lose his life.

loose (rhymes with *noose*)—not tight; not bound together or fastened down: *The girl carried a bundle of loose clothing;* careless about morals or conduct: *a loose character.*

214

marital—martial

marital (three syllables)—pertaining to marriage: *marital vows, marital obligations. The judge ruled that Mr. Niles had not discharged his marital obligations.*

martial *(MAR-shul)*—pertaining to, or suitable for war: *martial music, martial law, the martial spirit. The new government declared a state of martial law until order could be restored.*

mode—mood

mode (rhymes with *road*)—prevailing style, fashion, or custom:
Short skirts became the mode about 1920.

mood (rhymes with *food*)—state of mind or feeling: *a sad mood, a cheerful mood.*

moral—morale

moral (rhymes with *quarrel*)—good or virtuous in character or conduct; according to civilized standards of right and wrong; right: *a moral man, a moral act;* dealing with the difference between right and wrong: *a moral question;* the lesson or inner meaning of a story, fable, or event, as:
The moral of the story is that you should be happy with what you have.

morale *(more-AL)*—mental or emotional condition as regards courage, confidence, enthusiasm, etc.:
Good working conditions produce good morale among employees.

overdo—overdue

overdo *(over-doo)*—to do too much:
Do your work conscientiously and thoroughly—but do not overdo it or you may put too great a strain on yourself.

overdue *(over-dyu)*—due some time ago but not yet arrived; not yet paid:
The 6:45 train is an hour overdue.
Payment on your account is a month overdue.

often—orphan

often *(OFF-n)*—many times:
We go to the opera quite often.

orphan (be sure to pronounce the *r*)—child whose parents are dead:
The orphan was adopted by his grandparents.

19 | Assignments

A For each word shown, write the **plural** form in the space provided.

1. belief	*beliefs*	11. loaf	*loaves*
2. calf	*et calves*	12. self	*selves*
3. chief	*chiefs*	13. sheep	*sheep*
4. cliff	*cliffs*	14. wife	*wives*
5. grief	*griefs*	15. thief	*thieves*
6. half	*halves*	16. brief	*briefs*
7. handkerchief	*handkerchiefs*	17. wolf	*wolves*
8. knife	*knives*	18. proof	*proofs*
9. leaf	*leaves*	19. reef	*reefs*
10. life	*lives*	20. roof	*roofs*

B For each word shown, write the **plural** form in the space provided.

1. auto — _autos_
2. piano — _pianos_
3. piccolo — _piccolos_
4. casino — _casinos_
5. contralto — _contraltos_
6. dynamo — _dynamos_ ~~dynamoes~~
7. Eskimo — _Eskimos_
8. soprano — _sopranos_
9. tobacco — _____
10. potato — _potatoes_
11. tomato — _tomatoes_
12. veto — _vetoes_
13. mosquito — _mosquitoes_
14. motto — _mottoes_
15. zero — _zeros_

16. domino — _dominoes_
17. radio — _radios_
18. solo — _solos_
19. bravo — _bravoes_
20. buffalo — _buffaloes_
21. hero — _heroes_
22. echo — _echoes_
23. embargo — _embargoes_
24. cargo — _cargoes_
25. innuendo — _innuendoes_
26. Negro — _Negroes_
27. torpedo — _torpedoes_
28. memento — _mementos_ ~~mementoes~~ ✓
29. halo — _halos_
30. bronco — _____ ✓

19 | Words Often Confused
Assignments

A Select from the following words the one that correctly fits into the blank in each of the sentences below. Then write it in the space provided.

lose	lightning	locale	legislature	martial
loose	lightening	local	legislator	marital

1. The state _____ convenes next Thursday. . . . .   *legislature*
2. _____, it is said, never strikes twice in the same place.   *lightning*
3. The _____ police were unable to cope with the rise in juvenile delinquency in the community. . . . .   *local*
4. The new tax relief measures should go a long way toward _____ the taxpayer's burden. . . . .   *lightening*
5. When you receive your loud-speaker, inspect it to see that the enclosure is not _____. . . . .   *loose*
6. _____ troubles often stem from incompatibility. . . . . . .   *Marital*
7. Hawaii is the _____ of Paramount's latest motion picture. . . . .   *locale*
8. _____ music makes most of us want to step out and march. . . . .   *Martial*
9. Senator Morris ranked high as a national _____. . . . . . .   *legislator*
10. Children are more apt to _____ things than adults. . . . . . .   *lose*

B In the following sentences underline the word in parentheses that makes the sentence correct. Then write it in the space provided.

1. When there is (lightening—lightning) one should not seek shelter under a tree. ....   *lightning*

2. Cypress Gardens, in Florida, provides an excellent working (local—locale) for the serious photographer. ....   *locale*

3. If you do not treat your customers fairly, you will (loose—lose) them. ....   *lose*

4. Haskell was a man of fine (moral—morale) character. ....   *moral*

5. We regret to inform you that payment is (overdo—overdue). ..   *overdue*

6. In most cases, the child who is in a sullen (mood—mode) wants attention. ....   *mood*

7. The newspaper was held (liable—libel) to pay damages for defaming the Mayor's reputation. ....   *libel*

8. The mentally-disturbed person is subject to sudden changes of (mode—mood). ....   *mood*

9. An employee's (morale—moral) will be high after he receives a promotion. ....   *morale*

10. In a partnership, each partner is (libel—liable) for the other's debts. ....   *liable*

C In some of the following sentences an incorrect word is used; cross it out and write the correct word in the space provided. Where there is no error write **C** in the space.

1. Well-paid employees generally have high moral. ....   *morale*

2. Despite his troubles, Hilary always managed to maintain an optimistic mode. ....   *mood*

3. Marital law is very rarely invoked except during wartime. ..   *Martial*

4. It is wise never to overdo in work or play. ....   *C*

5. People who are overtired are libel to make mistakes. ......   *liable*

6. The morale of the story is to be prompt. ....   *moral*

7. The washing machine failed to start because a bolt was lose.   *loose*

8. Printing a libel is a serious offense. ....   *C*

9. Most states have two-house legislators. ....   *legislatures*

10. Mr. Clark maintained that his bill was not overdo.   *overdue*

220

Plurals 3: Compound Words, Letters, Figures, Titles, etc.

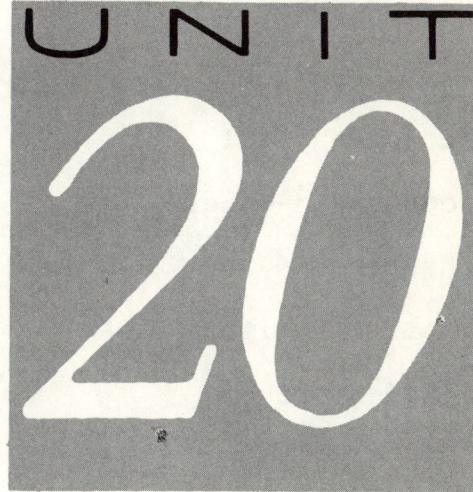

UNIT 20

A. A compound word is a word that is really composed of two or more words strung together: **brother-in-law.** In some compound words, the most important word in the compound takes the plural form. The rest of the word remains unchanged.

SINGULAR	PLURAL
mother-in-law	**mothers-in-law**

The principal or most important part of the word is **mother.** In forming the plural of mother-in-law, only **mother** changes to the plural.
The same holds true for the following:

SINGULAR	PLURAL
attorney-at-law	attorneys-at-law
brother-in-law	brothers-in-law
commander-in-chief	commanders-in-chief
consul general	consuls general
court-martial	courts-martial
editor-in-chief	editors-in-chief
hanger-on	hangers-on
maid-in-waiting	maids-in-waiting
maid-of-honor	maids-of-honor
man-of-war	men-of-war
notary public	notaries public

B. Words of measure ending in **ful,** add **s** to form the plural.

cupful	cupfuls
handful	handfuls
spoonful	spoonfuls

C. Titles form their plurals in the regular manner.

Captain	Captains Hold and Brown
Doctor	Doctors Jones and Smith

SINGULAR	PLURAL
Judge	Judg<u>es</u> Hare and Hotchkiss
Master	Master<u>s</u> Harry and Tom
Miss	Miss<u>es</u> Jane and Mary
Professor	Professor<u>s</u> Howard and Lane

D. The plurals of *letters, figures, signs, symbols* are formed by adding **'s** to the singular.

Your 5<u>'s</u> look like 3<u>'s</u>.

How many r<u>'s</u> in embarrass?

You use too many etc.<u>'s</u> in your letters.

There are six Ph.D<u>'s</u> in this class.

Conrad was much admired in the 1890<u>'s</u>.

Cross out all the t<u>'s</u>.

E. The following abbreviations do not follow any set rule in forming their plurals.

SINGULAR	PLURAL
Dr.	Drs.
Mr.	Messrs.
Mrs.	Mesdames

F. The following nouns are *always* used in the singular even though they end in s and seem to have a plural feeling or meaning.

aeronautics	molasses
arthritis	news
civics	phonetics*
economics	physics (science)
ethics	politics
logistics*	rickets
mathematics	
measles	

G. The following nouns are rarely or never used in the singular. They are almost invariably plural.

acoustics*	pants (trousers)	statistics
annals*	proceeds	suds
barracks	remains	tactics
belongings	riches	thanks
cattle	scissors	trousers
goods	shears	tweezers

H. Some nouns have the same form in the singular and the plural.

---

corps	sheep	fish
deer	salmon	means (methods)
gross	series	grouse
	trout	

I. FOREIGN ENDINGS

SINGULAR	PLURAL
alumna (feminine)	alumnae
alumnus (masculine)	alumni
analysis	analyses
appendix	appendices
automaton*	automata
bacillus*	bacilli
bacterium*	bacteria
crisis	crises
criterion*	criteria
diagnosis	diagnoses
formula	formulas, formulae
fungus	fungi
index	indices, indexes

SINGULAR	PLURAL
larva*	larvae
libretto*	librettos, libretti
maximum	maxima
medium	media, mediums
memorandum	memoranda
minimum	minima
neurosis*	neuroses
phenomenon*	phenomena
psychosis*	psychoses
stratum*	strata
synopsis*	synopses

20 | Words Often Confused

partition—petition

partition—division into parts: *partition an empire;* wall between rooms: *to separate by a wooden partition.*

petition—noun—a formal request to a superior or one in higher authority for some privilege, right, benefit:
The people sent the governor a petition for a new lighting system.

petition—verb—to make a formal request to a superior:
The people must petition the governor to make the change.

persecute—prosecute

persecute—to bring undeserved suffering or unhappiness upon someone; to plague, to hunt down, to annoy:
Throughout history, men have been persecuted for unorthodox opinions.

prosecute—to bring before a court of law:
Traffic violators will be prosecuted to the limit of the law.

pastor—pasture

pastor—clergyman in charge of a church or congregation:
The pastor delivered an inspiring sermon.

pasture—grazing field for cattle or horses:
The cattle were grazing in the pasture.

perspective—prospective

perspective (note the *per*)—the art of drawing objects as they appear to the eye with respect to relative depth and distance; a proper evaluation with relative importance given to the component parts:
A good secretary has a proper perspective concerning the relative importance of her various tasks.

prospective (note the *pro*)—looking to the future, the expected, the likely:
The prospective upturn in business encouraged many people to invest because they thought their prospects for profit were good.

personal—personnel

personal (PER-son-al)—done in person directly by oneself: *a personal visit, a personal call;* of the body or bodily appearance: *personal beauty;* about or against a person: *personal remarks.*

personnel (per-son-NEL)—persons employed in any work, business, or service:
Our Employment Director chooses the personnel for our office.

plaintive—plaintiff

plaintive *(PLANE-tiv)*—sad, melancholy:
The child uttered a plaintive cry when her mother left.

plaintiff *(PLANE-tiff)*—one who brings a suit into a court of law:
The plaintiff accused the defendant of striking him.

poplar—popular

poplar *(POP-lar)*—a type of tree.

popular *(POP-u-lar)*—liked by many people: *a popular play, a popular girl.*

portion—potion

portion—allotted part of anything:
A generous portion of food.

potion (rhymes with *lotion*)—drink, especially of medicine or poison:
Socrates drank a potion made from hemlock bark.

practical—practicable

practical—useful, having to do with action or practice rather than theory:
Edison's approach to science was always a practical one.

practicable *(PRAK-ti-ka-bl)*—workable, capable of being put into practice:
Von Braun was convinced that his plans for the satellite EXPLORER *were practicable.*

precedent—president

precedent *(PRESS-ih-dent)*—a case or instance that may serve as an example or reason for a later case:
If we permit overtime pay on this job, we shall be setting a precedent for the future.

president *(PREZ-ih-dent)*—the elected head of a nation, firm, association:
The President will soon confer with his Cabinet.

preposition—proposition

preposition—a part of speech that shows relationship between other words:
e.g., on, with, at, in.

proposition—a proposal:
We find your proposition most interesting.

precede—proceed—proceeds

precede—to go before:
The scouts will precede the battalion by about fifty feet.

proceed—to go forward, to carry on after having been stopped:
You may proceed with the work as soon as you receive notification.

proceeds (always used as a plural form)—money received from sale of merchandise:
The proceeds from today's sales are over one thousand dollars.

20 | Assignments

A For each word shown, write the **plural** form in the space provided. If the word has no plural form, put a check (√) in the space.

1. Jack-of-all-trades   *Jacks-of-all-trades*
2. editor-in-chief   *editors-in-chief*
3. lieutenant general   *lieutenant generals*
4. handful   *handfuls*
5. doctor   *doctors*
6. 5   *5's*
7. S   *S's*
8. Mr.   *Messrs.*
9. Mrs.   *Mesdames*
10. medium   *media*
11. ethic   *ethics*
12. mumps   √
13. cattle   √
14. sheep   √
15. fish   √ *(or fishes)*

16. economics   √
17. mathematics   √
18. civics   √
19. corps   √ *same*
20. salmon   √ *same*
21. deer   √ *same*
22. front   *fronts*
23. physics   √
24. molasses   √.
25. measles   √.
26. judge   *judges*
27. cupful   *cupfuls*
28. rickets   √
29. news   √
30. tactic   *tactics*

B For each word shown, write the **singular** form in the space provided. If the word has no singular form, put a check (✓) in the space.

1. hangers-on — _hanger-on_
2. courts-martial — _court-martial_
3. annals — _✓_
4. proceeds — _✓_
5. links — _link_
6. consuls-general — _consul-general_
7. spoonfuls — _spoonful_
8. remains — _✓_
9. pants — _✓_
10. tactics — _tactic_

11. notaries public — _notary public_
12. men-of-war — _man-of-war_
13. goods — _✓_
14. shears — _✓_
15. scissors — _✓_
16. tweezers — _✓_
17. pliers — _✓_
18. trousers — _✓_
19. grouse — _grouse_
20. gross —

C For each word shown, write the **plural** form in the space provided. If the word has no plural form, put a check (✓) in the space. If you are in doubt, look up the plural in your dictionary.

1. maximum — _maximus_
2. criterion — _criteria_
3. alumnus — _alumni_
4. alumna — _alumnae_
5. cargo — _cargoes_
6. crisis — _crises_
7. formula — _formulae / formulas_
8. boss — _bosses_
9. Mr. — _Messrs._
10. sheep — _sheep_

11. appendix — _appendices_
12. deer — _deer_
13. minimum — _minima_
14. phenomenon — _phenomena_
15. index — _indexes, indices_
16. medium — _media_
17. occurrence — _occurrences_
18. sister-in-law —
19. editor-in-chief —
20. spoonful —

Score_____

20 Assignments

(continued)

D For each word shown, write the **singular** form in the space provided. If there is no singular form, put a check (√) in the space.

1. data — *datum*

2. salmon — *salmon*

3. geese — *geese (goose)*

4. Mesdames — *Mrs.*

5. editors-in-chief — *editor-in-chief*

6. hangers-on — *hanger-on*

7. crises — *crisis*

8. gross — *gross*

9. men-of-war — *man-of-war*

10. wolves — *wolf*

11. alumni — *alumnus*

12. alumnae — *alumna*

13. indices — *index*

14. notaries public — *notary public*

15. tallies — *tally*

16. tales — *tale*

17. trolleys — *trolley*

18. harnesses — *harness*

19. mice — *mouse*

20. goods — *goods* √
(no singular)

E For each word shown, write the **plural** form in the space provided.

1. child	children	16. class	classes
2. leaf	leaves	17. bus	buses
3. folio	folios	18. veto	vetoes
4. company	companies	19. duty	duties
5. memento	mementos	20. box	boxes
6. safe	safes	21. business	businesses
7. baby	babies	22. auto	autos
8. tomato	tomatoes	23. proof	proofs
9. key	keys	24. fix	fixes
10. life	~~lif~~ lives	25. man	men
11. secretary	secretaries	26. group	groups
12. cargo	cargoes	27. piano	pianos
13. policy	policies	28. lady	ladies
14. valley	valleys	29. debt	debts
15. radio	radios	30. attorney	attorneys

F In the following sentences, insert **is** or **are**, whichever is correct:

1. Mathematics __is__ difficult for most students. . . . . _is_
2. His trousers __are__ at the cleaners. . . . . _are_
3. Measles __is__ a serious disease when contracted by adults. . . . . _is_
4. Ethics __is__ the study of the motives and values in human conduct. . . . . _is_
5. The remains of the late Mr. Tynan __are__ buried at Warrensburg. . . . . _are_

20 | Words Often Confused
Assignments

A Select from the following words the one that correctly fits into the blank in each of the sentences below. Then write this word in the space provided.

prospective	partition	personnel	precede	portions
perspective	petition	personal	proceed	potions

1. The people drew up a _____ demanding equal rights. — *petition*

2. The employees were pleased with the new employment director's enlightened _____ policies. .... — *personnel*

3. Anyone who enters your store is a _____ customer. ... — *prospective*

4. The _____ was made of a sound-proof material. ...... — *partition*

5. We will take _____ care in handling your checking account. .... — *personal*

6. Johnny will _____ Michael in the church procession... — *precede*

7. Many witch doctors' _____ kill their patients rather than cure them. .... — *potions*

8. Some modern artists intentionally distort the _____ in their paintings. .... — *perspective*

9. When the bell sounds you may _____ to your next class. — *proceed*

10. If you want to lose weight, stop eating extra _____ of food. .... — *portions*

B In the following sentences underline the word in parentheses that makes the sentence correct. Then write it in the space provided.

1. (Precede—Proceed) 50 feet, then turn left. . . . . _____

2. The word "to" is usually a (proposition—preposition). . . . . . . _____

3. All offenders will be (persecuted—prosecuted) to the full extent of the law. . . . . _____

4. He made an attractive (proposition—preposition) for the sale of the property. . . . . _____

5. We hire only (practicable—practical) men in our organization. . . . . _____

6. Any attempt to (prosecute—persecute) a minority group constitutes a danger to all citizens. . . . . _____

7. Besides Robert Fulton himself, not many people believed his steamboat to be (practicable—practical). . . . . _____

8. The (president—precedent) of the club called the meeting to order. . . . . _____

9. Roger suggested that a (petition—partition) be drawn up to amend the state Constitution. . . . . _____

10. Of all the (prepositions—propositions) submitted, Baldwin's seemed to be most practicable. . . . . _____

C In the following sentences, find each word improperly used, cross it out, and write the correct word in the space provided. If the sentence has no error, write **C** in the space.

1. Roman mobs prosecuted early Christians. . . . . *persecuted*

2. Gifts with a personnel touch are appreciated by those who receive them. . . . . *personal*

3. The policeman had to persecute him for going through the red light. . . . . *prosecute*

4. He set a president for us to follow. *precedent*

5. Jones was a practicable man. . . . . *practical*

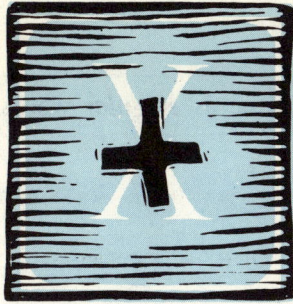

The Apostrophe
and the Possessive

UNIT 21

There's nothing difficult or mysterious about forming the possessive case of nouns. You're doing this all the time. In fact, you couldn't speak or write without using the possessive case. Be sure that you know the simple rules governing the formation of the possessive case. Then you won't be making errors when you speak or write or when you transcribe your notes.

I. The Singular Possessive

A. Add 's to the singular.

SINGULAR	SINGULAR POSSESSIVE
girl	girl's coat
boy	boy's hat
dog	dog's paw

Always treat *one, anyone, everyone*, etc., as *singular* words.

SINGULAR	SINGULAR POSSESSIVE
one	one's possessions
anyone	anyone's clothing
everyone	everyone's affairs

B. If the singular ends in **s**, modern usage says: simply add an apostrophe (') to form the possessive:

SINGULAR	SINGULAR POSSESSIVE
bass	bass' voice
Dickens	Dickens' books
lass	lass' blouse

Some authorities prefer the following:

Dickens's books

II.   The Plural Possessive

A. Add only the apostrophe if the plural ends in **s**:

PLURAL	PLURAL POSSESSIVE
girls	girls' hairdo
ladies	ladies' waists
waiters	waiters' tips

B. Add **'s** to the plural when the plural does not end in **s**:

PLURAL	PLURAL POSSESSIVE
children	children**'s** books
men	men**'s** clothing
women	women**'s** coats

III. At one time the possessive case of inanimate objects was generally shown by using a phrase beginning with **of** instead of **'s**:

> The corner of the street—(*not* the street's corner)
> The sleeve of my jacket—(*not* my jacket's sleeve)

This usage is no longer held by all authorities. Certainly all agree on the use of the following possessives:

a month**'s** journey	a day**'s** trip	for pity**'s** sake
an hour**'s** ride	sixty days**'** notice	a week**'s** delay

IV. *Never* use an *apostrophe* with the possessive case of the following *pronouns*:

its yours ours theirs his hers

V. Put an apostrophe s (**'s**) after the last period in an abbreviation of a singular noun:

Y.M.C.A.**'s** building

G.L.S.**'s** new safety measures

Standard Oil Co.**'s** profit-sharing plan

21

VI. To show *joint* ownership or authorship by two or more individuals, put *only the last named person* in the possessive case.

Robertson and Smith**'s** new market closed last week.

(Here Mr. Robertson and Mr. Smith are partners.)

Smith, Dutton, and Randle**'s** Modern Democracy is widely used in

American schools.   (Refers to *one* book.)

VII. To show *separate* ownership or authorship, put each name in the possessive case:

The American Steel Company**'s** and the Graybar Corporation**'s**

new plants were opened a week ago.

(Here there are *two* plants, each separately owned.)

VIII. The possessive case of a compound word is formed by putting the *last word* in the compound in the possessive case.

SINGULAR	SINGULAR POSSESSIVE
father-in-law	father-in-law**'s**
editor-in-chief	editor-in-chief**'s**
attorney general	attorney general**'s**

PLURAL	PLURAL POSSESSIVE
fathers-in-law	fathers-in-law**'s**
editors-in-chief	editors-in-chief**'s**
attorneys general	attorneys general**'s**

21 | Words Often Confused

prophecy—prophesy

prophecy *(PROF-eh-see)*—a foretelling of future events:
Economists ventured a prophecy that we would be passing through an economic recession within a year.

prophesy *(PROF-eh-sie)*—to foretell the future:
The Secretary of State said, "If you follow this plan, I can safely prophesy that there will be no war in our time."

recent—resent

recent *(REE-sint)*—done or made not long ago, modern: *recent events.*

resent *(ree-ZENT)*—feel insulted, indignant:
We resent the lies that have been spread about our product.

respectfully—respectively

respectfully—showing respect or honor:
To talk respectfully to elders.

respectively—a number of items taken as individual units in the order mentioned:
Jackson, Abel, and Wilkins were elected respectively president, secretary, and treasurer of the company. (In the order mentioned: *Jackson—president; Abel—secretary; Wilkins—treasurer.)*

rout—route—root

rout (rhymes with *shout*)—to disperse in disorderly defeat, to defeat completely:
The British routed the French in the Battle of Waterloo.

root (rhymes with *shoot*)—the part of a plant that grows in the ground:
The roots of a tree.

route (rhymes with *shoot*)—a road: *Route 66;* to send by way of a certain road or route: *Because the bridges were down, all traffic was routed through Centerdale.*

salvage—selvage

salvage (*a* as in *cat*)—to rescue and restore property damaged by fire or other disaster.

selvage (*e* as in *end*)—woven edge which prevents cloth or fabric from raveling:
Cheap cloth very often has no selvage.

statue—stature—statute

statue *(STAT-tyu)*—a carved or cast image: *the Statue of Liberty.*

stature *(STAT-tyur)*—height of an animal, especially man; development attained:

In stature, Barton was a giant. The President gained in stature with every diplomatic victory.

statute *(STAT-tyoot)*—law enacted by a legislative body:

The governor has just signed the latest statute designed to control the sale of securities in this state.

suit—suite

suit (rhymes with *cute*)—a set of outer garments: *a winter suit;* act of bringing legal action: *a law suit;* one of four sets of cards: *a suit of clubs, diamonds, hearts, or spades;* to satisfy or please:

The arrangements suit my taste.

suite (pronounced *sweet*)—connected series of rooms: *the Bridal Suite;* a set of matching furniture: *a living room suite;* a musical composition: *Grand Canyon Suite.*

treaties—treatise

treaties *(TREE-teez)*—formal agreements among nations:
The United States has special treaties with most of the nations of the world.

treatise *(TREE-tiss)*—systematic essay or book on some subject:
Bertrand Russell has written a famous treatise on philosophy.

undo—undue

undo *(un-DOO)*—unfasten: *to undo a knot;* destroy: *to undo a year's efforts in one careless moment.*

undue *(un-DYOU)*—not fitting, not proper; too great, too much; unwarranted:
The lobbyists were shown to have exercised undue influence in trying to get legislators to vote for their special bills.
Many authorities condemn the undue rigor of some of our tax laws.

21 | Assignments

For each word shown, write the **possessive** form in the space provided.

1. woman — *woman's*

2. firm — *firm's*

3. employees — *employees'*

4. men — *men's*

5. month — *month's*

6. U.S.A. — *U.S.A.'s*

7. secretaries — *secretaries'*

8. sister-in-law — *sister-in-law's*

9. Charles — *Charles's*

10. notebooks — *notebooks'*

11. winners — *winners'*

12. days — *days'*

13. oxen — *oxen's*

14. U.C.L.A. — *U.C.L.A.'s*

15. offices — *offices'*

16. General Motors — *General Motors's*

17. week — *week's*

18. children — *children's*

19. attorney general — *attorney general's*

20. typewriter — *typewriter's*

21. manager — *manager's*

22. Jones — *Jones's*

23. authors — *authors'*

24. telephones — *telephones'*

25. playwright — *playwright's*

26. lady — *lady's*

27. committee — *committee's*

28. editor-in-chief — *editor-in-chief's*

29. it — *its*

30. everyone — *everyone's*

B

In some of the following sentences, the possessive form is incorrectly written. Cross out each error and write it correctly in the space provided. If the sentence has no error, write **C** in the space.

1. In business, as elsewhere, there is such a thing as beginner's luck. .... _C_

2. There will be a sensational mens clothing sale at Owen Jones downtown store. .... _men's, Jones's_

3. I heard the story "straight from the horses mouth." .... _horse's_

4. We shall send you ten days notice before we ship your order. _days'_

5. The blouse's you mention in your last letter are our's. We have written to Gorley's New York office telling them that the blouse's are not their's. .... _ours, theirs_

6. You may count on our making a contribution to the U. S. O.s drive for funds. .... _U. S. O.'s_

7. Robert and Browns fall line is refreshingly original. .... _Brown's_

8. Chrysler Corporations net profit for the first quarter of the year was down. .... _Corporation's_

9. Bills father's-in-law investments proved very profitable. _Bill's father-in-law's_ ✗

10. Macys store and Gimbels store face each other. .... _Macy's, Gimbels_

11. I don't like it's looks. .... _its_

12. The childrens' party was spoiled by the rain. .... _children's_

13. There will be a months delay before our material reaches you. _months_

14. Hartford is just a days trip from Mr. Hartleys home. .... _day's_

15. It is clearly every citizens duty to support his governments position at home and abroad. .... _citizen's, governments_

16. My only coats' sleeves are too long. .... _coat's_

17. "For pitys sake!" the old man exclaimed. .... _pity's_

18. No employee may be discharged unless he has received at least two weeks notice. .... _C_

19. Men's clothing tends to be more conservative than womens wear. .... _women's_

20. We discovered that the errors were our's, not yours. .... _ours_

21 | Words Often Confused
Assignments

A Select from the following words the one that correctly fits into the blank in each of the sentences below. Then write it in the space provided.

rout	resent	undo	Suit	treatise	respectively
root	recent	undue	Suite	treaties	respectfully
route					

1. Children should behave _____ to their elders. .... *respectfully*

2. The boy earned several dollars weekly on his newspaper _____. .... *route*

3. The visitors occupied the Presidential_____at the hotel. *Suite*

4. The citizens felt that the laws constituted _____ restriction of their rights. .... *undue*

5. The _____ of the problem lies in our lack of advertising. *root*

6. The soldiers cheered when they learned of the complete _____ of the enemy. .... *rout*

7. Try not to _____ all the good you have done. .... *undo*

8. Throughout our history, we have signed many _____ with foreign countries. .... *treaties*

9. The most _____ census showed an increase in population. .... *recent*

10. John, Philip, and Bob were _____ graded A, B, and C on the spelling exam. .... *respectively*

B In the following sentences underline the word in parentheses that makes the sentence correct. Then write it in the space provided.

1. The (Statute—Statue—Stature) of Liberty is a symbol of freedom to most of the world. . . . .   *statue*

2. During the war, every person tried to (selvage—salvage) reusable metal. . . . .   *salvage*

3. Time proved that his (prophecy—prophesy) was accurate. . . .

4. Compared with Goliath, David was a pigmy in (stature—statue—statute). . . . .   *stature*

5. It may take many years to (undue—undo) the damage caused by the storm. . . . .   *undo*

6. The bedroom (suit—suite) consisted of three pieces of furniture.   *suite*

7. It took only fifteen minutes to completely (route—rout—root) the enemy. . . . .   *rout*

8. A commonly used complimentary close for business letters is "(Respectively—Respectfully) yours." . . . .   *Respectfully*

9. (Recent—Resent) strides achieved in automation have not put many people out of jobs. . . . .   *Recent*

10. His (treatise—treaties) on the subject of mathematics was given immediate attention. . . . .   *treatise*

C In some of the following sentences an incorrect word is used; cross out this word and write the correct word in the space provided. Where there is no error write **C** in the space.

1. Undo worrying never helped anyone. . . . .   *Undue*

2. The A.A.A. mapped out the rout for our car trip to Canada. . . . .   *route*

3. In resent months we have found an increased need for added personnel. . . . .   *recent*

4. He would not venture a prophesy in such a delicate matter. . . . .

5. Adults maintain that they treated their parents more respectively than do children today. . . . .   *respectfully*

244

The Apostrophe In Contractions

When we speak, we tend quite naturally to follow certain short cuts. We say:

I'll	for	I will or I shall
don't	for	do not
could've	for	could have
I'd	for	I would or should

There's nothing at all wrong in using these short cuts. Actually, if we did not streamline our spoken language this way, we would soon be sounding stilted and artificial.

When we run words together, as I'll (I will), we create *contractions*—and quite often, spelling problems, too. So when we write these contractions, we must be careful to indicate what words we've run together and what letter or letters we've left out. The apostrophe (') tells us what we want to know:

<u>aren't</u>   for   <u>are</u> <u>not</u>

(The apostrophe shows us that a letter (**o**) has been omitted.)

<u>I've</u>   for   <u>I</u> <u>have</u>

(The apostrophe shows us that **h** and **a** have been left out.)

The following list contains the most common contractions. Look at each of these very carefully. Note where the apostrophe is placed. Note, too, what letter or letters have been omitted.

aren't	– are not	isn't	– is not
can't	– can not	I've	– I have
couldn't	– could not	let's	– let us
could've	– could have	mustn't	– must not
don't	– do not	she'd	– she would
doesn't	– does not	she's	– she is
hadn't	– had not	shouldn't	– should not
hasn't	– has not	should've	– should have
haven't	– have not	there's	– there is
he'd	– he would	they'd	– they did or they would
he'll	– he will or he shall	they'll	– they will
he's	– he is	they're	– they are
I'd	– I would	they've	– they have
I'll	– I will or I shall	we'd	– we would
weren't	– were not	would've	– would have
won't	– will not	you'd	– you would
wouldn't	– would not	you're	– you are
		you've	– you have

22 | Assignments

A Supply the missing apostrophes in the following sentences: Cross out the word or words that are incorrect. Then write them correctly in the space provided. If the sentence is correct, mark **C** in the space.

1. If ~~youll~~ look in the cellar, youll find what youre looking for. _youll, youll, youre_

2. ~~Hes~~ taking his' and Joe's hats with him. .... _He's_

3. Barkan said he wouldnt and couldnt do the job for only one weeks salary. .... _wouldn't, couldn't_

4. Your C's look like O's. .... _C_

5. ~~Youve~~ used too many buts in your talk. .... _you've, but's_

6. Hes not interested in anybodys money—not yours, mine, or Sams. .... _He's, Sam's_

7. When its time to get up, the train with its ten cars goes noisily by our house. .... _it's_

8. Jack and Eddie's diner is enjoying a flourishing business. .... _C_

9. Hartleys mother-in-laws house was a gathering place for the whole family. .... _Hartley's, laws_

10. The Federal governments road-building program will ultimately cost billions of taxpayers dollars. ....

B In the following sentences, there are some words that should be written with apostrophes. Cross out these words and rewrite them correctly in the space provided.

1. The banks ~~arent~~ as easy with credit as they were last year. — *aren't*

2. ~~Ive~~ told you that I ~~cant~~ possibly open the store before ~~weve~~ taken our inventory. — *I've, can't, we've*

3. ~~Couldnt~~ you tell us what we shouldve done? — *Couldn't, should've*

4. ~~Im~~ sure he ~~doesnt~~ know what ~~hes~~ supposed to do. — *I'm, doesn't, he's*

5. We ~~wont~~ guarantee this fabric against shrinkage. — *won't*

6. ~~Werent~~ you aware that you ~~hadnt~~ enclosed the order blanks? — *Weren't, hadn't*

7. ~~Ill~~ agree with you that there ~~isnt~~ anything he ~~wont~~ do to win his point. — *I'll, isn't, won't*

8. ~~Dont~~ you think ~~hed~~ have been more willing to talk if ~~hed~~ known ~~wed~~ listen more sympathetically? — *Don't, he'd, he'd, we'd*

9. ~~Lets~~ be frank with our employees and tell them what they ~~mustnt~~ do. — *Let's, mustn't*

10. If I ~~havent~~ heard from you by noon, I'll call you and let you know whether ~~theres~~ any point in waiting for the late plane. — *haven't, there's*

C Place apostrophes where they belong in the following sentences. Also cross out any misspelled words you find and spell them correctly in the space provided. If the sentence needs no correction, mark it **C**.

1. The five creditors accounts were found in the files. — *creditors'*

2. Yours is the first of our customers names listed. —

3. James Wilson and Companys address is 54 Worth Street. — *Company's*

4. ~~Theres~~ where we placed our Accounts Receivable ledgers. — *There's*

5. ~~Smiths~~ and ~~Grahams~~ names are both in that folder. — *Smith's, Graham's*

6. Smiths and Grahams purchase is noted on that invoice. — *Graham's*

7. Hers is the neatest of the costumes worn by the six girls in our office. —

8. The secretaries desks were moved from the bosses offices. — *secretaries', bosses'*

9. Are the carpets in Mr. and Mrs. Gladstones home properly cleaned? — *Gladstone's*

10. All 5s must be changed to 0s. — *5's, 0's*

22 | Vocabulary Enrichment Exercise

Below is a list of words with which you should be fully familiar. In the space provided, fill in the word that best completes the meaning of the sentence.

annals	**fallacy**	**innuendo**
acoustics	**facilitate**	**concede**
conceive	**subtle**	**alleviate**
dilemma	**absurd**	**supersede**

1. The excellent _____ in the concert hall added much to the enjoyment of the music. .... *acoustics*

2. In the _____ of history there has never been such an age of scientific enlightenment as the 20th Century. ...... *annals*

3. If you try this new method, it may _____ your completing the job sooner. .... *facilitate*

4. It was a serious _____ because the two alternatives were equally controversial. .... *dilemma*

5. Your employer's urgent request will often _____ any other work assigned previously. .... *supersede*

6. A _____ approach is sometimes more successful than a direct attack on a problem. .... *subtle*

7. When a person has made a mistake, it denotes moral courage for him to _____ his error honestly. .... *concede*

8. He looked _____ dressed in a green jacket, pink shirt, and red tie. .... *absurd*

9. It is a _____ to believe that good fortune comes without hard work. .... *fallacy*

10. New drugs are being invented every day to _____ the pain and suffering of the injured. *alleviate*

22

Review Exercise *Score*_____

In some of the following sentences a misspelled word is used; cross it out and write the correct spelling in the space provided. Where there is no error write **C** in the space.

1. I was surprised to learn that we had sent cataloges to only a few of our ~~customer~~'s. . . . .   *customers*

2. Thank you for the ~~courtesys~~ extended to our representative during his three-day visit at your plant.   *courtesies*

3. Our agent will be glad to assist you in determining the amount of insurance you will need to cover ~~todays~~ higher costs. . . . . .   *today's*

4. You should see this years model at ~~you~~ dealers without delay.   *your, year's*

5. Plane travel will make it possible for your salesman to spend more time in their customer's ~~officies~~ or ~~factorys.~~ . . . .   *offices, factories*

6. Representatives from many ~~companys~~ will talk to our students explaining the job opportunities open to them. . . . .   *companies*

7. ~~Taxs~~ are not included in the costs shown on the rate ~~chartes.~~   *Taxes, charts*

8. Lewis and ~~Blacks~~ store handles complete lines of mens, womens, and childrens clothing. . . . .   *Black's, men's, women's, children's*

9. Our best advertising medium are newspapers and television. *C*

10. No office machine can produce ~~it's~~ best work if the quality of ~~supplys~~ used on it is poor. . . . .   *its, supplies*

11. If you will give us a few days notice in the future, I am sure we shall be able to take care of all of ~~you'r~~ customers. . . . .   *your*

12. These ~~policys~~ contain no provisions for benefits if you're partially disabled. . . . .   *policies*

13. ~~Wont~~ you let us know what disposition has been made of the case. . . . .   *Won't*

14. This pamphlet was designed to answer students questions on the operations of banks. . . . .   *student's*

15. ~~Lady's~~ hats are on the second floor; mens' are on the third. . . . .   *ladies'*

The Demons

UNIT **23**

Here is a list of almost 400 words very frequently misspelled all the way from first grade through college! And yet, as you examine these words, you'll be struck with the fact that they are all very simple—so simple that you'll wonder why people should be baffled by them. The latest research, on which this list is based, proves beyond a doubt that these are *the spelling demons* that bother most people.

Lists of demons are generally presented alphabetically or in approximate order of difficulty. To make this list more *useful* to you, we've *grouped* the words according to the *special problems* they present. In most cases, you are referred directly to the chapter in this book where the particular spelling problem is treated in detail. Don't be surprised if you've already studied some of these words elsewhere in the book. They are repeated here for special emphasis.

251

THE DEADLY DOZEN

its	there	too	whose
it's	they're	two	your
their	to	who's	you're

PRONUNCIATION

a<u>c</u>cept	exp<u>eri</u>ment	lab<u>o</u>ratory	stri<u>ct</u>
ac<u>cur</u>ate	Feb<u>ru</u>ary	<u>per</u>form	<u>sur</u>prise
ath<u>l</u>ete	fo<u>r</u>ward	pr<u>eju</u>dice	temper<u>a</u>ment
disa<u>strou</u>s	gove<u>rn</u>ment	prob<u>abl</u>y	temper<u>a</u>ture
envi<u>ron</u>ment	hin<u>d</u>rance	quan<u>ti</u>ty	tra<u>g</u>edy
e<u>x</u>cept	hun<u>dred</u>	rec<u>og</u>nize	tr<u>e</u>men<u>dou</u>s
	i<u>rre</u>l<u>e</u>vant	remem<u>bra</u>nce	undoub<u>ted</u>ly

DOUBLING THE FINAL CONSONANT

admi<u>tt</u>ed	admi<u>tt</u>ing	occu<u>rr</u>ed	occu<u>rr</u>ing
begi<u>nn</u>er	begi<u>nn</u>ing	pla<u>nn</u>ed	pla<u>nn</u>ing
bi<u>gg</u>er	bi<u>gg</u>est	prefe<u>rr</u>ed	prefe<u>rr</u>ing
contro<u>ll</u>ed	contro<u>ll</u>ing	refe<u>rr</u>ed	refe<u>rr</u>ing
dro<u>pp</u>ed	dro<u>pp</u>ing	ste<u>pp</u>ed	ste<u>pp</u>ing
equi<u>pp</u>ed	equi<u>pp</u>ing	transfe<u>rr</u>ed	transfe<u>rr</u>ing

Adding Suffixes to Words Ending in Silent E

advantageous	coming
arguing	losing
argument	noticeable
becoming	shining
changeable	using
changing	writing

Words With Ei-Ie

achieve	financier	piece
achievement	foreign	receipt
belief	friend	receive
believe	height	relieve
conceive	leisure	seize
deceive	mischief	weird
field	niece	yield

Words Ending In Cede, Sede, Ceed

accede	proceed
concede	succeed
precede	supersede

PREFIXES

<u>di</u>sappoint	<u>di</u>sillusioned	<u>dis</u>satisfied
<u>inter</u>rupt	<u>un</u>necessary	

SUFFIXES

accident<u>ally</u>	evident<u>ly</u>	incident<u>ally</u>
actua<u>lly</u>	extreme<u>ly</u>	individua<u>lly</u>
annua<u>lly</u>	fina<u>lly</u>	mora<u>lly</u>
basic<u>ally</u>	financia<u>lly</u>	rea<u>lly</u>
complete<u>ly</u>	genera<u>lly</u>	sincere<u>ly</u>
crue<u>lly</u>	idea<u>lly</u>	who<u>lly</u>

cc

a<u>cc</u>ident	a<u>cc</u>omplish	a<u>cc</u>ustom
a<u>cc</u>laim	a<u>cc</u>urate	o<u>cc</u>asion
a<u>cc</u>ompany	a<u>cc</u>use	o<u>cc</u>ur

ff

di<u>ff</u>erence	di<u>ff</u>icult
di<u>ff</u>erent	su<u>ff</u>icient

gg

aggravate   aggressive   exaggerate

ll

alleviate	collect	intellect
allot	fallacy	parallel
allowed	illusion	

mm

commercial	dilemma	recommend
committee	immediate	roommate
Communism	immense	summary

nn

annual   connote   manner   tyranny

pp

apparatus	appreciate	opportunity
appear	approach	oppose
applies	approximate	opposite

rr

a<u>rr</u>ange	cu<u>rr</u>iculum	su<u>rr</u>ounding
co<u>rr</u>elate	i<u>rr</u>itable	wa<u>rr</u>ant

Silent Letters

pla<u>yw</u>right	<u>p</u>sy<u>ch</u>ology	<u>rh</u>ythm	su<u>b</u>tle

Words Ending in Ance-Ence

appear<u>ance</u>	exist<u>ence</u>	magnific<u>ence</u>
conveni<u>ence</u>	guid<u>ance</u>	occurr<u>ence</u>
dilig<u>ence</u>*	independ<u>ence</u>	sent<u>ence</u>
		tend<u>ency</u>

Words Ending In Ant-Ent

abund<u>ant</u>	differ<u>ent</u>	excell<u>ent</u>
conveni<u>ent</u>	domin<u>ant</u>	magnific<u>ent</u>
depend<u>ent</u>	effici<u>ent</u>	persist<u>ent</u>
		promin<u>ent</u>

Words Ending in Yze

anal<u>yze</u>	paral<u>yze</u>

WORDS OFTEN CONFUSED

advice – advise	ingenious – ingenuous
affect – effect	later – latter
all together – altogether	led – lead
already – all ready	lose – loose
breath – breathe	maybe – may be
choose – chose	moral – morale
conscience – conscious	personal – personnel
desert – dessert	prophecy – prophesy
device – devise	quiet – quite

The final group of demons just refuse to be classified. So we call them *Tough Spots*.

The particular letters in the words which cause the most trouble have been underlined.

For example: fascinate is frequently misspelled because people have difficulty with the **sc.** So we print the word as follows:

fas<u>c</u>inate

We know from experience that this is where the problem is likely to be. So it becomes clear at once that this is the spot on which you must concentrate.

TOUGH SPOTS

a<u>b</u>sence	criti<u>c</u>ize	f<u>e</u>licitate	parl<u>i</u>ament
ab<u>sur</u>d	cr<u>ue</u>l	fictit<u>ious</u>	parti<u>c</u>ular
a<u>cc</u>uracy	cur<u>ious</u>	ga<u>ie</u>ty	p<u>er</u>suade
a<u>cq</u>uaint	curt<u>ain</u>	gen<u>ius</u>	pl<u>e</u>asant
a<u>c</u>quire	de<u>al</u>t	gen<u>uine</u>	pres<u>ence</u>

23

TOUGH SPOTS

adequate	definite	grammar	prestige
advertisement	describe	humor	prevalent
afraid	description	humorous	privilege
against	desire	influential	pursue
amateur	despair	ingredient	recipe
appreciate	destruction	initiative	recognize
article	disciple	inquisitive	resources
author	discipline	interest	ridiculous
bargain	discuss	interpret	schedule
benefit	disease	irrelevant	separate
boundary	disgusted·	knowledge	sergeant
brilliant	divide	length	shoulder
Britain	divine	likelihood	significance
calendar	eighth	liveliest	speech
captain	eliminate	livelihood	strength
certain	endeavor	loneliness	symbol
challenge	entirely	luxury	synonym
character	escape	maintenance	technique
cigarette	expense	marriage	thorough
comparative	facilitate	meant	tragedy
concentrate	fascinate	minute	villain
concern	familiar	ninety	woman (sing.)
criticism	favorite	paid	women (plural)

23 | Assignments

A Cross out all misspelled words. Spell them correctly in the spaces provided. If the word is correctly spelled, write **C** in the space.

1. incidently — *incidentally*
2. accidently — *accidentally*
3. sincerely — *C*
4. finaly — *finally*
5. disastrous — *C*

11. Febuary — *February*
12. tradegy — *tragedy*
13. dissappoint — *disappoint*
14. preceed — *precede*
15. proceed — *C*

6. enviorment — *environment*
7. government — *C*
8. temperment — *temperament*
9. secretary — *C*
10. probaly — *probably*

16. supercede — *supersede*
17. rythm — *rhythm*
18. vacum — *vacuum*
19. separate — *C*
20. criticism — *C*

21. definate — *definite* ~~definate~~ *definite*
22. alright — all right
23. facinate — fascinate
24. grammer — grammar
25. prejudice — C

26. privelege — privilege
27. Britian — Britain
28. humerous — humorous
29. certain — C
30. sergeant — C

31. divide — C
32. ninty — ninety
33. familiar — C
34. speach — speech
35. irrevelant — irrelevant

36. liklihood — likelihood
37. parliment — parliament
38. reconize — recognize
39. miniature — C
40. sacrifice — C

41. strength — C
42. livelihood — C
43. concede — C
44. excede —
45. rememberance — remembrance

46. modren — modern
47. evidently — C
48. ideally — C
49. basicaly — idea basically
50. suprise — surprise

51. labortory — laboratory
52. tremendous — C
53. parelel — parallel
54. allot — C
55. ilusion — illusion

56. falasy — fallacy
57. tyrany — Tyranny
58. dilema —
59. roomate —
60. accurate —

23 | Assignments
(continued)

B In each of the following words one or more key letters have been omitted. Insert the proper letters; then rewrite the complete word correctly in the space provided.

1. arg____ment   _____

2. notic____ble   _____

3. advantag__us   _____

4. contro____ed   _____

5. refe____ing   _____

6. benefi____ed   _____

7. indep____nce   _____

8. magnif__nce   _____

9. exis____nce   _____

10. anal____e   _____

11. bel_____ve   _____

12. h_____ght   _____

13. dec_____ve   _____

14. ac__ompany   _____

15. para_____el   _____

16. tyra_____y   _____

17. incident__ly   _____

18. financ____ly   _____

19. disast_____us   _____

20. rememb__nce   _____

21. pre____udice   _____

22. rec____nize   _____

23. temp__ment   _____

24. dis____lusion   _____

25. inter____pt   _____

26. super____ede   _____

27. excel____nt   _____

28. advert__ment   _____

29. ad____quate   _____

30. bound____ry   _____

31. cigar____te   _____

32. dis____ipline   _____

33. compar__tive   _____

34. calend____r   _____

35. d____vide   _____

36. ficti____ous   _____

37. ga____ty   _____

38. hum____rous   _____

39. influen____l   _____

40. init____tive   _____

41. len____th   _____

42. maint____nce   _____

43. live____hood   _____

44. parti____lar   _____

45. p____suade   _____

46. priv____ge   _____

47. r____culous   _____

48. sh____lder   _____

49. signif____nce   _____

50. s____edule   _____

51. aud____nce   _____

52. pat____nce   _____

53. bel____f   _____

54. p____ce   _____

55. sc____nce   _____

56. rel____ve   _____

57. suffic____nt   _____

58. rev____w   _____

59. f____ld   _____

60. defic____nt   _____

Summary Review

U N I T 24

We've come a long way together.

In addition to becoming familiar with the use of the dictionary and overcoming the common spelling demons, you have mastered the basic rules governing the spelling of words with double letters and silent letters; for adding various endings; for using prefixes and suffixes; dropping of the silent e and ei-ie words; the forming of plurals, possessives and contractions.

You've learned a great deal—and we're sure you've learned it well, but the most important step is yet to come. You must now apply what you have learned towards everything you do, in order to retain and profit from what you have studied.

Remember, good spelling is one of the requirements for success in any occupation. Whether transcribing or proofreading letters, you must, at all times, use and be aware of correct spelling. If you're not sure—*check the dictionary*.

Using the knowledge you have acquired through BUSINESS SPELLING AND WORD POWER will help you be certain that your letters will be read, well-received and acted upon, because they will create the right impression.

The following assignments will exercise your ability to apply what you have learned.

24 | SUMMARY REVIEW EXERCISE 1

There are misspelled words in some of the following sentences. Cross out each misspelled word and write the correct spelling in the space provided. If there are no misspelled words, write **C** in the space next to the sentence.

1. The fragrent aroma of boiling coffee seemed to come from a distance. . . . . _____

2. During his convalescence from the flu, Harry read all day long. _____

3. We are reluctent to recommend this man to you. We have serious doubts about his competence. . . . . _____

4. If you encounter any resistance or interference, call the main office immediately. . . . . _____

5. Insect repellants stupify the insects with which they come in contact. . . . . _____

6. With a little more study and training, you should be able to qualify for promotion. . . . . _____

7. The general ordered his field lieutenants to fortefy their positions against the numerically superior enemy. . . . . _____

8. There is a growing feeling that society must find some permanent protection against the incorrigable criminal. . . . . _____

9. Please check those debts that are still collectable. . . . . _____

10. Oxygen liquifies at a very low temperature. . . . . _____

SUMMARY REVIEW EXERCISE 2

There are misspelled words in the following letter. Cross out each misspelled word and write the correct spelling in the space provided to the right of the line. If there are no misspelled words in a line, write **C** in the space.

Dear Sir:

The booklet which you requested

resently is enclosed. It will show you

an easy, pleasent way to make extra money.

You dont need expereince, and you dont

have to be a salesman.

After you have read the booklet

carefuly, fill in the card which youll

find on page 9 and mail it to us. It

will bring you two beautifull assortments

of greeting cards. Your freinds will be

amazed to see such high-quality cards at

such low prices.

If you belong to an organization

that wants to make money, you will want

to introduse these cards to the group. Hun-

dreds of organizations have used this plan.

We have been in business for fourty

years, so you can be sure that you will

recieve fine service and high quality.

           Cordually your's,

1. _____

2. _____

3. _____

4. _____

5. _____

6. _____

7. _____

8. _____

9. _____

10. _____

11. _____

12. _____

13. _____

14. _____

15. _____

16. _____

17. _____

18. _____

19. _____

20. _____

24 SUMMARY REVIEW EXERCISE 3

There are misspelled words in some of the following sentences. Cross out each misspelled word and write the correct spelling in the space provided. If there are no misspelled words, write **C** in the space next to the sentence.

1. Many offices are changeing from manual to electric type-writers. . . . . _____

2. Our firm celebrated it's fiftieth anniversary last year. . . . . . . _____

3. An experienced worker is naturaly faster than a beginner. . . . _____

4. The hotel allotted its most luxurious suite to the foreign soveriegn and his staff. . . . . _____

5. There are many men's washable suits on the market this year. _____

6. After a long seige of illness, the patient was finally released from the hospital. . . . . _____

7. Conceit is not a likeable quality. . . . . _____

8. The temperture was well over the hundred degree mark in the shade. . . . . _____

9. Every day America imports a larger and larger volume of European cars. . . . . _____

10. Don't waste valuable time in unnecessary arguements. . . . . . . _____

SUMMARY REVIEW EXERCISE 4

There are misspelled words in the following letter. Cross out each misspelled word and write the correct spelling in the space provided to the right of the line. If there are no misspelled words in a line, write **C** in the space.

Gentlemen:

We were glad to recieve your resent

request for our insurence booklet. This

booklet outlines our special plan. We

hope you will examine it throughly.

Before we divised this plan, we sent

questionares to several hundred companys

like your's to determine what there prob-

lems were. There answers showed that

they all carried fire insurence which

covered only the equippment. There pol-

icys did nothing about the benifits they

would loose while there buildings were

being repared.

Lets give a moments consideration to

the cost of this protection. Does it

suprise you to learn that the total cost

of such a polisy is only 3 cents a day?

Read the booklet that is enclosed;

than fill out and mail the application.

Sincerely yours,

1. _____
2. _____
3. _____
4. _____
5. _____
6. _____
7. _____
8. _____
9. _____
10. _____
11. _____
12. _____
13. _____
14. _____
15. _____
16. _____
17. _____
18. _____
19. _____
20. _____

24 | SUMMARY REVIEW EXERCISE 5

There are misspelled words in some of the following sentences. Cross out each misspelled word and write the correct spelling in the space provided. If there are no misspelled words, write **C** in the space next to the sentence.

1. If you have done your job well, our representative will inter-sede on your behalf. .... _____

2. We have been unable to disuade Mr. Crowley from coming here today; he is determined to attend. .... _____

3. We are well on the way to educating all iliterates. .... _____

4. When you hire imature personnel, you are taking unecessary chances. .... _____

5. You'll have to inspect the contents of all the unnumbered boxes. .... _____

6. Some people develope a distaste for underdone meat. .... _____

7. It is a mistake to undertake more than you can accomplish in a given time. .... _____

8. One mistep and you are lost! .... _____

9. The senator was publicly accused of failure to live up to his responsibilities. .... _____

10. Actually, Johnston was basicaly well qualified for the job. ... _____

SUMMARY REVIEW EXERCISE 6

There are misspelled words in the following letter.
Cross out each misspelled word and write the correct
spelling in the space provided to the right of the line.
If there are no misspelled words in a line, write **C** in
the space.

Dear Mr. Allen:

Your letter in which you tell us that

you have been charged for sevral items of

stationary that you did not purchace has

been refered to me. We are sorry this

error occured, and we are enclosing a

corrected bill.

As you know, there is a Mr. Sam Allen

in your town; and on sevral ocassions you

have been charged for puchaces he made. We

are taking defenite steps to be sure that

this does not ocur again.

We now have in stock the carbon paper

which you wanted. The enclosed leaflet

discribes the various weights and the

uses for which they are recomended.

We are greatful for the business you

have given us in the past and hope that we

shall continue to have the pleazure of filling

your stationary needs.

Respectively yours,

1. _____
2. _____
3. _____
4. _____
5. _____
6. _____
7. _____
8. _____
9. _____
10. _____
11. _____
12. _____
13. _____
14. _____
15. _____
16. _____
17. _____
18. _____
19. _____
20. _____

24 | SUMMARY REVIEW EXERCISE 7

There are misspelled words in some of the following sentences. Cross out each misspelled word and write the correct spelling in the space provided. If there are no misspelled words, write **C** in the space next to the sentence.

1. Every parent must be sure to have his children immunized against polio. .... _____

2. Do not do anything until you receive official permission which will authorize you to circularise all the merchants in the neighborhood. .... _____

3. During World War II our soldiers abroad were forbidden to fraternise with civilians of the conquered countries. .... _____

4. All receipts must be itemized. .... _____

5. At the first sign of trouble abroad, the army began to mobilise its forces. .... _____

6. On July 20 we obtained judgement against The Carter Corporation. .... _____

7. The debter was represented by his counsel at the court cession. _____

8. The court's ruling will have the affect of reducing the total amount of the debt. .... _____

9. As a competant secretary, you should be concerned with accurate transcription. .... _____

10. Personal traits play an important part in helping you acheive business success. .... _____

SUMMARY REVIEW EXERCISE 8

There are misspelled words in the following letter. Cross out each misspelled word and write the correct spelling in the space provided to the right of the line. If there are no misspelled words in a line, write **C** in the space.

Dear Madam:

I know you are busy, but wont you   1. _____

take time to revue this valuble book   2. _____

called "Effective Letters." Any person   3. _____

who follows the suggestions in this book   4. _____

will be able to write more affectively   5. _____

when replying to inquirys or when making   6. _____

sales by direct mail.   7. _____

All we ask is that you examine this   8. _____

useful book at our expence.   9. _____

Is your situation similer to that   10. _____

of many other companys? Are you getting   11. _____

satisfactery results from you're collec-   12. _____

tion letters? Follow the suggestions on   13. _____

page 32 and note the results.   14. _____

Their are 200 pages of practicle,   15. _____

useable information in this book. See   16. _____

the enclosed sumary of the contents.   17. _____

Remember, "Effective Letters" is   18. _____

your's with our complements.   19. _____

Very truely your's,   20. _____

Dictionary Section

*The definitions on the following pages are from
WEBSTER'S NEW WORLD DICTIONARY
of the American Language, College Edition.
Reprinted with the permission of
The World Publishing Company.*

a·bey·ance (ə-bā'əns), *n.* [Anglo-Fr. *abeiance;* OFr. *abeance,* expectation < *bayer,* to gape, wait expectantly < LL. *badare,* to gape], **1.** temporary suspension, as of an activity or function. **2.** in *law,* a state of not having been determined or settled, as of lands awaiting proof of ownership.

ab·hor·rent (əb-hôr'ənt, ab-hor'ənt), *adj.* [L. *abhorrens,* ppr. of *abhorrere;* see ABHOR], **1.** causing fear, disgust, hatred, etc.; loathsome; detestable. **2.** feeling abhorrence. **3.** opposed (*to* one's principles, reason, etc.). —*SYN.* see hateful.

a·bridge (ə-brij'), *v.t.* [ABRIDGED (-brijd'), ABRIDGING], [ME. *abregen;* OFr. *abregier;* L. *abbreviare;* < *ad-,* to + *breviare* < *brevis,* short], **1.** to reduce in scope, extent, etc.; shorten. **2.** to shorten by lessening the number of words but keeping the main contents. **3.** to lessen; curtail. **4.** to deprive of (rights, privileges, etc.). Abbreviated **abr.** —*SYN.* see shorten.

ab·sti·nence (ab'stə-nəns), *n.* [ME.; OFr.; L. *abstinentia* < ppr. of *abstinere;* see ABSTAIN], **1.** an abstaining from some or all food, drink, or other pleasures. **2.** the act of giving up drinking any alcoholic liquors: also called *total abstinence.*

ac·a·dem·i·cal·ly (ak'ə-dem'i-k'l-i), *adv.* **1.** in relation to an academy. **2.** in an academic manner; pedantically. **3.** from an academic point of view.

ac·cess (ak'ses), *n.* [ME. & OFr. *acces;* L. *accessus,* pp. of *accedere;* see ACCEDE], **1.** a coming toward or near to; approach. **2.** a way or means of approach. **3.** the right to come into, approach, or use (with *to*); admittance. **4.** increase; growth. **5.** an outburst; paroxysm: as, an *access* of anger. **6.** in *medicine,* the onset of a disease; attack.

ac·com·mo·date (ə-kom'ə-dāt'), *v.t.* [ACCOMMODATED (-id), ACCOMMODATING], [< L. *accommodatus,* pp. of *accommodare* < *ad-,* to + *commodare,* to fit < *com-,* with + *modus,* a measure], **1.** to make fit; adjust; adapt (often used reflexively). **2.** to reconcile. **3.** to supply or help by supplying (*with* something). **4.** to do a service or favor for. **5.** to have space for; find room for; lodge. *v.i.* to become adjusted, as the lens of the eye in focusing on objects at various distances. —*SYN.* see adapt, contain.

a·cous·tics (ə-kōōs'tiks, ə-kous'tiks), *n.pl.* **1.** the qualities of a room, theater, etc. that have to do with how clearly sounds can be heard or transmitted in it. **2.** [construed as sing.], the science of heard sound.

ac·quit·tal (ə-kwit'l), *n.* **1.** an acquitting; discharge (of duty, obligation, etc.). **2.** in *law,* a setting free or being set free.

a·cu·men (ə-kū'mən), *n.* [L., a point, sting, mental acuteness < *acuere,* to sharpen], keenness and quickness of mind; sharp insight.

ad·her·ence (əd-hēr'əns, ad-hēr'əns), *n.* [Fr.; L. *adhaerentia* < ppr. of *adhaerere;* see ADHERE], an adhering; attachment (*to* a person, cause, party, idea, etc.); devotion and support.

ad·ja·cent (ə-jā's'nt), *adj.* [L. *adjacens,* ppr. of *adjacere,* to lie near; *ad-,* to + *jacere,* to lie, lit., cast oneself down], near or close (*to* something); adjoining. *SYN.*—**adjacent** things may or may not be in actual contact with each other but they are not separated by things of the same kind (*adjacent* angles, *adjacent* farmhouses); that which is **adjoining** something else touches it at some point or along a line (*adjoining* rooms); things are **contiguous** when they touch along the whole or most of one side (*contiguous* farms); **tangent** implies contact at a single, nonintersecting point with a curved line or surface (a line *tangent* to a circle); **neighboring** things lie near to each other (*neighboring* villages).

ad·mis·si·ble (əd-mis'ə-b'l, ad-mis'ə-b'l), *adj.* [Fr.; ML. *admissibilis* < L. *admissus,* pp. of *admittere;* see ADMIT], **1.** that can be accepted or allowed: as, *admissible* evidence. **2.** having the right to be admitted.

af·fa·ble (af'ə-b'l), *adj.* [Fr.; L. *affabilis* < *ad-,* to + *fari,* to speak < base *fa-,* as in *fable*], easy to approach and talk to; pleasant and polite. —*SYN.* see amiable.

af·fi·da·vit (af'ə-dā'vit), *n.* [ML., he has made oath; perf. tense of *affidare;* see AFFIANCE], in *law,* a written statement made on oath, usually before a notary public or other authorized person.

af·fil·i·ate (ə-fil'i-āt'), *v.t.* [AFFILIATED (-id), AFFILIATING], [< L. *affiliatus,* pp. of *affiliare,* to adopt as a son < *ad-,* to + *filius,* son], **1.** to take in as a member or branch. **2.** to connect or associate (oneself). **3.** to decide legally who is the father of; hence, **4.** to trace the source and connections of (a language, etc.). *v.i.* to associate oneself; join. *n.* (ə-fil'i-it), an affiliated individual or organization; member.

af·flu·ent (af'lōō-ənt), *adj.* [Fr. < L. *affluens,* ppr. of *affluere;* see AFFLUENCE], **1.** flowing freely. **2.** plentiful; abundant. **3.** wealthy; rich. *n.* a stream flowing into a river; tributary. —*SYN.* see rich.

ag·gre·gate (ag'rə-git; for *v.,* ag'ri-gāt'), *adj.* [L. *aggregatus,* pp. of *aggregare,* to lead to a flock, add to < *ad-,* to + *gregare,* to herd < *grex, gregis,* a herd], **1.** gathered into a whole or mass; total. **2.** in *botany,* clustered. **3.** in *geology,* composed of mineral fragments or crystals mixed in one rock. *n.* **1.** a total or whole; group or mass of distinct things gathered together. **2.** the sand and pebbles used in making concrete. *v.t.* [AGGREGATED (-id), AGGREGATING], **1.** to gather into a whole or mass. **2.** to amount to; total. —*SYN.* see sum.

in the aggregate, taken all together; on the whole.

al·bi·no (al-bī'nō), *n.* [*pl.* ALBINOS (-nōz)], [Port., lit., whitish < *albo;* L. *albus,* white], **1.** a person whose skin, hair, and eyes lack normal coloration: albinos have a white skin, whitish hair, and pink eyes. **2.** any animal or plant abnormally lacking in color.

al·ien (āl'yən, ā'li-ən), *adj.* [ME.; OFr.; L. *alienus* < *alius,* other], belonging to another country or people; foreign; strange. *n.* **1.** a foreigner. **2.** a foreign-born resident in a country who has not become a naturalized citizen. **3.** an outsider. *v.t.* to transfer (land, etc.). **alien to,** strange to; not natural to. *SYN.*—**alien** is applied to a resident who bears political allegiance to another country; **foreigner,** to a visitor or resident from another country whose language, cultural pattern, etc. are different from one's own; **stranger,** to a person who comes from another region and is unacquainted with local people, customs, etc.; **immigrant,** to a person who comes to a new country to settle there; **émigré,** to one who has left his country to take political refuge in a new land. See also **extrinsic.** —*ANT.* citizen, subject, national.

a·lign (ə-līn'), *v.t.* [Fr. *aligner* < *à,* to + *ligne,* line], **1.** to bring into a straight line; adjust by line. **2.** to bring into agreement, close co-operation, etc.: as, he *aligned* himself with the liberals. *v.i.* to come or fall into line; line up. Also spelled **aline.**

al·ka·lize (al'kə-līz'), *v.t. & v.i.* [ALKALIZED (-līzd'), ALKALIZING], [Fr. *alcaliser* < *alcali;* see ALKALI], to make alkaline.

al·lege (ə-lej'), *v.t.* [ALLEGED (-lejd'), ALLEGING], [ME. *aleggen,* to produce as evidence; OFr. *eslegier* < ML. *exlitigare;* L. *ex,* out of + *litigare;* see LITIGATE], **1.** to assert positively; declare; affirm. **2.** to assert or declare without proof: as, Hitler *alleged* that he was saving Europe. **3.** to give as a plea, excuse, etc.: as, in his defense he *alleged* temporary insanity.

al·le·vi·ate (ə-lē'vi-āt'), *v.t.* [ALLEVIATED (-id), ALLEVIATING], [< L. *alleviatus,* pp. of *alleviare* < *allevare* < *ad-,* to + *levis,* light], to make less hard to bear; lighten or relieve (pain, suffering, etc.). —*SYN.* see relieve.

al·lo·cate (al'ə-kāt', al'ō-kāt'), *v.t.* [ALLOCATED (-id), ALLOCATING], [< ML. *allocatus,* pp. of *allocare* < L. *ad,* to + *locare,* to place < *locus,* a place], **1.** to set apart for a specific purpose: as, they will *allocate* funds for housing. **2.** to distribute by a plan; allot; assign. **3.** to locate. —*SYN.* see allot.

al·to (al'tō), *n.* [*pl.* ALTOS (-tōz)], [It. < L. *altus,* high], in *music,* **1.** the range of the lowest female voice (contralto) or the highest male voice. **2.** a voice or singer with such a range. **3.** an instrument having a similar range, as an althorn. **4.** a part for such a voice or instrument. *adj.* **1.** singing or playing within this range. **2.** for this range. Abbreviated **alt., a.**

a·me·na·ble (ə-mē'nə-b'l, ə-men'ə-b'l), *adj.* [Anglo-Fr. < Fr. *amener,* to lead; *a-* (L. *ad*), to + *mener* < L. *minare,* to drive < *minari,* to threaten], **1.** responsible or answerable. **2.** willing to follow advice; open to suggestion; responsive; submissive. **3.** that can be tested by (with *to*): as, *amenable* to the laws of physics. —*SYN.* see obedient.

am·i·ca·ble (am'i-kə-b'l), *adj.* [L. *amicabilis;* see AMIABLE], friendly; peaceable.

a·mor·tize (am'ẽr-tīz', ə-môr'tīz'), *v.t.* [AMORTIZED (-tīzd'), AMORTIZING], [ME. *amortisen* < OFr. *amortir,* to extinguish, deaden, sell in mortmain (< ML. *amortire*); or < ML. *amortizare;* both ML. forms < L. *ad,* to + *mors,* death], **1.** to put money aside at intervals, as in a sinking fund, for gradual payment of (a debt, etc.). **2.** in *accounting,* to write off (expenditures) by prorating over a fixed period. **3.** in *law,* to transfer or sell (property) in mortmain.

am·pli·fi·er (am'plə-fī'ĕr), *n.* **1.** a person or thing that amplifies. **2.** in *electricity* & *radio*, a circuit, electronic tube, apparatus, etc. for increasing the strength of electrical impulses.

an·nals (an''lz), *n.pl.* [*sing.* ANNAL (an''l)], [L. *annalis*, pl. *annales* < *annus*, year], **1.** a written account of events year by year in chronological order. **2.** historical records or chronicles; history. **3.** *sing.* the record of a single year or event. **4.** any journal containing reports of discoveries in some field, meetings of a society, etc.

an·no·tate (an'ō-tāt'), *v.t.* & *v.i.* [ANNOTATED (-id), ANNOTATING], [< L. *annotatus*, pp. of *annotare* < *ad-*, to + *notare*, to note, mark < *nota*, a mark, sign], to provide critical or explanatory notes for (a literary work, etc.).

an·nu·i·ty (ə-nū'ə-ti, ə-nōō'ə-ti), *n.* [*pl.* ANNUITIES (-tiz)], [Fr. *annuité*; ML. *annuitas* < L. *annus*, year], **1.** a yearly payment of money. **2.** the right to receive such a payment. **3.** an investment yielding fixed payments during the holder's lifetime or for a stated number of years. Abbreviated **ann.**

an·nul (ə-nul'), *v.t.* [ANNULLED (-nuld'), ANNULLING], [Fr. *annuler* < L. *annullare*, to bring to nothing < *ad-*, to + *nullum*, nothing, neut. of *nullus*, none], to do away with; make of no effect; invalidate; make null and void; cancel. —*SYN.* see **abolish.**

a·non (ə-non'), *adv.* [ME.; AS. *on an*, acc., in one, together, straightway], **1.** soon; shortly. **2.** at another time. **3.** [Archaic], immediately; at once.
  ever and anon, now and then; once in a while.

an·thol·o·gy (an-thol'ə-ji), *n.* [*pl.* ANTHOLOGIES (-jiz)], [L. & Gr. *anthologia*, a flower gathering, garland, collection of short poems < *anthologos* < *anthos*, flower + *legein*, to gather], a collection of poems, stories, etc.

an·thro·poph·a·gous (an'thrə-pof'ə-gəs), *adj.* [see ANTHROPOPHAGI], cannibalistic; eating human flesh.

ap·praise (ə-prāz'), *v.t.* [APPRAISED (-prāzd'), APPRAISING], [OFr. *apreiser* < LL. *appretiare* < L. *ad*, to + *pretium*, value; influenced by *praise*], **1.** to set a price for; decide the value of. **2.** to estimate the quantity of. **3.** to judge the quality or worth of. —*SYN.* see **estimate.**

ap·prise, ap·prize (ə-prīz'), *v.t.* [APPRISED OR APPRIZED (-prīzd'), APPRISING OR APPRIZING], [Fr. *appris*, pp. of *apprendre*, to teach, inform < L. *apprehendere*; see APPREHEND], to inform; notify. —*SYN.* see **notify.**

ar·bi·trar·y (är'bə-trer'i), *adj.* [L. *arbitrarius* < ARBITER], **1.** discretionary. **2.** based on one's preference, notion, or whim: hence, **3.** capricious. **4.** absolute; despotic. —*SYN.* see **dictatorial.**

as·sail (ə-sāl'), *v.t.* [ME. *assailen*; OFr. *asaillir*; LL. *assilire*, to leap on < L. *ad*, to + *salire*, to leap], **1.** to attack physically and violently; assault. **2.** to attack with arguments, ridicule, etc. **3.** to face (a difficulty, task, etc.) with determination. —*SYN.* see **attack.**

as·sim·i·late (ə-sim''l-āt'), *v.t.* [ASSIMILATED (-id), ASSIMILATING], [< L. *assimilatus*, pp. of *assimilare* < *ad-*, to + *similare*, to make similar to < *similis*, like], **1.** to take up and make part of itself or oneself; absorb and incorporate; digest: as, the body *assimilates* food. **2.** to compare or liken. **3.** to make like or alike; cause to resemble (with *to*): as, *assimilate* the final sound of a prefix to the initial sound of a word. *v.i.* **1.** to become like or alike. **2.** to be absorbed and incorporated: as, minority groups often *assimilate* by intermarriage.

as·suage (ə-swāj'), *v.t.* [ASSUAGED (-swājd'), ASSUAGING], [ME. *aswagen*; OFr. *asouagier* < L. *ad*, to + *suavis*, sweet], **1.** to lessen (pain, distress, etc.); allay; mitigate. **2.** to pacify; calm (passion, anger, etc.). **3.** to satisfy or quench (thirst, etc.). —*SYN.* see **relieve.**

at·tri·bute (ə-trib'yoot; *for n.*, at'rə-būt'), *v.t.* [ATTRIBUTED (-id), ATTRIBUTING], [< L. *attributus*, pp. of *attribuere*, to assign < *ad-*, to + *tribuere*, to assign], to set down or think of as belonging to, produced by, or resulting from; assign or ascribe (*to*): as, the play is *attributed* to Shakespeare, he *attributes* his poverty to bad luck. *n.* **1.** a characteristic or quality of a thing. **2.** an object used in literature or art as a symbol for a person, position, etc.: as, winged feet are the *attribute* of Mercury. **3.** in *grammar*, a word or phrase used as an adjective. Abbreviated **attrib.** —*SYN.* see **ascribe, quality.**

au·di·tor (ô'də-tĕr), *n.* [L., hearer < *audire*, to hear], **1.** a hearer; listener. **2.** a person who audits accounts: abbreviated **aud.** **3.** a person who audits classes.

au·tom·a·ton (ô-tom'ə-ton', ô-tom'ə-tən), *n.* [*pl.* AUTOMATONS (-tonz', -tənz), AUTOMATA (-tə)], [Gr. *automaton*, neut. of *automatos*; see AUTOMATIC], **1.** anything that can move or act of itself. **2.** an apparatus with a concealed mechanism that enables it to move or work of itself. **3.** a person or animal acting in an automatic or mechanical way.

ba·cil·lus (bə-sil'əs), *n.* [*pl.* BACILLI (-ī)], [Mod. L. < L. *bacillum*, dim. of *baculus*, a stick], **1.** any of a genus of rod-shaped bacteria which occur in chains, produce spores, and are active only in the presence of oxygen: abbreviated **B.** **2.** any rod-shaped bacterium: distinguished from *coccus, spirillum:* see **bacteria,** illus. **3.** *usually pl.* loosely, any of the bacteria, especially those causing disease.

bac·te·ri·a (bak-têr'i-ə), *n.pl.* [*sing.* BACTERIUM (-əm)], [Mod. L., pl. of *bacterium* < Gr. *baktērion*, dim. of *baktron*, a staff], typically one-celled microorganisms which have no chlorophyll, multiply by simple division, and can be seen only with a microscope: they occur in three main forms, spherical (cocci), rod-shaped (bacilli), and spiral (spirilla); some bacteria cause diseases such as pneumonia, tuberculosis, and syphilis, but others are necessary for fermentation, nitrogen fixation, etc.

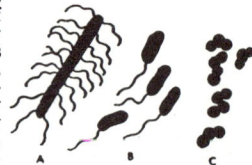

TYPES OF BACTERIA
A, rod (bacillus); B, spiral (spirillum); C, sphere (coccus)

bal·last (bal'əst), *n.* [LG.; D. *barlast; bar*, bare, waste + *last*, a load], **1.** anything heavy carried in a ship or vehicle to give stability or in an aircraft to help control altitude. **2.** anything giving stability and firmness to character, human relations, etc. **3.** crushed rock or gravel, as that placed between and below the ties of a railroad. *v.t.* **1.** to furnish with ballast; stabilize. **2.** to fill in (a railroad bed, etc.) with ballast.

bank·rupt·cy (baŋk'rupt-si, baŋk'rəp-si), *n.* [*pl.* BANKRUPTCIES (-siz)], state or instance of being bankrupt.

bar·ba·rous (bär'bə-rəs), *adj.* [L. *barbarus*; Gr. *barbaros*, foreign, strange, ignorant; prob. < **barbar*, echoic word used for description of strange tongues], **1.** originally, different from one's own language or customs; foreign; alien: in the ancient world, any person or thing that was non-Greek, non-Roman, or non-Christian was called barbarous. **2.** characterized by words and phrases that are substandard in usage; also, not classical: said of language. **3.** characteristic of barbarians; primitive or lacking in civilization. **4.** crude, coarse, rough, etc. **5.** cruel; brutal. **6.** harsh in sound; raucous. —*SYN.* see **barbarian.**

bel·lig·er·ent (bə-lij'ĕr-ənt), *adj.* [Fr. *belligérant*, waging war < L. *belligerans*, ppr. of *belligerare*, to wage war < *bellum*, war + *gerere*, to carry on], **1.** at war. **2.** of war; of fighting. **3.** seeking war; warlike. *n.* any person, group, or nation engaged in war or fighting. *SYN.*—**belligerent** implies a taking part in war or fighting or in actions that are likely to provoke fighting (*belligerent* nations); **bellicose** implies a warlike or hostile nature, suggesting a readiness to fight (a *bellicose* mood); **pugnacious** and **quarrelsome** both connote aggressiveness and a willingness to initiate a fight, but **quarrelsome** more often suggests pettiness and eagerness to fight for little or no reason (he is *quarrelsome* when drunk); **contentious** suggests an inclination to argue or quarrel, usually with annoying persistence. —*ANT.* peaceful, friendly.

ben·e·fi·cial (ben'ə-fish'əl), *adj.* [Fr.; LL. *beneficialis* < L. *benefacere*; see BENEFACTION], **1.** productive of benefits; advantageous; favorable. **2.** receiving benefit. **3.** in *law*, for one's own benefit: as, *beneficial* interest.

be·nev·o·lent (bə-nev'ə-lənt), *adj.* [OFr. *benivolent*; L. *benevolens; bene*, well + *volens*, ppr. of *volere*, to wish], doing or inclined to do good; kindly; benignant; charitable: opposed to *malevolent.* —*SYN.* see **kind.**

be·nign (bi-nīn'), *adj.* [ME. & OFr. *benigne*; L. *benignus*, good < *bene*, well + *genus*, type], **1.** good-natured; kindly. **2.** favorable; beneficial. **3.** in *medicine*, doing little or no harm; not malignant. —*SYN.* see **kind.**

bi·en·ni·al (bī-en′i-əl), *adj.* [L. *biennalis* < *biennium*, period of two years < *bis*, twice + *annus*, year], 1. happening every two years. 2. lasting or living for two years. *n.* 1. a biennial event or occurrence. 2. in *botany*, a plant that lasts two years, usually producing flowers and seed the second year.

boss·y (bôs′i, bos′i), *adj.* [< *boss* (employer)], [Colloq.], domineering.

boss·y (bôs′i, bos′i), *adj.* [< *boss* (raised ornament)], decorated with bosses; studded.

boss·y (bos′i, bôs′i), *n.* [dim. of *boss* (cow)], a cow or calf.

Brah·min (brä′min), *n.* 1. a Brahman. 2. a cultured person from a long-established upper-class family, especially one regarded as haughty or conservative.

bul·lion (bool′yən), *n.* [D. *bulioen*; Fr. *billon*, small coin, alloy of copper with silver < *bille*, a stick, bar < Gallic *bilia*, tree trunk], 1. gold and silver regarded as raw material. 2. ingots of gold or silver, as before coinage.

bul·lion (bool′yən), *n.* [Fr. *bouillon* < L. *bulla*, a bubble], a heavy fringe or lace of twisted gold or silver thread.

buoy·ant (boi′ənt, boo′yənt), *adj.* [? < Sp. *boyante* < *boyar*, to float], having or showing buoyancy.

bur·sar (bûr′sẽr), *n.* [LL. *bursarius*, treasurer < *bursa*; see BURSA], 1. a college treasurer or similar official in charge of the college funds. 2. in Scotland, a university student who has a scholarship.

bust (bust), *n.* [Fr. *buste*; It. *busto*], 1. a piece of sculpture representing the head, shoulders, and upper chest of a human body. 2. the bosom, especially of a woman. —*SYN.* see **breast**.

bust (bust), *v.t. & v.i.* [orig., dial. var. of *burst*], [Slang], 1. to burst; break. 2. to make or become bankrupt. 3. to demote or become demoted. 4. to tame: said of broncos, etc. 5. to hit or punch. *n.* [Slang], 1. a failure. 2. a blow or punch. 3. a spree.

C/A, 1. capital accountant. 2. credit account. 3. current account.

caf·fe·ine, caf·fe·in (kaf′i-in, kaf′ēn′), *n.* [Fr. *caféine* < *café*, coffee], the alkaloid C₈H₁₀N₄O₂, present in coffee, tea, and kola: it is a stimulant to the heart and central nervous system: the methyl derivative of theobromine.

‡car·pe di·em (kär′pi dī′em), [L., lit., seize the day], seize present opportunities; make the most of today.

caulk (kôk), *v.t.* to stop up (a crack or joint), as with tar, oakum, etc.: see **calk**.

cen·sure (sen′shẽr), *n.* [L. *censura* < *censor*; see CENSOR], 1. a blaming; condemnation; adverse opinion or judgment. 2. [Archaic], a judicial sentence, especially by church law. *v.t.* [CENSURED (-shẽrd), CENSURING], to blame; condemn as wrong; criticize adversely; express disapproval of. —*SYN.* see **criticize**.

cen·ten·ni·al (sen-ten′i-əl), *adj.* [< L. *centum*, a hundred + *annus*, year], 1. of 100 years. 2. happening once in a period of 100 years. 3. 100 years old. 4. lasting 100 years. 5. of a 100th anniversary. *n.* 1. a 100th year of existence or duration; 100th anniversary. 2. the celebration of this.

chas·tise (chas-tīz′), *v.t.* [CHASTISED (-tīzd′), CHASTISING], [ME. *chastisen*, extended form of *chastien*; see CHASTEN], 1. to punish in order to correct, usually by beating. 2. [Archaic], to chasten. —*SYN.* see **punish**.

co·de·ine (kō′di-ēn′, kō′dēn), *n.* [< Gr. *kodeia*, poppy head; + -*ine*], an alkaloid, C₁₈H₂₁O₃N·H₂O, derived from opium and resembling morphine, but milder in its action and less habit-forming: used for the relief of pain and as a sedative.

col·lab·o·rate (kə-lab′ə-rāt′), *v.i.* [COLLABORATED (-id), COLLABORATING], [< L. *collaboratus*, pp. of *collaborare*, to work together. < *com-*, with + *laborare*, to work], 1. to work together: especially in reference to literary, artistic, or scientific work. 2. to co-operate with the enemy; be a collaborationist.

col·league (kol′ēg), *n.* [Fr. *collègue*; L. *collega*, one chosen at the same time with another, partner in office < *com-*, with + base *leg-* (to pick, choose) of *legare*, to appoint as deputy, send as ambassador; cf. LEGATE], a fellow worker in the same profession; associate in office: abbreviated **coll.** —*SYN.* see **associate**.

com·mence (kə-mens′), *v.i. & v.t.* [COMMENCED (-menst′), COMMENCING], [OFr. *comencer*; LL. *cominitiare*; L. *com-*, together + *initiare*, to begin], to begin; start; originate. —*SYN.* see **begin**.

com·pa·ra·ble (kom′pẽr-ə-b'l), *adj.* [L. *comparabilis*], 1. that can be compared; having characteristics in common. 2. worthy of comparison.

com·pen·sate (kom′pən-sāt′), *v.t.* [COMPENSATED (-id), COMPENSATING], [< L. *compensatus*, pp. of *compensare*, to weigh together, weigh one thing against another; *com-*, with + *pensare*, freq. of *pendere*, to weigh], 1. to make up for; be a counterbalance to in weight, force, etc. 2. to make equivalent return to; recompense; pay: as, the government *compensated* the owners for the land taken from them. 3. in *mechanics*, to counteract or make allowance for (a variation). 4. in *psychology*, to disguise (an undesired trait) by exaggerating a desired or socially approved one. *v.i.* to make compensation; make amends. —*SYN.* see **pay**.

com·pe·tence (kom′pə-təns), *n.* [Fr. *compétence*; L. *competentia*, a meeting, agreement < *competens*, ppr. of *competere*; see COMPETE], 1. sufficient means for one's needs or for a comfortable existence. 2. ability; skill; fitness. 3. in *law*, legal qualification, power, or jurisdiction.

com·pli·ance (kəm-plī′əns), *n.* 1. a complying, or giving in to a request, wish, demand, etc.; acquiescence. 2. a tendency to give in to others.
in compliance with, in accordance with.

com·prise (kəm-prīz′), *v.t.* [COMPRISED (-prīzd′), COMPRISING], [< Fr. *compris*, pp. of *comprendre*; see COMPREHEND], 1. to include; contain. 2. to consist of; be composed of. Also spelled **comprize**. —*SYN.* see **include**.

comp·trol·ler (kən-trōl′ẽr), *n.* [< *controller*, by association with Fr. *compt*, an account], an official in charge of expenditures; controller.

con·cede (kən-sēd′), *v.t.* [CONCEDED (-id), CONCEDING], [L. *concedere* < *com-*, with + *cedere*, to go, cede, grant], 1. to yield, as in argument; admit the truth of; acknowledge. 2. to admit the justice of; grant as a right: as, he *conceded* the victory. *v.i.* to make a concession.

con·coct (kon-kokt′, kən-kokt′), *v.t.* [< L. *concoctus*, pp. of *concoquere*, to boil together, prepare < *com-*, together + *coquere*, to cook], 1. to make by combining various ingredients; compound. 2. to devise; plan.

con·do·lence (kən-dō′ləns; *rarely*, kon′də-ləns), *n.* [< LL. *condolens*; see CONDOLE], expression of sympathy with another in grief. —*SYN.* see **pity**.

con·stit·u·ent (kən-stich′oo-ənt), *adj.* [< L. *constituens*, ppr. of *constituere*; see CONSTITUTE], 1. necessary in the formation of the whole; component: as, a *constituent* part. 2. that can or does appoint or vote for a representative. 3. authorized to make or revise a political constitution: as, a *constituent* assembly. *n.* 1. a person who helps appoint another as his representative, especially by voting in an election. 2. a necessary part or element; component. 3. in *linguistics*, an element of a construction: in "they painted signs" the main elements *they* and *painted signs* are called *immediate constituents*; the further indivisible elements *they*, *paint*, -*ed*, *sign*, and -*s* are called *ultimate constituents*. —*SYN.* see **element**.

con·tin·gent (kən-tin′jənt), *adj.* [L. *contingens*, ppr. of *contingere*, to touch, meet, happen < *com-*, together + *tangere*, to touch; see CONTACT], 1. that may or may not happen; possible. 2. happening by chance; accidental; fortuitous. 3. dependent (*on* or *upon* something uncertain); conditional. 4. [Archaic], touching; tangential. 5. in *logic*, true only with certain conditions or contexts; not always or necessarily true. *n.* 1. an accidental or chance happening. 2. a share, proportion, or quota, as of troops, ships, laborers, delegates, etc. 3. a group or body forming part of a larger one.

con·tral·to (kən-tral′tō), *n.* [*pl.* CONTRALTOS (-tōz), CONTRALTI (-ti)], [It.; see CONTRA- & ALTO], 1. the part sung by the lowest female voice or, formerly, the highest male voice. 2. a female voice of the lowest range. 3. a woman or girl who sings in this range. *adj.* of or for a contralto. Symbol, C (no period). Abbreviated **contr.**

con·triv·ance (kən-trīv′əns), *n.* 1. the act, way, or power of contriving. 2. something contrived, as an invention, mechanical device, plan, etc.

con·va·les·cence (kon′və-les′'ns), *n.* [Fr.; L. *convalescens*, ppr. of *convalescere*; see CONVALESCE], 1. gradual recovery after illness. 2. the period of such recovery.

con·vey·ance (kən-vā′əns), *n.* 1. a conveying; transportation; transmission. 2. means of conveying; carrying device, especially a vehicle. 3. the transfer of the ownership of real property from one person to another. 4. the document by which this is effected; deed.

cor·pu·lence (kôr′pyoo-ləns), *n.* [Fr.; L. *corpulentia*; see CORPULENT], fleshiness of body; obesity.

coun·ter·sign (koun′tĕr-sīn′; *also, for v.,* koun′tĕr-sīn′), *n.* 1. a signature added to a previously signed piece of writing in order to authenticate or confirm it. 2. a secret sign or signal in answer to another, as in a secret society. 3. in *military usage,* a secret word or signal, usually changed daily, which must be given to a guard or sentry by someone wishing to pass; password. *v.t.* to authenticate or confirm (a previously signed piece of writing) by signing.

cov·e·nant (kuv′ə-nənt), *n.* [ME.; OFr. *covenant,* later *covenant,* agreement, ppr. of *covenir* < L. *convenire;* see CONVENE], 1. a binding and solemn agreement made by two or more individuals, parties, etc. to do or keep from doing a specified thing; compact. 2. an agreement among members of a church to hold to points of doctrine, faith, etc. 3. [C-], an agreement of Presbyterians in Scotland in 1638 to oppose episcopacy: also called *National Covenant.* 4. [C-], an agreement between the parliaments of Scotland and England in 1643 to extend and preserve Presbyterianism in England: also called *Solemn League and Covenant.* 5. [C-], the Covenant of the League of Nations. 6. in *law,* *a)* a formal, sealed contract. *b)* a clause of such a contract. *c)* a suit for damages for violation of such a contract. 7. in *theology,* the promises made by God to man, as recorded in the Bible. *v.i. & v.t.* to promise by or in a covenant.

cred·i·ble (krẹd′ə-b'l), *adj.* [L. *credibilis* < *credere;* see CREED], that can be believed; worthy of belief or trust; trustworthy; reliable. —*SYN.* see plausible.

cri·te·ri·on (krī-tēr′i-ən), *n.* [*pl.* CRITERIA (-ə), CRITERIONS (-ənz)], [< Gr. *kritērion,* means of judging < *kritēs,* judge; cf. CRITIC], a standard, rule, or test by which a judgment of something can be formed. —*SYN.* see standard.

cru·ci·ble (krōō′sə-b'l), *n.* [ML. *crucibulum,* lamp, cresset, melting pot, crucible; prob. < MHG. *kruse,* earthen pot (akin to Eng. *cruse*) + L. suffix -*ibulum* (as in *thuribulum,* censer), but often associated with L. *crux, crucis* (see CROSS) as if lamp burning before cross], 1. a container made of graphite, porcelain, platinum, or other substance that can resist great heat, for melting and calcining ores, metals, etc. 2. the hollow at the bottom of an ore furnace, where the molten metal collects. 3. a severe test; hard trial.

cu·ri·o (kyoor′i-ō′), *n.* [*pl.* CURIOS (-ōz′)], [contr. of *curiosity*], an art object valued as a curiosity or rarity.

de·duct (di-dukt′), *v.t.* [< L. *deductus,* pp. of *deducere;* see DEDUCE], to take away or subtract (a quantity).

de·fer (di-fũr′), *v.t. & v.i.* [DEFERRED (-fũrd′), DEFERRING], [ME. *differren;* OFr. *differer;* see DIFFER], to put off to a future time; postpone; delay.

de·fer (di-fũr′), *v.i.* [DEFERRED (-fũrd′), DEFERRING], [Fr. *déférer,* to yield, impeach in court, pay deference to; L. *deferre,* to bring down; *de-,* down + *ferre,* to bear], to submit in opinion or judgment; yield with courtesy; be respectful: as, he *defers* to his father's decisions. —*SYN.* see yield.

deign (dān), *v.i.* [ME. *deignen;* OFr. *deigner;* L. *dignare, dignari,* to deem worthy < *dignus,* worthy], to think befitting one's dignity (*to do* something); condescend; lower oneself. *v.t.* 1. to condescend to give; vouchsafe: as, will you *deign* no answer? 2. [Obs.], to condescend to accept. —*SYN.* see stoop.

de·mise (di-mīz′), *n.* [Fr. *démis, démise,* pp. of *démettre,* to dismiss, put away; L. *demittere;* see DEMIT], 1. the transfer of an estate by will or lease. 2. the transfer of sovereignty by death or abdication; hence, 3. death; decease. *v.t.* [DEMISED (-mīzd′), DEMISING], 1. to give, grant, or transfer (an estate) by will or lease. 2. to transfer (sovereignty) by death or abdication. *v.i.* to be passed on by bequest or inheritance.

de·pre·ci·ate (di-prē′shi-āt′), *v.t. & v.i.* [DEPRECIATED (-id), DEPRECIATING], [L. *depretiatus,* pp. of *depretiare,* to lower the price of, make light of; *de-,* from + *pretiare,* to value < *pretium,* price], 1. to lessen in value or price. 2. to belittle; disparage. —*SYN.* see disparage.

des·pi·ca·ble (des′pik-ə-b'l, di-spik′ə-b'l), *adj.* [LL. *despicabilis;* see DESPISE], that is or should be despised; contemptible.

de·ter (di-tũr′), *v.t.* [DETERRED (-tũrd′), DETERRING], [L. *deterrere; de-,* from + *terrere,* to frighten], to keep (a person) from doing something through fear, anxiety, doubt, etc.; discourage: as, the weather *deterred* them from going on a picnic.

de·vel·op (di-vel′əp), *v.t.* [Fr. *développer* < *dé-* (L. *dis-*), apart + OFr. *voluper,* to wrap; cf. Pr. *desvolopar,* Fr. *envelopper,* It. *inveluppare,* to wrap up; see ENVELOP], I. to cause to grow gradually in some way; cause to become gradually fuller, larger, better, etc.; especially, 1. to expand, as a business. 2. to strengthen, as muscles. 3. to bring into activity, as an idea. 4. to unfold gradually, as a bud. 5. to make more available or extensive, as electric power. 6. in *music,* to elaborate (a theme). 7. in *photography,* *a)* to put (an exposed film, plate, or printing paper) in various chemical solutions in order to make the picture visible. *b)* to make (a picture) visible by doing this. II. to show or work out by degrees; reveal; disclose; especially, 1. to make known gradually, as a plot. 2. to explain more clearly; enlarge upon. 3. in *mathematics,* to work out in detail or expand (a function or expression). *v.i.* 1. to come into being or activity. 2. to become larger, fuller, better, etc.; grow; evolve. 3. to become known or apparent; be disclosed. Also spelled **develope.**

de·vise (di-vīz′), *v.t. & v.i.* [DEVISED (-vīzd′), DEVISING], [ME. *devisen;* OFr. *deviser,* to distribute, direct, regulate, talk; LL. *divisare* < L. *divisus,* pp. of *dividere;* see DIVIDE], 1. to think out; contrive; plan; invent. 2. in *law,* to bequeath (real property) by will. 3. [Obs.], to divide. 4. [Obs.], to guess; divine. *n.* in *law,* 1. a gift of real property by will. 2. a will, or clause in a will, granting such a gift. 3. the property so granted.

dif·fi·dent (dif′i-dənt), *adj.* [L. *diffidens;* see DIFFIDENCE], lacking confidence in oneself; hesitant to assert oneself; shy. —*SYN.* see shy.

di·lem·ma (di-lem′ə), *n.* [LL.; Gr. *dilēmma; di-,* two + *lēmma,* proposition or assumption < *lambanein,* to take], 1. an argument necessitating a choice between equally unfavorable or disagreeable alternatives; hence, 2. any situation necessitating a choice between unpleasant alternatives; perplexing or awkward situation. —*SYN.* see predicament.
on the horns of a dilemma, faced with a choice between equally disagreeable alternatives.

dil·i·gence (dil′ə-jəns), *n.* [ME.; OFr.; L. *diligentia* < *diligens,* ppr. of *diligere,* to esteem highly, select < *dis-,* apart + *legere,* to choose], 1. the quality of being diligent. 2. constant, careful effort; perseverance.

dil·i·gence (dil′ə-jəns; Fr. dē′lē′zhäns′), *n.* [Fr. < *carrosse de diligence,* lit., coach of diligence, i.e., fast coach < *faire diligence,* to hurry], a public stagecoach formerly much used in France and other European countries.

dis·ap·point (dis′ə-point′), *v.t.* [OFr. *desapointer;* see DIS- & APPOINT], 1. to fail to satisfy the hopes or expectations of. 2. to break one's promise to. 3. to prevent or undo the intended result of; balk; thwart: as, the weather *disappointed* their plans.

dis·bar (dis-bär′), *v.t.* [DISBARRED (-bärd′), DISBARRING], to expel (a lawyer) from the bar; deprive of the right to practice law. —*SYN.* see exclude.

dis·cern·i·ble (di-zũrn′ə-b'l, di-sũrn′ə-b'l), *adj.* [LL. *discernibilis*], that can be discerned; perceptible.

dis·course (dis′kôrs, dis′kōrs; *also, and for v. always,* dis-kôrs′, dis-kōrs′), *n.* [OFr. *discours;* LL. *discursus,* discourse < L., pp. of *discurrere,* to run to and fro; *dis-,* from, in different directions + *currere,* to run], 1. communication by talking; conversation. 2. communication in general, especially as a subject of study. 3. a long and formal treatment of a subject, in speech or writing; lecture; sermon; treatise; dissertation. 4. [Archaic], ability to reason; rationality. *v.i.* [DISCOURSED (-kôrst′, -kōrst′), DISCOURSING], 1. to carry on conversation; talk; confer. 2. to speak or write (*on* or *upon* a subject) formally and at some length. *v.t.* 1. to utter. 2. [Archaic], to tell. —*SYN.* see speak.

dis·il·lu·sion (dis′i-lōō′zhən, dis′i-lū′zhən), *v.t.* to tree from illusion; disenchant. *n.* disillusionment.

dis·pel (dis-pel′), *v.t.* [DISPELLED (-peld′), DISPELLING], [L. *dispellere; dis-,* apart, away + *pellere,* to drive], to scatter and drive away; cause to vanish; disperse. —*SYN.* see scatter.

dis·sect (di-sekt′), *v.t.* [< L. *dissectus,* pp. of *dissecare,* to cut apart, cut up; *dis-,* apart + *secare,* to cut], 1. to cut apart piece by piece; separate into parts, as a body for purposes of study; anatomize. 2. to examine or analyze closely.

dis·sem·ble (di-sem′b'l), *v.t.* [DISSEMBLED (-b'ld), DISSEMBLING], [earlier *dissimule* < OFr. *dissimuler;* L. *dissimulare* (see DISSIMULATE); re-formed after *re-*

semble], **1.** to conceal under a false appearance: as, he *dissembled* his hatred by pretending to be friendly. **2.** to resemble falsely; simulate; feign: as, vice sometimes *dissembles* virtue. **3.** to pretend not to observe; feign ignorance of. *v.i.* to conceal one's true feelings, motives, etc. by pretense; behave hypocritically.

dis·sem·i·nate (di-sem'ə-nāt'), *v.t.* [DISSEMINATED (-id), DISSEMINATING], [< L. *disseminatus*, pp. of *disseminare*, lit., to scatter seed, hence disseminate; *dis-*, apart + *seminare*, to sow < *semen*, seed], to scatter far and wide; spread abroad, as if sowing; promulgate widely.

dis·ser·ta·tion (dis'ər-tā'shən), *n.* [LL. *dissertatio;* see DISSERTATE], a formal and lengthy discussion in speech or writing; a discourse or treatise, especially one required by colleges and universities as partial fulfillment of requirements for a degree; thesis.

dis·si·dent (dis'ə-dənt), *adj.* [L. *dissidens*, ppr. of *dissidere;* see DISSIDENCE], not agreeing; dissenting. *n.* a dissident person; dissenter.

dis·si·pate (dis'ə-pāt'), *v.t.* [DISSIPATED (-id), DISSIPATING], [< L. *dissipatus*, pp. of *dissipare*, to scatter, disperse; *dis-*, apart + *sipare, supare*, to throw], **1.** to scatter; dispel; disperse. **2.** to drive completely away; make disappear. **3.** to waste; squander. *v.i.* **1.** to be dissolved or dispelled; vanish. **2.** to waste one's time and energy on frivolities; indulge in pleasure, especially drinking, gambling, etc., to the point of harming oneself; be dissolute. —*SYN.* see **scatter.**

dis·sol·u·ble (di-sol'yoo-b'l), *adj.* [L. *dissolubilis* < *dissolvere;* see DISSOLVE], that can be dissolved.

dis·so·lute (dis'ə-lōōt', dis'ə-lūt'), *adj.* [L. *dissolutus*, loosened, lax, unrestrained; pp. of *disolvere;* see DISSOLVE], dissipated and immoral; profligate; debauched.

dis·so·nance (dis'ə-nəns), *n.* [Fr.; LL. *dissonantia* < L. *dissonans*, ppr. of *dissonare*, to be discordant, disagree in sound < *dis-*, apart + *sonus*, a sound], **1.** an inharmonious sound or combination of sounds; discord. **2.** any lack of harmony or agreement; incongruity. **3.** in *music*, a chord that sounds harsh and incomplete until resolved to a harmonious chord.

dis·suade (di-swād'), *v.t.* [DISSUADED (-id), DISSUADING], [L. *dissuadere; dis-*, away, from + *suadere*, to persuade], to turn (a person) aside (*from* a course, etc.) by persuasion or advice.

dis·tance (dis'təns), *n.* [ME.; OFr.; L. *distantia* < *distans*, ppr. of *distare*, to stand apart, be separate < *dis-*, apart + *stare*, to stand], **1.** the fact or condition of being separated or removed in space or time; remoteness. **2.** a gap or space between two points. **3.** an interval between two points in time. **4.** the measure of a space or interval: as, the *distance* was one mile. **5.** a remoteness in relationship: as, the *distance* between health and illness. **6.** a remoteness in behavior; coolness of manner; reserve. **7.** a far-away place: as, the bird flew away into the *distance*. **8.** a far-away point of time: as, at this *distance* we cannot know Neanderthal man. **9.** in *music*, an interval between two tones. **10.** in *painting*, the depicting of distance, as in a landscape. **11.** in *racing*, a space that is a certain distance back from the finish line: in order to be qualified for future heats, a horse must have reached this space by the time the winner has completed the course. Abbreviated **dis., dist.** *v.t.* [DISTANCED (-tənst), DISTANCING], **1.** to place or hold at some distance. **2.** to make appear to be far away: as, he *distances* his landscapes well. **3.** to do better or more than; leave behind; outdo; best.

  keep at a distance, to treat aloofly; be reserved or cool toward (someone).

  keep one's distance, to be or remain aloof or reserved.

dys·en·ter·y (dis''n-ter'i), *n.* [OFr. *dysenterie;* L. *dysenteria;* Gr. *dysenteria* < *dys-*, bad + *enteron*, pl. *entera*, bowels], any of various intestinal diseases characterized by inflammation, abdominal pain, toxemia, and diarrhea with bloody, mucous feces.

ec·cen·tri·cal·ly (ik-sen'tri-k'l-i, ek-sen'trik-li), *adv.* in an eccentric manner.

ed·i·fy (ed'ə-fī'), *v.t.* [EDIFIED (-fīd'), EDIFYING], [ME. *edifien;* OFr. *edifier;* L. *aedificare*, to build, construct, edify < *aedes*, a dwelling, house, temple, orig., hearth, fireplace (akin to Gr. *aithein*, to burn, AS. *ad*, pyre < IE. base **ai-dh-*, to burn) + *-ficare*, to make; see -FY], **1.** to instruct; especially, to instruct or improve morally or spiritually. **2.** [Archaic], to build; establish.

em·i·nent (em'ə-nənt), *adj.* [L. *eminens;* see EMINENCE], **1.** rising above other things or places; high; lofty. **2.**

projecting; prominent; protruding. **3.** standing high by comparison with others; renowned; exalted; distinguished. **4.** outstanding; remarkable; noteworthy: as, a man of *eminent* good sense. —*SYN.* see **famous.**

em·is·sar·y (em'ə-ser'i), *n.* [*pl.* EMISSARIES (-iz)], [L. *emissarius* < pp. of *emittere*, see EMIT], a person or agent, especially a secret agent, sent on a specific mission. *adj.* of, or serving as, an emissary or emissaries.

en·thuse (in-thōōz', in-thūz'), *v.t. & v.i.* [ENTHUSED (-thōōzd', -thūzd'), ENTHUSING], [back-formation < *enthusiasm*], [Colloq.], **1.** to make or become enthusiastic. **2.** to show or cause to show enthusiasm.

e·nu·mer·ate (i-nōō'mə-rāt', i-nū'mə-rāt'), *v.t.* [< L. *enumeratus*, pp. of *enumerare; e-*, out + *numerare*, to count < *numerus*, number], **1.** to count; count one by one. **2** to name one by one; specify, as in a list.

en·vi·ron·ment (in-vi'rən-mənt; *sometimes* in-vī'ērn-mənt), *n.* [*environ* + *-ment*], **1.** a surrounding or being surrounded. **2.** something that surrounds; surroundings. **3.** all the conditions, circumstances, and influences surrounding, and affecting the development of, an organism or group of organisms: often contrasted with *heredity*.

e·pit·o·mize (i-pit'ə-mīz'), *v.t.* [EPITOMIZED (-mīzd'), EPITOMIZING], to make or be an epitome of.

eq·ui·ta·ble (ek'wi-tə-b'l), *adj.* [Fr. *équitable* < *équité*], **1.** characterized by equity; fair; just: said of actions, results of actions, etc. **2.** in *law*, *a*) having to do with equity, as distinguished from common or statute law. *b*) valid in equity.

e·soph·a·gus (i-sof'ə-gəs), *n.* [*pl.* ESOPHAGI (-jī')], [L. *oesophagus* < Gr. *oisophagos*, lit., passage for food < *oisein*, fut. inf. of *pherein*, to carry + *phagein*, to eat], the passage for food from the pharynx to the stomach; gullet: also spelled **oesophagus:** see **alimentary canal,** illus.

es·sence (es''ns), *n.* [Fr.; L. *essentia* < ppr. of *esse*, to be], **1.** something that is, or exists; entity. **2.** that which makes something what it is; intrinsic, fundamental nature (of something); essential being. **3.** a substance that keeps, in concentrated form, the flavor, fragrance, or other properties of the plant, drug, food, etc. from which it is extracted; essential oil. **4.** a solution of such a substance or oil in alcohol. **5.** a perfume. **6.** in *philosophy*, the inward nature of anything, underlying its manifestations; true substance.

eth·i·cal·ly (eth'i-k'l-i, eth'ik-li), *adv.* **1.** in an ethical manner. **2.** according to ethics.

ex·cise (ik-sīz'; *for n., also* ek'sīz), *n.* [earlier *accise;* prob. < MD. *accijs;* OFr. *aceis* < LL. **accensus* < *accensare*, to tax < L. *ad-*, to + *census*, a tax], **1.** a tax; a tax or duty on the manufacture, sale, or consumption of various commodities within a country, as liquor, tobacco, etc.: also **excise tax.** **2.** a fee paid for a license to carry on certain occupations, sports, etc. *v.t.* [EXCISED (-sīzd'), EXCISING], to force payment of an excise from.

ex·cise (ik-sīz'), *v.t.* [EXCISED (-sīzd'), EXCISING], [< L. *excisus*, pp. of *excidere;* see EXCIDE], to cut out or away; remove, as a tumor.

ex·em·pla·ry (ig-zem'plə-ri), *adj.* [LL. *exemplaris;* see EXEMPLAR], **1.** serving as a model or example; worth imitating: as, *exemplary* behavior. **2.** serving as a warning or deterrent: as, *exemplary* punishment. **3.** serving as a sample, instance, type, etc.; typical.

ex·on·er·ate (ig-zon'ə-rāt'), *v.t.* [EXONERATED (-id), EXONERATING], [< L. *exoneratus*, pp. of *exonerare*, to disburden; *ex-*, out + *onerare*, to load < *onus, oneris*, a load, burden], **1.** originally, to relieve of (a burden, obligation, etc.); unload; hence, **2.** to free (a person) from a charge or the imputation of guilt; declare or prove blameless; exculpate. —*SYN.* see **absolve.**

ex·or·bi·tant (ig-zôr'bə-tənt), *adj.* [L. *exorbitans*, ppr. of *exorbitare*, to go out of the track < *ex-*, out + *orbita*, a track, orbit], going beyond what is reasonable, just, proper, usual, etc.; excessive; extravagant; immoderate: said of charges, prices, etc. —*SYN.* see **excessive.**

ex·or·cise (ek'sôr-sīz'), *v.t.* [EXORCISED (-sīzd'), EXORCISING], [OFr. *exorciser;* LL. *exorcizare;* New Testament Gr. *exorkizein*, to drive away an evil spirit by adjuration, (earlier) to swear a person, administer an oath < Gr. *ex-*, out + *horkizein*, to make one swear < *horkos*, an oath; cf. CONJURE], **1.** to drive (a supposed evil spirit or spirits) out or away by ritual charms or incantation.

2. to summon or command (such a spirit or spirits).
3. to free from such a spirit or spirits. Also spelled **exorcize**.

ex·pe·di·ent (ik-spē'di-ənt), *adj.* [ME.; OFr.; L. *expediens*, ppr. of *expedire*; see EXPEDITE], 1. useful for effecting a desired result; suited to the circumstances or the occasion; advantageous; convenient. 2. based on or offering what is of use or advantage rather than what is right or just; guided by self-interest; advisable; politic. *n.* 1. an expedient thing; means to an end. 2. a device used in an emergency; makeshift; resource. —*SYN.* see **resource.**

ex·po·nent (ik-spō'nənt), *adj.* [L. *exponens*, ppr. of *exponere*; see EXPOUND], setting forth; explaining; expounding; interpreting. *n.* 1. a person who sets forth, expounds, or interprets (principles, methods, etc.). 2. a person or thing that is an example or symbol (*of* something). 3. in *algebra*, a small figure or symbol placed above and at the right of another figure or symbol to show how many times the latter is to be multiplied by itself (e.g., $b^3 = b \times b \times b$).

ex·u·ber·ant (ig-zōō'bĕr-ənt, ig-zū'bĕr-ənt), *adj.* [L. *exuberans*; see EXUBERANCE], 1. growing profusely; luxuriant; prolific: as, *exuberant* vegetation. 2. overflowing; lavish; effusive: as, *exuberant* spirits. 3. overflowing with good health and spirits: said of a person.

fa·cil·i·tate (fə-sil'ə-tāt'), *v.t.* [FACILITATED (-id), FACILITATING], [Fr. *faciliter*, after It. *facilitare* < L. *facilis*; see FACILE], 1. to make easy or easier. 2. to lighten the work of; assist; help.

Fahr·en·heit (far'ən-hīt', fär'ən-hīt'), *adj.* [< Gabriel Daniel *Fahrenheit* (1686–1736), G. physicist who devised the scale], designating or of a thermometer on which the boiling point of pure water is 212° and the freezing point 32°, under standard atmospheric pressure. *n.* this thermometer or its scale. Abbreviated **F.**, **Fah.**, **Fahr.**

fal·li·ble (fal'ə-b'l), *adj.* [ME.; ML. *fallibilis* < L. *fallere*, to deceive], 1. liable to be mistaken or deceived. 2. liable to be erroneous or inaccurate.

FCIC, Federal Crop Insurance Corporation.

fea·si·ble (fē'zə-b'l), *adj.* [OFr. *faisible, faisable* < *faire*, to make, do; L. *facere*], 1. capable of being done or carried out; practicable; possible: as, a *feasible* scheme. 2. likely; reasonable; probable: as, a *feasible* story. 3. capable of being used or dealt with successfully; suitable: as, land *feasible* for cultivation. —*SYN.* see **possible.**

feign (fān), *v.t.* [ME. *feinen*; OFr. *feindre* (ppr. *feignant*) < L. *fingere*, to touch, handle, shape; cf. FICTION, FIGURE], 1. originally, to form; shape. 2. to make up (a story, excuse, etc.); invent; fabricate. 3. to imagine. 4. to make a false show of; pretend; imitate; simulate. *v.i.* to pretend; dissemble. —*SYN.* see **assume.**

flab·ber·gast (flab'ĕr-gast'), *v.t.* [18th-c. slang; prob. < *flabby* + *aghast*], [Colloq.], to make speechless with amazement; astonish. —*SYN.* see **surprise.**

flex·i·ble (flek'sə-b'l), *adj.* [L. *flexibilis* < *flexus*; see FLEX], 1. able to bend without breaking; not stiff or rigid; pliant; easily bent. 2. easily persuaded or influenced; tractable. 3. adjustable to change; capable of modification: as, a *flexible* voice. —*SYN.* see **elastic.**

for·bear·ance (fôr-bâr'əns, fēr-bâr'əns), *n.* 1. the act of forbearing. 2. the quality of being forbearing; self-control; patient restraint. 3. in *law*, an extension of time for the payment of a debt. —*SYN.* see **patience.**

for·mi·da·ble (fôr'mi-də-b'l), *adj.* [Fr.; L. *formidabilis* < *formidare*, to fear, dread < *formido*, fear], 1. causing dread, fear, or awe. 2. hard to handle or overcome: as, a *formidable* job.

fran·chise (fran'chīz), *n.* [ME.; OFr. < *franc*, free; see FRANK, adj.], 1. originally, freedom from some restriction, servitude, etc.; hence, 2. *a)* any special right or privilege granted by the government, as to be a corporation, operate a public utility, etc. *b)* the jurisdiction over which this extends. 3. the right to vote; suffrage. 4. the right

to market a product, often exclusive for a specified area, as granted by the manufacturer.

fran·chised (fran'chīzd), a *franchised* dealer.

frat·er·nize (frat'ĕr-nīz), *v.i.* [FRATERNIZED (-nīzd'), FRATERNIZING], [Fr. *fraterniser* < L. *fraternus*; see FRATERNAL], 1. to associate in a brotherly manner; be on friendly terms. 2. [Colloq.], to have sexual relations with one of the enemy: said of soldiers in and after World War II. *v.t.* [Rare], to bring into fraternal association.

fraud·u·lent (frô'jə-lənt), *adj.* [ME.; OFr.; L. *fraudulentus < fraus*; see FRAUD], 1. acting with fraud; deceitful. 2. based on or characterized by fraud. 3. done or obtained by fraud.

fluc·tu·ate (fluk'chōō-āt'), *v.i.* [FLUCTUATED (-id), FLUCTUATING], [< L. *fluctuatus*, pp. of *fluctuare* < *fluctus*, a flowing, wave < pp. stem of *fluere*, to flow], 1. to move back and forth or up and down; rise and fall, as waves. 2. to be continually changing or varying in an irregular way: as, the cost of sugar *fluctuates*. *v.t.* to cause to fluctuate. —*SYN.* see **swing.**

gal·va·nize (gal'və-nīz'), *v.t.* [GALVANIZED (-nīzd'), GALVANIZING], [Fr. *galvaniser* < *galvanisme*; see GALVANISM], 1. to apply an electric current to. 2. to stimulate as if by electric shock; startle; excite. 3. to plate (metal) with zinc, originally by galvanic action. —*SYN.* see **swing.**

glos·sa·ry (glos'ĕr-i, glôs'ĕr-i), *n.* [*pl.* GLOSSARIES (-iz)], [L. *glossarium* < *glossa*; see GLOSS (explanation)], a list of foreign, difficult, or technical terms with explanations or translations, as for some particular author, field of knowledge, etc., often included in alphabetical listing at the end of a textbook: abbreviated **gloss.**

gnarled (närld), *adj.* [< ME. *knarre*, knot], knotty, as a tree trunk; contorted; twisted; knobby; rugged.

griev·ous (grēv'əs), *adj.* [ME. *grevous*; OFr. *grevous* < *grever*; see GRIEVE], 1. causing grief. 2. showing or characterized by grief: as, a *grievous* cry. 3. causing physical suffering; hard to bear; severe: as, *grievous* pain. 4. deplorable; atrocious: as, a *grievous* crime.

grot·to (grot'ō), *n.* [*pl.* GROTTOES, GROTTOS (-ōz)], [It. *grotta* < LL. *grupta*; L. *crypta*; see CRYPT], 1. a cave. 2. a cavelike summerhouse, shrine, etc.

gul·li·ble (gul'ə-b'l), *adj.* [*gull, v.* + *-ible*], easily cheated or tricked; credulous: also spelled **gullable.**

hag·gard (hag'ĕrd), *adj.* [MFr. *hagard*, untamed, untamed hawk; prob. < MHG. *hag*, a hedge; see HAG (witch)], 1. in *falconry*, designating a hawk captured after reaching maturity; hence, 2. untamed; unruly; wild. 3. *a)* wild-eyed. *b)* having a wild, wasted, worn look, as from sleeplessness, grief, illness, hunger, etc.; gaunt; drawn. *n.* in *falconry*, a haggard hawk.

har·ass (har'əs, hə-ras'), *v.t.* [Fr. *harasser* < OFr. *harer*, to set a dog on], 1. to trouble, worry, or torment, as with cares, debts, repeated questions, etc. 2. in *military usage*, to trouble (the enemy) by constant raids or attacks, continual fire, etc.; harry.

haugh·ty (hô'ti), *adj.* [HAUGHTIER (-ti-ĕr), HAUGHTIEST (-ti-ist)], [ME. *haut*, high, haughty < OFr. *haut*, high < L. *altus* (with *h-* after OHG. *hoh*, high); + *-y*; influenced by ME. *hautein*; OFr. *hautain < haut*; *gh* prob. inserted by analogy with *naughty* (cf. DELIGHT, SPRIGHTLY)], 1. having or showing great pride in oneself and disdain, contempt, or scorn for others; proud; arrogant; supercilious. 2. [Archaic], lofty; noble. —*SYN.* see **proud.**

hei·nous (hā'nəs), *adj.* [ME. *hainous, heinous*; OFr. *hainös* (Fr. *haineux*) < *haine*, hatred < *hair*, to hate < same LG. base as Eng. *hate*], hateful; odious; extremely wicked; abominable. —*SYN.* see **outrageous.**

hi·er·arch·y (hī'ĕr-är'ki), *n.* [*pl.* HIERARCHIES (-kiz)], [Early Mod. Eng. *yerarchy*; ME. *gerarchie*; OFr. *jerarchie*; LL. *ierarchia*, for *hierarchia*; Gr. *hierarchia*, power or rule of a hierarch < *hierarchēs* (see HIERARCH); now spelled after LL. & Gr.], 1. a system of church government by priests or other clergy in graded ranks. 2. the group of officials in such a system. 3. a group of persons or things arranged in order of rank, grade, class, etc. 4. in *theology*, *a)* any of the three divisions of angels. *b)* all the angels.

hi·er·o·glyph·ic (hī'ĕr-ə-glif'ik, hī'rə-glif'ik), *adj.* [Fr.

hiéroglyphique; LL. *hieroglyphicus;* Gr. *hieroglyphikos < hieros,* sacred + *glyphein,* to carve, hollow out], 1. of, or having the nature of, hieroglyphics. 2. written in hieroglyphics. 3. symbolical; emblematic. 4. hard to read or understand. *n.* 1. a picture or symbol representing a word, syllable, or sound, used by the ancient Egyptians and others instead of alphabetic letters. 2. *usually pl.* a method of writing using hieroglyphics; picture writing. 3. a symbol, sign, etc. hard to understand. 4, *pl.* writing hard to decipher.

HIEROGLYPHICS
(Translation:"Isent:Iorder that you reduce and crush all the high officers of Tsahi. I cast them together with all their possessions at thy feet.")

hin·drance (hin′drəns), *n.* [ME.], 1. **a** hindering. 2. any person or thing that hinders; obstacle; impediment; obstruction. —*SYN.* see **obstacle.**

hos·pi·ta·ble (hos′pi-tə-b'l; *occas.* hos-pit′ə-b'l), *adj.* [MFr. < L. *hospitare,* to receive as a guest < *hospes,* host, guest], 1. entertaining, or fond of entertaining, guests in a friendly, generous manner. 2. caused or characterized by generosity and friendliness to guests: as, a *hospitable* act. 3. liberal and generous in disposition and mind; receptive or open, as to new ideas.

ig·no·min·y (ig′nə-min′i), *n.* [*pl.* IGNOMINIES (-iz)], [Fr. *ignominie;* L. *ignominia < in-,* without, not + *nomen,* name, renown], 1. loss of one's reputation; shame and dishonor; infamy. 2. disgraceful, shameful, or contemptible quality, behavior, or act. —*SYN.* see **disgrace.**

il·leg·i·ble (i-lej′ə-b'l), *adj.* [*il-* (not) + *legible*], very difficult or impossible to read because badly written or printed, obscured by age, etc.

il·lic·it (i-lis′it), *adj.* [Fr. *illicite;* L. *illicitus,* not allowed; see IN- (not) & LICIT], not allowed by law, custom, etc.; unlawful; prohibited; unauthorized; improper.

im·mi·nent (im′ə-nənt), *adj.* [L. *imminens,* ppr. of *imminere,* to project over, overhang, threaten < *in-,* on + *minere,* to project], 1. [Rare], overhanging. 2. likely to happen without delay; impending; threatening: said of danger, evil, misfortune, etc.

im·pair (im-pâr′), *v.t.* [ME. *empaire, empeire;* OFr. *empeirer* < L. *in-,* intens. + LL. *pejorare,* to make worse < L. *pejor,* worse], to make worse, less, weaker, etc.; damage; reduce; deteriorate. —*SYN.* see **injure.**

im·passe (im′pas, im-pas′; Fr. an′päs′), *n.* [*pl.* IMPASSES (-iz; Fr. an′päs′)], [Fr.], 1. a passage open only at one end; blind alley; hence, 2. a situation from which there is no escape; difficulty without solution; deadlock.

im·pec·ca·ble (im-pek′ə-b'l), *adj.* [LL. *impeccabilis* < L. *in-,* not + *peccare,* to sin], 1. not liable to sin or wrongdoing. 2. without defect or error; faultless; flawless. *n.* an impeccable person.

im·pede (im-pēd′), *v.t.* [IMPEDED (-id), IMPEDING], [L. *impedire,* to entangle, ensnare, lit., to hold the feet < *in-,* in + *pes, pedis,* foot], to bar or hinder the progress of; obstruct; retard. —*SYN.* see **delay, hinder.**

im·per·vi·ous (im-pûr′vi-əs), *adj.* [L. *impervius;* see IN- (not) & PERVIOUS], 1. incapable of being passed through or penetrated: as, a fabric *impervious* to moisture. 2. not affected or influenced by (with *to*): as, a man *impervious* to reason.

im·pla·ca·ble (im-plā′kə-b'l, im-plak′ə-b'l), *adj.* [Fr.; L. *implacabilis*], 1. not placable; not to be appeased or pacified; relentless; inexorable. 2. [Obs.], that cannot be eased, lessened, or allayed. —*SYN.* see **inflexible.**

im·pro·vise (im′prə-vīz′, im′prə-vīz′), *v.t.* & *v.i.* [IMPROVISED (-vīzd′, -vīzd′), IMPROVISING], [Fr. *improviser;* It. *improvisare* < *improviso,* unprepared; L. *improvisus,* unforeseen < *in-,* not + *provisus,* pp. of *providere,* to foresee, anticipate; see PROVIDE], 1. to compose, or simultaneously compose and perform, sing, etc., on the spur of the moment and without any preparation; extemporize. 2. to make, provide, or do with the tools and materials at hand, usually to fill an unforeseen and immediate need: as, he *improvised* a bed out of leaves.

im·pu·dent (im′pyoo-dənt), *adj.* [ME.; Fr.; L. *impudens* < *in-,* not + *pudens,* modest, orig. ppr. of *pudere,* to feel shame], 1. originally, immodest; shameless. 2. shamelessly bold; saucy; insolent. —*SYN.* see **impertinent.**

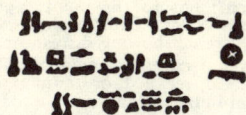

in·can·des·cent (in′kən-des′'nt), *adj.* [L. *incandescens,* ppr. of *incandescere;* see IN- (in) & CANDESCENT], 1 glowing with intense heat; red-hot or, especially, white-hot. 2. very bright; shining brilliantly; gleaming.

in·cin·er·a·tor (in-sin′ə-rā′tēr), *n.* a person or thing that incinerates; specifically, *a*) a furnace or other device for burning trash. *b*) a crematory.

in·cise (in-sīz′), *v.t.* [INCISED (-sīzd′), INCISING], [Fr. *inciser* < L. *incisus,* pp. of *incidere,* to cut into < *in-,* into + *caedere,* to cut], 1. to cut into with a sharp tool. 2. to make (figures, inscriptions, etc.) by cutting; engrave; carve.

in·co·her·ent (in′kō-hēr′ənt), *adj.* not coherent; specifically, *a*) lacking cohesion; not sticking together. *b*) not logically connected; disjointed; rambling. *c*) characterized by incoherent speech, thought, etc.

in·com·pe·tent (in-kom′pə-tənt), *adj.* [Fr. *incompétent;* LL. *incompetens;* see IN- (not) & COMPETENT], 1. without adequate ability, knowledge, fitness, etc.; failing to meet requirements; incapable; unskillful. 2. not legally qualified. *n.* an incompetent person; especially, one who is mentally deficient.

in·com·pre·hen·si·ble (in′kom-pri-hen′sə-b'l, in-kom′pri-hen′sə-b'l), *adj.* 1. not comprehensible; that cannot be understood; unintelligible. 2. [Archaic], illimitable.

in·cor·ri·gi·ble (in-kôr′i-jə-b'l, in-kor′i-jə-b'l), *adj.* [ME. *incorygibile;* OFr.; LL. *incorrigibilis*], not corrigible; that cannot be corrected, improved, or reformed, especially because firmly established, as a habit, or set in bad habits, as a child. *n.* an incorrigible person.

in·cum·bent (in-kum′bənt), *adj.* [L. *incumbens,* ppr. of *incumbere,* to recline or rest on < *in-,* on + *cubare,* to lie down], 1. lying, resting, or pressing with its weight on something else; hence, 2. [Poetic], impending; imminent. *n.* the holder of a benefice or office.
    incumbent on (or **upon**), resting or coming upon as a duty or obligation.

in·de·fat·i·ga·ble (in′di-fat′i-gə-b'l), *adj.* [MFr. *indéfatigable;* L. *indefatigabilis* < *in-,* not + *defatigare,* to tire out, weary; see DE- & FATIGUE], that cannot be tired out; tireless; untiring.

In·di·an·a (in′di-an′ə), *n.* a Middle Western State of the United States: area, 36,291 sq. mi.; pop., 3,934,000; capital, Indianapolis: abbreviated **Ind.**: nicknamed *Hoosier State.*

in·dis·creet (in′dis-krēt′), *adj.* not discreet; lacking prudence, as in speech or action; unwise.

in·dom·i·ta·ble (in-dom′i-tə-b'l), *adj.* [LL. *indomitabilis* < L. *indomitus,* untamed, ungoverned < *in-,* not + *domitus,* pp. of *domitare,* to tame, intens. < *domere,* to tame, subdue], not easily discouraged, defeated, or subdued; unyielding; unconquerable.

in·duce (in-dōōs′, in-dūs′), *v.t.* [INDUCED (-dōōst′, -dūst′), INDUCING], [ME. *enducen;* L. *inducere; in-,* in + *ducere,* to lead], 1. to lead on to some action, condition, belief, etc.; prevail on; persuade. 2. to bring on; bring about; cause; effect: as, indigestion is *induced* by overeating. 3. to draw (a general rule or conclusion) from particular facts; infer by induction. 4. in *physics,* to bring about (an electric or magnetic effect) in a body by exposing it to the influence or variation of a field of force. —*SYN.* see **persuade.**

in·ex·o·ra·ble (in-ek′sēr-ə-b'l), *adj.* [L. *inexorabilis;* see IN- (not) & EXORABLE], that cannot be moved or influenced by persuasion or entreaty; unrelenting; inflexible.

in·fer (in-fûr′), *v.t.* [INFERRED (-fûrd′), INFERRING], [L. *inferre,* to bring or carry in, infer; *in-,* in + *ferre,* to bring, carry], 1. originally, to bring on or about; cause; induce. 2. to conclude or decide from something known or assumed; derive by reasoning; draw as a conclusion. 3. to lead to as a conclusion; indicate; imply: generally regarded as a loose usage. *v.i.* to draw inferences.
SYN.—**infer** suggests the arriving at a decision or opinion by reasoning from known facts or evidence (from your smile, I *infer* that you're pleased); **deduce,** in strict discrimination, implies inference from a general principle by logical reasoning (the method was *deduced* from earlier experiments); **conclude** strictly implies an inference that is the final logical result in a process of reasoning (I must, therefore, *conclude* that you are wrong); **judge** stresses the careful checking and weighing of premises, etc. in arriving at a conclusion; **gather** is an informal substitute for **infer** or **conclude** (I *gather* that you don't care).

in·i·tial·ly (i-nish′əl-i), *adv.* at the beginning; at first.

in·no·va·tion (in′ə-vā′shən), *n.* [LL. *innovatio*], 1. the act or process of innovating. 2. something newly introduced; new method, custom, device, etc.; change in the way of doing things.

in·nu·en·do (in′ū-en′dō), [L., by nodding to, abl. of gerund of *innuere*, to nod to, intimate, hint; *in-*, in + *-nuere* (in comp.), to nod], meaning; that is to say: Latin formula for introducing explanatory material in legal documents; hence, *n.* [*pl.* INNUENDOES (-dōz)], 1. in *law*, the explanatory material so introduced; especially, that part of a complaint in an action for libel or slander which explains the expressions alleged to be libelous or slanderous. 2. an indirect remark, gesture, or reference, usually implying something derogatory; hint; insinuation.

in·nu·mer·a·ble (i-nōō′mĕr-ə-b'l, in-nū′mĕr-ə-b'l), *adj.* [ME.; L. *innumerabilis*; see IN- (not) & NUMERABLE], too numerous to be counted; very many; countless. —*SYN.* see **many**.

in·scru·ta·ble (in-skrōō′tə-b'l), *adj.* [LL. *inscrutabilis* < L. *in-*, not + *scrutari*, to search carefully, examine], that cannot be learned or understood; completely obscure or mysterious; incomprehensible; unfathomable; enigmatic. —*SYN.* see **mysterious**.

in·sin·u·ate (in-sin′ū-āt′), *v.t.* [INSINUATED (-id), INSINUATING], [< L. *insinuatus*, pp. of *insinuare*, to introduce by windings and turnings, insinuate < *in-*, in + *sinus*, curved surface], 1. to get in, push, or introduce slowly, indirectly, and skillfully. 2. to hint or suggest (something) indirectly; imply: as, he *insinuated* his doubt of her ability. —*SYN.* see **introduce**, **suggest**.

in·so·lent (in′sə-lənt), *adj.* [ME.; OFr.; L. *insolens*; *in-*, not + *solens*, ppr. of *solere*, to be accustomed], disrespectful of custom or established authority; impertinent; impudent. —*SYN.* see **impertinent**, **proud**.

in·sol·vent (in-sol′vənt), *adj.* 1. not solvent; unable to pay debts; bankrupt. 2. not enough to pay all debts: as, an *insolvent* inheritance. 3. of insolvents or insolvency. *n.* an insolvent person.

in·still, in·stil (in-stil′), *v.t.* [INSTILLED (-stild′), INSTILLING], [Fr. *instiller*; L. *instillare*; *in-*, in + *stillare*, to drop < *stilla*, a drop], 1. to put in drop by drop. 2. to put (a notion, principle, feeling, etc.) *in* or *into* little by little; impart gradually.

SYN.—**instill**, in this figurative connection, implies a gradual imparting of knowledge over an extended period of time (he had *instilled* honesty in his children); **implant** suggests the imparting of knowledge as if by planting it in the mind, with the implication that it will develop there; **inculcate** implies frequent or insistent repetition so as to impress upon the mind (prejudice is *inculcated* in one during childhood); **infuse** suggests the imparting of qualities as if by pouring in (he *infused* life into the play); **inseminate** implies the spreading of ideas throughout a group, nation, etc. as if by sowing seeds.

in·sur·gent (in-sūr′jənt), *adj.* [L. *insurgens*, ppr. of *insurgere*, to rise up, rise up against; *in-*, in, upon + *surgere*, to rise], rising up against political or governmental authority; rebellious. *n.* an insurgent person.

in·tan·gi·ble (in-tan′jə-b'l), *adj.* [ML. *intangibilis*; see IN- (not) & TANGIBLE], 1. that cannot be touched; incorporeal; impalpable. 2. that cannot be easily defined, formulated, or grasped; vague. *n.* something intangible, as good will or a similar asset.

in·tel·li·gi·ble (in-tel′i-jə-b'l), *adj.* [ME.; L. *intelligibilis*, *intellegibilis* < *intelligere*; see INTELLECT], 1. that can be understood; clear; comprehensible. 2. in *philosophy*, understandable by the intellect only; conceptual.

in·ter·cede (in′tĕr-sēd′), *v.i.* [INTERCEDED (-id), INTERCEDING], [L. *intercedere*; *inter-*, between + *cedere*, to go], 1. to plead or make a request in behalf of another or others: as, his colleagues *interceded* with the president for a hearing. 2. to intervene for the purpose of producing agreement; mediate. 3. in ancient Rome, to interpose a *veto*: said of a tribune or other magistrate. —*SYN.* see **interpose**.

in·ter·mit·tent (in′tĕr-mit′'nt), *adj.* [L. *intermittens*, pp. of *intermittere*; see INTERMIT], stopping and starting again at intervals; pausing from time to time; periodic. *SYN.*—**intermittent** and **recurrent** both apply to something that stops and starts, or disappears and reappears, from time to time, but the former usually stresses the breaks or pauses, and the latter, the repetition or return (an *intermittent* fever, *recurrent* attacks of the hives); **periodic** refers to something that recurs at more or less regular intervals (*periodic* economic crises); **alternate** is usually used of two recurrent things that follow each other in regular order (a life of *alternate* sorrow and joy).—*ANT.* continued, continuous.

ir·rel·e·vant (i-rel′ə-vənt), *adj.* not relevant; not pertinent: not to the point; not relating to the subject.

ir·rev·er·ent (i-rev′ĕr-ənt), *adj.* [OFr.; L. *irreverens*], not reverent; showing disrespect.

ir·rev·o·ca·ble (i-rev′ə-kə-b'l), *adj.* that cannot be revoked, recalled, or undone; unalterable.

i·tal·i·cize (i-tal′ə-sīz), *v.t.* [ITALICIZED (-sīzd′), ITALICIZING], 1. to print in italics. 2. to underscore (written matter) with a straight line to indicate that it is to be printed in italics.

jeop·ard·ize (jep′ĕr-dīz′), *v.t.* [JEOPARDIZED (-dīzd′), JEOPARDIZING], to put in jeopardy; risk loss, damage, or failure of; endanger.

judg·ment (juj′mənt), *n.* [ME. *jugement*; OFr. *jugement*; LL. *judicamentum* < L. *judicare*; see JUDGE, *v.*], 1. a judging; deciding. 2. a legal decision; order or sentence given by a judge or law court. 3. a debt resulting from a court order. 4. a misfortune looked on as a punishment from God. 5. an opinion or estimate. 6. criticism or censure. 7. the ability to come to opinions of things; power of comparing and deciding; understanding; good sense. 8. in the *Bible*, justice; right. 9. [J-], in *theology*, *a*) God's final sentence as judge of all things. *b*) the time of this: often called *the Last Judgment*. Also spelled **judgement**.

ju·di·ci·ar·y (jōō-dish′i-er′i, jōō-dish′ĕr-i), *adj.* [L. *judiciarius* < *judicium*, judgment, court of justice < *judex*; see JUDGE], of judges, law courts, or their functions. *n.* [*pl.* JUDICIARIES (-iz)], 1. the part of government whose work is the administration of justice; system of law courts. 2. judges collectively.

lam·en·ta·ble (lam′ən-tə-b'l), *adj.* [ME.; L. *lamentabilis*], 1. to be lamented; grievous; deplorable; distressing. 2. expressing sorrow; mournful. 3. of poor quality; wretched: as, a *lamentable* piece of acting.

lar·va (lär′və), *n.* [*pl.* LARVAE (-vē)], [L. *larva*, *larua*, ghost, specter; akin to *lar*, household spirit], 1. an insect in the earliest stage of development, after it is hatched and before it is changed into a pupa; caterpillar, maggot, or grub. 2. the early form of any animal that changes structurally when it becomes an adult: as, the tadpole is the *larva* of the frog.

li·bret·to (li-bret′ō), *n.* [*pl.* LIBRETTOS (-ōz), LIBRETTI (-i)], [It., dim. of *libro* (< L. *liber*), a book; see LIBRARY], 1. the words, or text, of an opera, oratorio, or other long choral work. 2. a book containing these words.

liq·ue·fy (lik′wə-fī′), *v.t.* & *v.i.* [LIQUEFIED (-fīd′), LIQUEFYING], [Fr. *liquefier* < L. *liquefacere* < *liquere*, to be liquid + *facere*, to make], to change into a liquid. —*SYN.* see **melt**.

liq·ui·date (lik′wi-dāt′), *v.t.* [LIQUIDATED (-id), LIQUIDATING], [< ML. *liquidatus*, pp. of *liquidare*, to make liquid or clear < L. *liquidus*, liquid], 1. to settle by agreement or legal process the amount of (indebtedness, damages, etc.). 2. to clear up the affairs of (a bankrupt business firm that is closing, etc.); settle the accounts of, by apportioning assets and debts. 3. to pay (a debt). 4. to convert into cash. 5. to dispose of; get rid of, as by killing. *v.i.* to liquidate one's debts.

lo·gis·tics (lə-jis′tiks), *n.pl.* [construed as sing.], [Fr. *logistique* < *loger*, to quarter; see LODGE], the branch of military science having to do with moving, supplying, and quartering troops.

lu·mi·nar·y (lōō′mə-ner′i, lū′mə-ner′i), *n.* [*pl.* LUMINARIES (-iz)], [OFr. *luminarie*; ML. *luminarium* for L. *luminare* < *lumen*, *luminis*, light], 1. a body that gives off light, such as the sun or moon. 2. a person who sheds light on some subject or enlightens mankind; famous intellectual.

ma·lign (mə-līn′), *v.t.* [ME. *malignen*; OFr. *malignier*, *maliner*, to plot, deceive; L. *malignare* < *malignus*, wicked, malicious < *male*, ill + base of *genus*, born], to speak evil of; defame; slander; traduce. *adj.* 1. malevolent; malicious. 2. evil; baleful: as, a *malign* influence. 3. very harmful; malignant. —*SYN.* see **sinister**.

ma·lig·nant (mə-lig′nənt), *adj.* [L. *malignans*, *malignantis*, ppr. of *malignare*; see MALIGN], 1. having an evil influence; malign. 2. wishing evil; very malevolent or malicious. 3. very harmful. 4. very dangerous or virulent; causing or likely to cause death; not benign: as, a cancer is a *malignant* tumor. 5. [Obs.], malcontent; rebellious; disaffected. *n.* [Obs.], a malcontent: term applied by the Roundheads to the Cavaliers.

mal·le·a·ble (mal'i-ə-b'l), *adj.* [ME. *malliable;* OFr. < L. *malleare;* see MALLEATE], 1. that can be hammered, pounded, or pressed into various shapes without breaking or returning to its original shape: said of metals. 2. yielding; amenable; adaptable. —*SYN.* see pliable.

M.Ed., Master of Education.

mis·chie·vous (mis'chi-vəs), *adj.* [Anglo-Fr. & OFr. *meschevous*], 1. causing mischief; specifically, *a*) injurious; harmful. *b*) prankish; teasing; full of tricks. 2. inclined to annoy or vex with playful tricks; naughty: said especially of a child.

mis·de·mean·or (mis'di-mēn'ēr), *n.* [*mis-* + *demeanor*], 1. [Rare], a misbehaving. 2. in *law,* any minor offense, as the breaking of a municipal ordinance, for which statute provides a lesser punishment than for a felony: the penalty is usually a fine or imprisonment for a short time in a local jail, workhouse, etc. British spelling, **misdemeanour.**

mis·hap (mis'hap', mis-hap'), *n.* [ME.; prob. after OFr. *mescheance*, mischance], 1. bad luck; adversity; misfortune. 2. an instance of this; unlucky accident.

Mo·lière (mō'lyâr'; Eng. mō'li-âr'), *n.* (pseudonym of *Jean Baptiste Poquelin*), French writer of comedies; lived 1622–1673.

mo·nop·o·lize (mə-nop'ə-līz'), *v.t.* [MONOPOLIZED (-līzd'), MONOPOLIZING], 1. to get, have, or exploit a monopoly of. 2. to get or occupy the whole of; acquire exclusive possession or control of.

nat·u·ral·ize (nach'ēr-ə-līz'), *v.t.* [NATURALIZED (-līzd'), NATURALIZING], [Fr. *naturaliser* < *naturel;* see NATURAL], 1. to confer the rights of citizenship upon (an alien). 2. to adopt and make common (a custom, word, etc.) from another locality. 3. to adapt (a plant or animal) to an environment not native; acclimate. 4. to explain (occurrences) by natural law, rejecting supernatural influence. 5. to make natural or less artificial; free from conventionality. *v.i.* 1. to become naturalized, or as if native. 2. to study nature.

neg·li·gence (neg'li-jəns), *n.* [ME. *neglygence, necligens;* OFr.; L. *negligentia*], 1. the quality or condition of being negligent; specifically, *a*) habitual failure to do the required thing. *b*) carelessness in manner or appearance; indifference. 2. an instance of such failure, carelessness, or indifference. 3. in *law,* failure to use a reasonable amount of care when such failure results in injury to another.

neg·li·gi·ble (neg'li-jə-b'l), *adj.* [< L. *negligere* (see NEGLECT); + *-ible*], that can be neglected or disregarded because small, unimportant, etc.; trifling.

ne·go·ti·a·ble (ni-gō'shi-ə-b'l, ni-gō'shə-b'l), *adj.* that can be negotiated; specifically, *a*) transferable to a third person: said of promissory notes, checks, etc. *b*) that can be passed, crossed, surmounted, etc.

neu·ro·sis (noo-rō'sis, nyoo-rō'sis), *n.* [*pl.* NEUROSES (-sēz)], [Mod. L. < Gr. *neuron*, nerve], 1. formerly, a functional disorder of the nervous system. 2. any of various psychic, or mental, disorders characterized by special combinations of anxieties, compulsions, obsessions, phobias, and motor or sensory manifestations, such as tics, without apparent organic or structural injury or change: it results only in partial disorganization of the personality and is less serious both in form and prognosis than a psychosis: also **psychoneurosis.**

neu·tral·ize (nōō'trə-līz', nū'trə-līz'), *v.t.* [NEUTRALIZED (-līzd'), NEUTRALIZING], [Fr. *neutraliser*], 1. to declare (a territory, nation, etc.) neutral; declare open to all nations and inviolable from attack; exempt from war or military operations. 2. to make ineffective; paralyze, destroy, or counteract the effectiveness, force, disposition, etc. of. 3. in *chemistry,* to destroy the distinctive or active properties of: as, an alkali *neutralizes* an acid. 4. in *electricity,* to make electrically neutral.

nev·er (nev'ēr), *adv.* [ME. *naefre;* AS. *næfre; ne,* not + *æfre,* ever; see EVER], 1. not ever; at no time. 2. not at all; by no chance; in no case; under no conditions.

no·ta·ble (nō'tə-b'l; *for adj.* 2, *also* not'ə-b'l), *adj.* [ME.; OFr.; L. *notabilis* < *notare,* to mark, note < *nota,* a mark], 1. worthy of notice; remarkable; striking; distinguished; eminent. 2. [Dial.], industrious, capable, or efficient in housekeeping: said of women. *n.* 1. a person of distinction; famous or well-known person. 2. [N-], formerly, in France, any of the persons of authority, rank, etc. summoned by the king as a deliberative assembly in emergencies.

no·ta·ry (nō'tēr-i), *n.* [*pl.* NOTARIES (-iz)], [ME. *notarye;* OFr. *notaire;* L. *notarius < notare,* to note], an official authorized to certify or attest documents, take depositions and affidavits, etc.

ope (ōp), *adj., v.t. & v.i.* [OPED (ōpt), OPING], [Late ME. < *open(en)*], [Poetic], open.

op·er·et·ta (op'ə-ret'ə), *n.* [It., dim. of *opera*], a short, amusing musical play.

ob·so·les·cence (ob'sə-les''ns), *n.* [< *obsolescent*], the process or state of becoming obsolete.

os·tra·cize (os'trə-sīz'), *v.t.* [OSTRACIZED (-sīzd'), OSTRACIZING], [Gr. *ostrakizein < ostrakon,* a shell, potsherd], to banish, bar, shut out, etc. by ostracism. —*SYN.* see banish.

pac·i·fy (pas'ə-fī'), *v.t.* [PACIFIED (-fīd'), PACIFYING], [Fr. *pacifier;* L. *pacificare < pax, pacis,* peace + *facere,* to make], 1. to make peaceful or calm; appease; tranquilize. 2. to establish or secure peace in (a nation, etc.). *SYN.*—**pacify** implies a making quiet and peaceful that which has become noisy or disorderly (to *pacify* a crying child); **appease** suggests a pacifying by gratifying or giving in to the demands of (to *appease* one's hunger); **mollify** suggests a soothing of wounded feelings or an allaying of indignation (his compliments failed to *mollify* her); **placate** implies the changing of a hostile or angry attitude to a friendly or favorable one (to *placate* an offended colleague); **propitiate** implies an allaying or forestalling of hostile feeling by winning the good will of (to *propitiate* a deity); **conciliate** implies the use of arbitration, concession, persuasion, etc. in an attempt to win over.—*ANT.* anger, enrage.

pal·pa·ble (pal'pə-b'l), *adj.* [ME.; LL. *palpabilis* < L. *palpare,* to touch], 1. that can be touched, felt, or handled; tangible. 2. easily perceived by the senses; audible, recognizable, perceptible, noticeable, etc.; hence, 3. clear to the mind; obvious; evident; plain. —*SYN.* see evident, perceptible.

par·al·lel (par'ə-lel'), *adj.* [Fr. *parallèle;* L. *parallelus;* Gr. *parallēlos < para-,* side by side + *allēlos,* one another < *allos,* other], 1. extending in the same direction and at the same distance apart at every point, so as never to meet; as lines, planes, etc.: in modern non-Euclidian geometry, such lines and planes are considered to meet at infinity. 2. having parallel parts or movements, as some machines, tools, etc. 3. closely similar or corresponding, as in purpose, tendency, time, or essential parts. 4. in *music,* having consistently equal intervals in pitch, as two parts of harmony, a series of chords, etc. *n.* 1. something parallel to something else, as a line or surface. 2. any person or thing essentially the same as, or closely similar or corresponding to, something else; counterpart. 3. the condition of being parallel; conformity in essential points. 4. any comparison showing the existence of similarity or likeness. 5. any of the imaginary lines parallel to the equator and representing degrees of latitude on the earth's surface; hence, 6. such a line drawn on a map or globe. 7. in *electricity,* a hookup of lights, cells, etc. in which all positive poles or terminals are connected in one conductor and all negatives in another: also called *multiple circuit.* 8. in *military science,* a trench, usually one of a series, running parallel to and opposing a position. 9. *pl.* in *printing,* a sign (∥) marking material referred to in a note. Abbreviated *par. v.t.* [PARALLELED or PARALLELLED (-leld'), PARALLELING or PARALLELLING], 1. *a*) to make (one thing) parallel to another. *b*) to make parallel to each other. 2. to be parallel with; extend parallel to: as, the highway *parallels* the river. 3. to compare (things, ideas, etc.) in order to show similarity or likeness. 4. to find a counterpart for; match. 5. to be a counterpart for; match; equal.

per·ceive (pēr-sēv'), *v.t. & v.i.* [PERCEIVED (-sēvd'), PERCEIVING], [ME. *perceyven* < (via OFr.) L. *percipere,* to take hold of, feel, comprehend < *per,* through + *capere,* to take], 1. to grasp mentally; take note (of); recognize; observe. 2. to become aware (of) through sight, hearing, touch, taste, or smell. —*SYN.* see discern.

per·i·pa·tet·ic (per'i-pə-tet'ik), *adj.* [ME. *parypatetik, n.;* L. *peripateticus;* Gr. *peripatētikos < peripatein,* to walk about; *peri-,* around + *patein,* to walk], 1. [P-], of the philosophy or the followers of Aristotle, who walked about in the Lyceum while he was teaching. 2. moving from place to place; walking about; itinerant. *n.* 1. [P-], a follower of Aristotle. 2. a person who walks from place to place. —*SYN.* see itinerant.

per·se·vere (pūr'sə-vēr'), *v.i.* [PERSEVERED (-vērd'), PERSEVERING], [ME. *perseveren;* OFr. *perseverer;* L. *perseverare < perseverus,* very severe, strict; *per-,* intens. + *severus,* severe, serious, grave, strict], to continue doing something in spite of difficulty, opposition, etc.; be steadfast in purpose; persist.

per·sist·ent (pĕr-sis'tənt, pĕr-zis'tənt), *adj.* [L. *persistens*, ppr. of *persistere;* see PERSIST], 1. refusing to relent; continuing, especially in the face of opposition, etc.; stubborn; persevering. 2. continuing to exist or endure; lasting without change. 3. constantly repeated; continued. 4. in *botany*, remaining attached for a long time, as some withered leaves. 5. in *zoology*, remaining for life: said of such parts which in other animals disappear or wither at an early stage.

per·tain (pĕr-tān'), *v.i.* [ME. *partenen;* OFr. *partenir;* L. *pertinere*, to stretch out, reach < *per-*, intens. + *tenere*, to hold], 1. to belong; be connected or associated; be a part or accessory. 2. to be appropriate or suitable: as, the conduct that *pertains* to a gentleman. 3. to have reference or relevance: as, his remark did not *pertain* to the question.
 pertaining to, having to do with; belonging to; of.

per·ti·nent (pŭr't'n-ənt), *adj.* [ME. *pertynent;* L. *pertinens*, ppr. of *pertinere;* see PERTAIN], of or connected with the matter in hand; relevant; to the point. —*SYN.* see relevant.

pet·u·lant (pech'oo-lənt), *adj.* [Fr. *pétulant;* L. *petulans, petulantis*, forward, petulant < base of *petere*, to make for, aim at, attack], 1. [Obs.], *a)* forward; immodest. *b)* pert; insolent. 2. impatient or irritable, especially over a petty annoyance; peevish; bad-tempered.

phe·nom·e·non (fi-nom'ə-non'), *n.* [*pl.* PHENOMENA (-nə); also, esp. for 3 & 4, PHENOMENONS (-nonz')], [LL. *phaenomenon;* Gr. *phainomenon*, neut. ppr. of *phainesthai*, to appear], 1. any fact, circumstance, or experience that is apparent to the senses and that can be scientifically described or appraised: as, an eclipse is a *phenomenon* of astronomy. 2. the appearance or observed features of something experienced as distinguished from reality or the thing in itself. 3. anything that is extremely unusual; extraordinary occurrence. 4. [Colloq.], a person with some extraordinary quality, aptitude, etc.; prodigy.

pho·net·ics (fə-net'iks, fō-net'iks), *n.pl.* [construed as sing.], [see PHONETIC], 1. the branch of language study dealing with speech sounds, their production and combination, and their representation by written symbols. 2. the phonetic system of a particular language. Abbreviated **phon., phonet.**

pla·gi·a·rize (plā'jə-rīz', plā'ji-ə-rīz'), *v.t.* [PLAGIARIZED (-rīzd'), PLAGIARIZING], [see PLAGIARISM], 1. to take and pass off as one's own (the ideas, writings, etc. of another). 2. to take ideas, writings, etc. from and pass them off as one's own.

plau·si·ble (plô'zə-b'l), *adj.* [L. *plausibilis* < *plaudere*, to applaud, clap hands], 1. seemingly true, acceptable, etc.: often implying disbelief; hence, 2. specious. 3. seemingly honest, trustworthy, etc.: often implying distrust, as, a *plausible* rogue.
 SYN.—**plausible** applies to that which at first glance appears to be true, reasonable, valid, etc. but which may or may not be so, although there is no connotation of deliberate deception (a *plausible* argument); **credible** is used of that which is believable because it is supported by evidence, sound logic, etc.; (a *credible* account); **specious** applies to that which is superficially reasonable, valid, etc. but is actually not so, and it connotes intention to deceive (a *specious* excuse).—**ANT.** genuine, actual.

pli·a·ble (plī'ə-b'l), *adj.* [Fr. < *plier*, to bend, fold < L. *plicare*, to fold, bend], 1. easily bent or molded; flexible. 2. easily influenced or persuaded; adaptable; tractable.
 SYN.—**pliable** and **pliant** both imply capability of being easily bent, physically suggesting the suppleness of a wooden switch and figuratively, a yielding nature or adaptability; **plastic** is used of substances, such as plaster or clay, that can be molded into various forms which are retained upon hardening, and figuratively suggests an impressionable quality; **ductile** literally and figuratively suggests that which can be finely drawn or stretched out (copper is a *ductile* metal); **malleable** literally or figuratively suggests that which can be hammered, beaten, or pressed into various shapes (copper is *malleable* as well as ductile).—**ANT.** inflexible, rigid, brittle.

pneu·mat·ic (noo-mat'ik, nū-mat'ik), *adj.* [L. *pneumaticus;* Gr. *pneumatikos* < *pneuma*, breath < *pnein*, to breathe], 1. of or containing wind, air, or gases. 2. worked by or filled with compressed air. 3. equipped with pneumatic tires. 4. in *theology*, having to do with the spirit or soul; spiritual. 5. in *zoology*, having hollows filled with air, as the bones of certain birds. *n.* 1. a pneumatic tire. 2. a vehicle with pneumatic tires.

pre·ced·ence (pri-sē'd'ns, pres'ə-dəns), *n.* [< *precedent*], 1. the act, right, privilege, or fact of preceding in time, place, order, or importance. 2. superiority in rank.

prej·u·dice (prej'oo-dis), *n.* [ME.; OFr. *prejudice* (Fr. *préjudice*); L. *praejudicium; prae-*, before + *judicium*, judgment < *judex, judicis*, a judge], 1. a judgment or opinion formed before the facts are known; preconceived idea, favorable or, more usually, unfavorable. 2. a judgment or opinion held in disregard of facts that contradict it; unreasonable bias: as, a *prejudice* against Northerners. 3. the holding of such judgments or opinions. 4. suspicion, intolerance, or hatred of other races, creeds, regions, occupations, etc. 5. injury or harm resulting as from some judgment or action of another or others. *v.t.* [PREJUDICED (-dist), PREJUDICING], 1. to injure or harm, as by some judgment or action: as, his mistake *prejudiced* the outcome. 2. to cause to have prejudice; cause to be prejudiced; bias.
 without prejudice to, in *law*, without dismissal of or detriment to a legal right, claim, or the like.
 SYN.—**prejudice** implies a preconceived and unreasonable judgment or opinion, usually an unfavorable one marked by suspicion, fear, intolerance, or hatred (the lynch mob was incited by race *prejudice*); **bias** implies a mental leaning in favor of or against someone or something (few of us are without *bias* of any kind); **partiality** implies an inclination to favor a person or thing because of strong fondness or attachment (the conductor has a *partiality* for the works of Brahms); **predilection** implies a preconceived liking, formed as a result of one's background, temperament, etc., that inclines one to a particular preference (he has a *predilection* for murder mysteries).

prev·a·lent (prev'ə-lənt), *adj.* [L. *praevalens*, ppr. of *praevalere;* see PREVAIL], 1. [Rare], predominant. 2. widely existing; generally practiced, occurring, or accepted. —*SYN.* see prevailing.

pro·fess (prə-fes'), *v.t.* [< ME. *professed*, pp.; OFr. *profes, professe*, bound by vows; L. *professus*, pp. of *profiteri*, to avow publicly < *pro-*, before + *fateri*, to avow], 1. to make an open declaration of; affirm: as, he *professed* his admiration of our ideals. 2. to lay claim to (some feeling) insincerely: as, she *professed* a gratitude she did not feel. 3. to practice as one's profession. 4. to declare one's belief in: as, to *profess* Christ. 5. to accept into a religious order. *v.i.* 1. to make profession. 2. to make one's profession (sense 5).

pro·fi·cient (prə-fish'ənt), *adj.* [L. *proficiens*, ppr. of *proficere*, to advance < *pro-*, forward + *facere*, to make], highly competent; skilled. *n.* an expert.

pro·gen·i·tive (prō-jen'ə-tiv), *adj.* [see PROGENITOR], capable of begetting offspring; reproductive.

prom·is·so·ry (prom'ə-sôr'i, prom'ə-sō'ri), *adj.* [ML. *promissorius* < L. *promissor*, one who promises], 1. containing a promise. 2. having the nature of a promise: as, a *promissory* representation in selling insurance.

pro·pel (prə-pel'), *v.t.* [PROPELLED (-peld'), PROPELLING], [L. *propellere; pro-*, forward + *pellere*, to drive], to push, drive, or impel onward, forward, or ahead.—*SYN.* see push.

pro·pri·e·tar·y (prə-prī'ə-ter'i), *n.* [*pl.* PROPRIETARIES (-iz)], [LL. *proprietarius* < L. *proprietas;* see PROPERTY], 1. a proprietor; owner. 2. a group of proprietors. 3. proprietorship. 4. in *American history*, the owner of a proprietary colony. 5. a proprietary medicine. *adj.* 1. belonging to a proprietor. 2. holding property. 3. of property or proprietorship. 4. held under patent, trade-mark, or copyright by a private person or company: as, a *proprietary* medicine.

pro·te·in (prō'tē-in, prō'tēn), *n.* [G. < Gr. *proteios*, prime, chief < *protos*, first: so called because of being a chief constituent of plant and animal bodies], any of a class of nitrogenous substances consisting of a complex union of amino acids and containing carbon, hydrogen, nitrogen, oxygen, and frequently sulfur: proteins occur in all animal and vegetable matter and are essential to the diet of animals.

pru·dent (proo'd'nt), *adj.* [ME.; OFr.; L. *prudens*, for *providens;* see PROVIDENT], 1. capable of exercising sound judgment in practical matters. 2. cautious or discreet in conduct; circumspect; sensible; not rash. —*SYN.* see careful, wise.

psy·cho·sis (sī-kō'sis), *n.* [*pl.* PSYCHOSES (-sēz)], [Mod. L.; Gr. *psychōsis*, a giving of life < *psychoun*, to animate, give life to < *psyche*, soul], 1. in *psychiatry*, any mental disorder in which the personality is very seriously disorganized: psychoses are of two sorts, *a)* functional (characterized by lack of apparent organic cause, and principally of a schizophrenic or manic-depressive type), and *b*) organic (characterized by a pathological organic condition, such as general paresis, brain tumor, alcoholism, etc.). 2. in *psychology*, any mental state or process. —*SYN*. see **insanity**.

psy·cho·log·i·cal·ly (si′kə-loj′i-k'l-i, si′kə-loj′ik-li), *adv.* 1. in a psychological manner. 2. from a psychological standpoint.

psy·cho·a·nal·y·sis (si′kō-ə-nal′ə-sis), *n.* [Mod. L.; *psycho-* + *analysis*], 1. a method, developed by Freud and others, of treating neuroses and some other disorders of the mind: it is based on the assumption that such disorders are the result of the rejection by the conscious mind of factors that then persist in the unconscious as dynamic repressions, causing conflicts which may be resolved by discovering and analyzing the repressions through the use of such techniques as free association, dream analysis, etc. 2. the theory or practice of this. Often shortened to **analysis**.

pto·maine, pto·main (tō′mān, tō-mān′), *n.* [It. *ptomaina* < Gr. *ptōma*, a corpse, dead body < *piptein*, to fall], any of a class of alkaloid substances, some of which are poisonous, found in decaying animal or vegetable matter.

pul·mo·nar·y (pul′mə-ner′i), *adj.* [L. *pulmonarius* < *pulmo, pulmonis*, a lung], 1. of, like, or affecting the lungs. 2. having lungs or lunglike organs. 3. designating the artery conveying blood from the heart to the lungs, and the vein conveying blood from the lungs to the heart.

pu·tre·fy (pū′trə-fī′), *v.t. & v.i.* [PUTREFIED (-fīd′), PUTREFYING], [ME. *putrifien* (prob. via OFr.) < L. *putrefacere* < *putris*, putrid + *facere*, to make], to make or become putrid or rotten; decompose. —*SYN*. see **decay**.

Que., Quebec.

quin·tes·sence (kwin-tes′'ns), *n.* [ME. *quynte(n)cense*; ML. *quinta essentia*], 1. the fifth essence, or ultimate substance, of which the heavenly bodies were thought to be composed, in ancient and medieval philosophy: distinguished from the four elements, air, fire, water, and earth. 2. the pure, concentrated essence of anything. 3. the most perfect manifestation or embodiment of a quality or thing.

quo·tient (kwō′shənt), *n.* [ME. *quocient*; L. *quoties, quotiens*, how often, how many times < *quot*, how many], in *arithmetic*, the number obtained when one quantity is divided by another: abbreviated q.

Ra·cine, Jean Bap·tiste (zhän bȧ′tēst′ rȧ′sēn′; Eng. rə-sēn′), 1639–1699; French poet and writer of tragedies.

rar·e·fy (râr′ə-fī′), *v.t. & v.i.* [RAREFIED (-fīd′), RAREFYING], [Fr. *raréfier*; L. *rarefacere* < *rarus*, rare + *facere*, to make], 1. to make or become thin, or less dense. 2. to make or become purer, or more refined.

rat·i·fy (rat′ə-fī′), *v.t.* [RATIFIED (-fīd′), RATIFYING], [Fr. *ratifier*; ML. *ratificare* < L. *ratus* (see RATE, *n.*) + *facere*, to make], to approve or confirm; especially, to give formal sanction to. —*SYN*. see **approve**.

ra·tion·al·ize (rash′ən-'l-īz′), *v.t.* [RATIONALIZED (-īzd′), RATIONALIZING], 1. to make rational; make conform to reason. 2. to explain or interpret on rational grounds. 3. to apply modern methods of efficiency to (an industry, agriculture, etc.). 4. in *mathematics*, to remove the radical signs from (an equation) without changing the value. 5. in *psychology*, to devise superficially rational, or plausible, explanations or excuses for (one's acts, beliefs, desires, etc.), usually without being aware that these are not the real motives. *v.i.* 1. to think in a rational or rationalistic manner. 2. to rationalize one's acts, beliefs, etc.

re·cip·i·ent (ri-sip′i-ənt), *n.* [< L. *recipiens*, ppr. of *recipere*; see RECEIVE], a person or thing that receives. *adj.* receiving, or ready, willing, or able to receive.

rec·on·cile (rek′ən-sīl′), *v.t.* [RECONCILED (-sīld′), RECONCILING], [ME. *reconcilen*, OFr. *reconciler*; L. *reconciliare*; see RE- & CONCILIATE], 1. to make friendly again or win over to a friendly attitude. 2. to settle (a quarrel, etc.) or compose (a difference, etc.). 3. to make (arguments, ideas, texts, etc.) consistent, compatible, etc.; bring into harmony. 4. to make content, submissive, or acquiescent (*to*): as, we became *reconciled* to our lot.

rec·ti·fy (rek′tə-fī′), *v.t.* [RECTIFIED (-fīd′), RECTIFYING], [ME. *rectifien*; OFr. *rectifier*; LL. *rectificare* < L. *rectus*, right + *facere*, to make], 1. to put or set

right; correct; amend. 2. to adjust, as in movement or balance; adjust by calculation. 3. in *chemistry*, to refine or purify by distillation, especially by distilling again and again. 4. in *electricity*, to change (alternating current) to direct current. 5. in *mathematics*, to find the length of (a curve).

re·cur·rence (ri-kûr′əns), *n.* [< *recurrent*], 1. a bringing up again, as in thought or discussion (with *to*). 2. a coming up or back; reappearance; return; repetition. 3. [Rare], resort; recourse.

re·it·er·ate (rē-it′ə-rāt′), *v.t.* [REITERATED (-id), REITERATING], [< L. *reiteratus*, pp. of *reiterare*; *re-*, again + *iterare*, to say again, repeat < *iterum*, again], to repeat (something done or said); say or do again or repeatedly. —*SYN*. see **repeat**.

rel·e·vant (rel′ə-vənt), *adj.* [ML. *relevans*, ppr. of *relevare*, to bear upon (in L., to lift up); see RELIEVE], bearing upon or relating to the matter in hand; pertinent; to the point: opposed to *irrelevant*.

SYN.—**relevant** implies close logical relationship with, and importance to, the matter under consideration (*relevant* testimony); **germane** implies such close natural connection as to be highly appropriate or fit (your reminiscences are not truly *germane* to this discussion); **pertinent** implies an immediate and direct bearing on the matter in hand (a *pertinent* suggestion); **apposite** applies to that which is both relevant and happily suitable or appropriate (an *apposite* analogy); **applicable** refers to that which can be brought to bear upon a particular matter or problem (your description is *applicable* to several people); **apropos** is used of that which is opportune as well as relevant (that remark was most *apropos*).—*ANT*. inappropriate, extraneous.

rem·i·nis·cence (rem′ə-nis′'ns), *n.* [< Fr.; see REMINISCENT], 1. a remembering; recollecting; recalling to mind. 2. memory; recollection. 3. *pl.* an account, written or spoken, of remembered events. 4. something that suggests or recalls something else; reminder. —*SYN*. see **memory**.

re·mit (ri-mit′), *v.t.* [REMITTED (-id), REMITTING], [ME. *remytten*; L. *remittere* (pp. *remissus*), to send back; *re-*, back + *mittere*, to send], 1. to forgive or pardon (sins, etc.). 2. *a*) to refrain from exacting (a payment, tax, etc.). *b*) to refrain from inflicting (a punishment) or enforcing (a sentence); cancel. 3. to decrease; let slacken: as, he *remitted* his efforts. 4. to submit or refer (a matter) for consideration, judgment, or action, especially to someone whose business it is to look after such things. 5. to put back, as into a state or position. 6. to put off; postpone. 7. to send or pay (money). 8. [Rare], to send back to jail; recommit. 9. [Obs.], to give up; surrender. 10. in *law*, to send back (a case) to a lower court for further action. *v.i.* 1. to slacken; moderate in force or intensity. 2. to send money, as in payment; pay.

re·pent·ant (ri-pen′tənt), *adj.* [ME.; OFr., ppr.], 1. repenting; penitent. 2. characterized by or indicative of repentance.

rep·re·hen·si·ble (rep′ri-hen′sə-b'l), *adj.* [ME. *reprehensyble*; LL. *reprehensibilis*], deserving to be reprehended.

re·prieve (ri-prēv′), *v.t.* [REPRIEVED (-prēvd′), REPRIEVING], [earlier *repry* < Fr. *repris*, pp. of *reprendre*, to take back; altered by association with ME. *repreven* < OFr. *reprover*, to reprove], 1. to postpone the punishment of (a person); especially, to postpone the execution of (a person condemned to death). 2. to give temporary relief to, as from pain. 3. to postpone; defer (something evil). *n.* a reprieving or being reprieved; specifically, *a*) postponement of a penalty, especially that of death, or a warrant ordering this. *b*) a temporary relief or escape, as from pain or evil.

re·pug·nant (ri-pug′nənt), *adj.* [ME. *repugnaunt*; OFr.; L. *repugnans*, ppr.; see REPUGN], 1. contradictory; inconsistent: as, actions *repugnant* to his words. 2. offering resistance; opposed; antagonistic: as, *repugnant* forces. 3. causing repugnance; distasteful; offensive; disagreeable: as, a *repugnant* odor. —*SYN*. see **hateful**.

res·o·nance (rez′ə-nəns), *n.* [OFr.; L. *resonantia*, an echo], 1. the quality or state of being resonant. 2. reinforcement and prolongation of a sound by reflection or by vibration of other bodies. 3. in *chemistry*, the property of certain molecules of having two or more structures in which only the positions of electrons differ. 4. in *electricity*, the condition of adjustment of a circuit that allows the greatest flow of current of a certain frequency. 5. in *medicine*, the sound produced in the percussion of some part of the body, especially of the chest. 6. in *phonetics*, relative audibility: it rises in inverse proportion to the amount of stricture during articulation. 7. in *physics*, the reinforced vibration of a body exposed to the vibration, at about the same frequency, of another body.

ret·i·cent (ret′ə-s'nt), *adj.* [L. *reticens*, ppr. of *reticere*, to be silent < *re-*, again + *tacere*, to be silent], habitually silent or uncommunicative; disinclined to speak readily; reserved; taciturn. —*SYN.* see **silent.**

rev·er·ence (rev′ĕr-əns), *n.* [ME. < OFr. *reverence* or L. *reverentia* < *reverens*, ppr. of *revereri*; see REVERE], 1. a feeling or attitude of deep respect, love, and awe, as for something sacred; veneration. 2. a manifestation of this; specifically, a bow, curtsy, or similar gesture of respect; obeisance. 3. the state of being revered. 4. [R-], a title used in speaking to or of a clergyman: preceded by *your* or *his*. *v.t.* [REVERENCED (-ənst), REVERENCING], to treat or regard with reverence: venerate. —*SYN.* see awe, honor, revere.

sal·u·tar·y (sal′yoo-ter′i), *adj.* [< Fr. or L.; Fr. *salutaire*; L. *salutaris* < *salus, salutis*, health], 1. promoting or conducive to health; healthful. 2. promoting or conducive to some good purpose; beneficial or wholesome.

sar·coph·a·gus (sär-kof′ə-gəs), *n.* [*pl.* SARCOPHAGI (-jī′), SARCOPHAGUSES (-gəs-iz)], [L.; Gr. *sarkophagos* < *sarx, sarkos*, flesh + *phagein*, to eat: so named because the limestone caused rapid disintegration of the contents], 1. among the ancient Greeks and Romans, a limestone coffin or tomb, often inscribed and elaborately ornamented. 2. any stone coffin, especially one exposed to view in the open air or in a large or monumental tomb.

scru·ti·nize (skrōo′t'n-īz′), *v.t.* [SCRUTINIZED (-īzd′), SCRUTINIZING], [< *scrutiny* + *-ize*], to look at very carefully; examine closely; inspect minutely.
SYN.—**scrutinize** implies a looking over carefully and searchingly in order to observe the minutest details (he slowly *scrutinized* the bank note); **inspect** implies a close, critical observation, especially in order to detect errors, flaws, etc. (he *inspected* the building for fire hazards); **examine** suggests a close observation or investigation in order to determine the condition, quality, validity, etc. of something (the doctor *examined* me thoroughly); **scan**, in its earlier, stricter sense, implies a close scrutiny and analysis, but in current, popular usage, it more frequently connotes a quick, rather superficial survey (he *scanned* the headlines).

seethe (sēth), *v.t.* [SEETHED (sēthd), SEETHING; *obs.* past tense SOD (sod), pp. SODDEN (sod′'n)], [ME. *sethen*; AS. *sēothan*; akin to G. *sieden*; prob. IE. base *sew-*, to cook, boil], 1. to cook by boiling. 2. to soak, steep, or saturate in liquid. *v.i.* 1. to boil; be boiling hot. 2. to surge, bubble, or foam, as boiling liquid. 3. to be violently agitated, excited, or disturbed. *n.* the act or condition of seething. —*SYN.* see boil.

skein (skān), *n.* [ME. *skeyn*; OFr. *esca(i)gne*], 1. a quantity of thread or yarn wound in a coil. 2. something like this, as a coil of hair. 3. a flock of wild fowl.

S O S (es′ō′es′), 1. the standard signal of distress (. . – – – . . .) used internationally in wireless telegraphy, as by ships, aircraft, etc.; hence, 2. [Colloq.], any call or appeal for help.

stat·ic (stat′ik), *adj.* [Mod. L. *staticus*; Gr. *statikos*, causing to stand < *histanai*, to cause to stand], 1. acting through weight only: said of the pressure exerted by a motionless body or mass; hence, 2. of bodies, masses, or forces at rest or in equilibrium: opposed to *dynamic*. 3. not moving or progressing; at rest; inactive; stationary. 4. in *electricity*, designating, of, or producing stationary electrical charges, as those resulting from friction. 5. in *radio*, of or having to do with static. *n.* 1. electrical discharges in the atmosphere that interfere with radio reception, etc. 2. interference or noises produced by such discharges.

stra·tum (strā′təm, strat′əm), *n.* [*pl.* STRATA (-tə, -ə), STRATUMS (-təmz, -əmz)], [L., a covering, quilt, blanket, pavement < *stratus*, pp. of *sternere*, to spread, stretch out, cover], 1. a horizontal layer or section of material, especially any of several lying one upon another; specifically, *a*) in *biology*, a layer of tissue. *b*) in *geology*, a single layer of sedimentary rock representing the deposition of a single geological period. 2. a section, level, or division regarded as like a stratum: as, the highest *stratum* of society.

strength (strenth, strenkth), *n.* [ME. *strengthe*; AS. *strengthu* < **strang-ithu*; see STRONG & -TH], 1. the

state or quality of being strong; force; power; vigor. 2. the power to resist strain, stress, etc.; toughness; durability. 3. the power to resist attack; impregnability. 4. legal, moral, or intellectual force or effectiveness. 5. *a*) capacity for producing a reaction or effect; potency, as of drugs, liquors, etc. *b*) great capacity for producing such effect. 6. intensity, as of sound, color, odor, etc. 7. force, as measured in numbers: as, the battalion is at full *strength*. 8. a source of strength; that which makes strong; support. 9. in the *stock exchange*, a tendency to rise or remain firm in prices.
  on the strength of, based or relying on.
SYN.—**strength** refers to the inherent capacity to act upon or affect something, to endure, to resist, etc. (the *strength* to lift something, tensile *strength*); **power**, somewhat more general, applies to the ability, latent or exerted, physical or mental, to do something (the *power* of the press, of a machine, etc.); **force** usually suggests the actual exertion of power, especially in producing motion or overcoming opposition (the *force* of gravity); **might** suggests great or overwhelming strength or power (with all one's *might*); **energy** specifically implies latent power for doing work or affecting something (the *energy* in an atom); **potency** refers to the inherent capacity or power to accomplish something (the *potency* of a drug). —*ANT.* weakness, impotence.

strin·gent (strin′jənt), *adj.* [L. *stringens*, ppr. of *stringere*, to draw tight; cf. STRICT, STRIKE], 1. strict; severe. 2. short in loan or investment money: said of a market. 3. compelling; convincing. —*SYN.* see strict.

stub·born (stub′ĕrn), *adj.* [ME. *stoburn, stiborne*; prob. < AS. *stubb, stybb*, a stub, stump; cf. STUB], 1. refusing to yield, obey, or comply; resisting doggedly; determined; obstinate. 2. done or carried on in a stubborn, obstinate, or persistent manner: as, a *stubborn* campaign. 3. hard to handle, treat, or deal with; intractable: as, a *stubborn* piece of oak.
SYN.—**stubborn** implies an innate fixedness of purpose, course, condition, etc. that is strongly resistant to change, manipulation, etc.(a *stubborn* child, belief, etc.); **obstinate** applies to one who adheres persistently, and often unreasonably, to his purpose, course, etc., against argument or persuasion (a panel hung by an *obstinate* juror); **dogged** implies a thoroughgoing determination or, sometimes, sullen obstinacy (the *dogged* pursuit of a goal); **pertinacious** implies a strong tenacity of purpose that is regarded unfavorably by others (a *pertinacious* critic). —*ANT.* compliant, tractable, pliant.

stu·pe·fy (stōo′pə-fī′, stū′pə-fī′), *v.t.* [STUPEFIED (-fīd′), STUPEFYING], [Fr. *stupéfier*; L. *stupefacere* < *stupere*, to be stunned or amazed + *facere*, to make], 1. to bring into a state of stupor; stun; make dull or lethargic. 2. to astound; amaze; astonish.

sub·si·dize (sub′sə-dīz′), *v.t.* [SUBSIDIZED (-dīzd′), SUBSIDIZING], [< *subsidy* + *-ize*], 1. to support with a subsidy. 2. to buy the aid or support of with a subsidy: now often implying bribery.

sub·sist·ence (səb-sis′təns), *n.* [ME.; LL. *subsistentia* < L. *subsister*; see SUBSIST], 1. existence; being; continuance. 2. the quality of being inherent. 3. the act of providing sustenance. 4. means of support or livelihood. 5. in *philosophy*, the status of something that subsists.

suc·cumb (sə-kum′), *v.i.* [OFr. *succomber*; L. *succumbere* < *sub-*, under + *cumbere*, nasalized form of *cubare*, to lie], 1. to give way; yield; submit (often with *to*): as, he *succumbed* to her persuasion. 2. to die (often with *to*): as, he *succumbed* to cancer. —*SYN.* see yield.

su·per·sede (sōo′pĕr-sēd′, sū′pĕr-sēd′), *v.t.* [SUPERSEDED (-id), SUPERSEDING], [OFr. *superseder, superceder*, to surcease, leave off, give over; L. *supersedere*, lit., to sit over, preside over, forbear, refrain, desist; *super-*, above + *sedere*, to sit], 1. to cause to be set aside or dropped from use as inferior or obsolete and replaced by something else. 2. to take the place or office of; succeed. 3. to remove or cause to be removed so as to make way for another; supplant. —*SYN.* see replace.

sur·feit (sûr′fit), *n.*
[ME. *surfet, surfait*;
OFr. *sorfait < surfaire*,
to overdo; *sur-* (< L.
super), over + *faire* (<
L. *facere*), to make], 1.
too great an amount or supply; excess (usually with *of*): as, a *surfeit* of complaints. 2. overindulgence, especially in food or drink. 3. discomfort or disorder resulting from overindulgence in food or drink. 4. disgust, nausea, etc. resulting from any kind of excess; satiety. *v.t.* [ME. *sorfeten*], to feed or supply to

satiety or excess. *v.i.* to indulge or be supplied to satiety or excess: overindulge. —*SYN.* see **satiate**.

sur·mise (sẽr-mīz′; *also, for n.,* sũr′mīz), *n.* [ME. *surmyse;* OFr. *surmise,* accusation, fem. of *surmis,* pp. of *surmettre,* lit., to put upon, hence to accuse; *sur-* (< L. *super*), above + *mettre,* to put < L. *mittere,* to send], 1. an idea or opinion formed from evidence that is neither positive nor conclusive; conjecture; guess. 2. the act or process of surmising; conjecture in general. *v.t. & v.i.* [SURMISED (-mīzd′), SURMISING], to imagine or infer (something) without conclusive evidence; conjecture; guess. —*SYN.* see **guess**.

sus·cep·ti·ble (sə-sep′tə-b'l), *adj.* [ML. *susceptibilis* < L. *suscipere,* to receive, undertake < *sus-* (for *sub-*), under + *capere,* to take], easily affected emotionally; having a sensitive nature or feelings; responsive.
  susceptible of, that can be affected with; admitting; allowing: as; testimony *susceptible of* error.
  susceptible to, easily influenced by or affected with; especially liable to: as, *susceptible to* tuberculosis.

sus·te·nance (sus′ti-nəns), *n.* [ME. *sustenaunce;* OFr. *soustenance;* LL. *sustinentia,* patience, endurance < L. *sustinere;* see SUSTAIN], 1. sustainment. 2. maintenance; support; means of livelihood. 3. that which sustains life: nourishment; food.

syn·chro·nize (siŋ′krə-nīz′), *v.i.* [SYNCHRONIZED (-nīzd′), SYNCHRONIZING], [Gr. *synchronizein* < *synchronos,* contemporary; *syn-,* together + *chronos,* time], to move or occur at the same time or rate; be synchronous. *v.t.* 1. to cause to agree in rate or speed; regulate (clocks, a flashgun and camera shutter, etc.) so as to make synchronous. 2. to assign (events, etc.) to the same date or period; represent as or show to be coincident or simultaneous. 3. in *motion pictures, a)* to add or adjust (sound effects or dialogue) so as to coincide with the action of a picture. *b)* to add or adjust such sound effects or dialogue to (a picture).

syn·op·sis (si-nop′sis), *n.* [*pl.* SYNOPSES (-sēz)], [LL.; Gr. *synopsis; syn-,* together + *opsis,* a sight], a statement giving a brief, general review or condensation; summary, as of a story. —*SYN.* see **abridgment**.

syn·the·size (sin′thə-sīz′), *v.t.* [SYNTHESIZED (-sīzd′), SYNTHESIZING], 1. to bring together into a whole by synthesis. 2. to form by bringing together separate parts. 3. to treat synthetically.

tan·ta·lize (tan′tə-līz′), *v.t.* [TANTALIZED (-līzd′), TANTALIZING], [< *Tantalus*], to promise or show something desirable to (a person) and then remove or withhold it: arouse hope and then disappointment in; tease.

Tan·ta·lus (tan′tə-ləs), *n.* [ME. *Tantale;* L.; Gr. *Tantalos*], 1. in *Greek mythology,* a king, son of Zeus, whose punishment in the lower world was eternal hunger and thirst: he was doomed to stand in water that always receded when he tried to drink it and under branches of fruit he could never reach; hence, 2. [t-], a stand with decanters that, although plainly visible, cannot be removed until the bar that locks them in place is raised.

tel·e·graph (tel′ə-graf′, tel′ə-gräf′), *n.* [Fr. *télégraphe;* see TELE- & -GRAPH: orig. used of a semaphore], 1. originally, any signaling apparatus. 2. an apparatus or system for transmitting messages by electric impulses sent through a wire or converted into radio waves: basically it in-

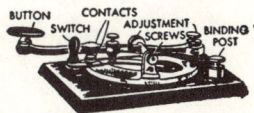
TELEGRAPH KEY

volves the use of a code of short and long signals, called *dots* and *dashes,* produced by the closing and opening of an electric circuit by means of a lever, or key: see also **telautograph, teletypewriter**. 3. a telegram. *v.t.* 1. to send (a message) by telegraph. 2. to send a telegram to. *v.i.* to send a telegram or telegrams. Abbreviated **tel., teleg.**

tem·per·a·ment (tem′prə-mənt, tem′pẽr-ə-mənt), *n.* [ME.; L. *temperamentum,* proper mixing < *temperare,* to mingle, qualify, temper], 1. originally, a tempering; proportionate mixture or balance of ingredients. 2. in medieval physiology, any one of the four conditions of body and mind, the *sanguine, phlegmatic, choleric* (or *bilious*), and *melancholic temperaments,* attributed to an excess of one of the four corresponding humors: see **humor**. 3. frame of mind; disposition; nature: as,

he has an excitable *temperament.* 4. a disposition that rebels at restraints and is often moody or capricious: as, many artists have *temperament.* 5. [Obs.], *a)* climate. *b)* temperature. 6. in *music,* a system of adjustment of the intervals between the tones of an instrument of fixed intonation: it may be *pure temperament,* in which the intervals are set exactly according to theory, or *equal temperament* (as in a piano), in which the pitch of the tones is slightly adjusted to make them suitable for all keys. —*SYN.* see **disposition**.

the·a·ter, the·a·tre (thē′ə-tẽr; *also formerly, now dial. or humorous,* thē-ā′tẽr), *n.* [OFr. *theatre* (Fr. *théâtre*); L. *theatrum;* Gr. *theatron* < base of *theasthai,* to see, view], 1. a place where plays, operas, motion pictures, etc. are presented; especially, a building expressly designed for such presentations. 2. any place resembling a theater, especially one having ascending rows of seats, as a lecture hall, surgical clinic, etc. 3. any place where events take place; scene of operations: as, the Pacific *theater* of war. 4. *a)* the dramatic art; drama. *b)* the theatrical world; people engaged in theatrical activity. 5. theatrical technique, production, etc. with reference to its effectiveness: as, the play was good *theater.*

tran·sient (tran′shənt), *adj.* [L. *transiens,* ppr. of *transire;* see TRANSIT], 1. *a)* passing away with time; not permanent; temporary; transitory. *b)* passing quickly or soon; fleeting; ephemeral. 2. transeunt. 3. staying only for a short time: as, a *transient* lodger. 4. in *music,* designating or of a temporary modulation. *n.* a transient person or thing, as a temporary lodger.
  SYN.—**transient** applies to that which lasts or stays but a short time (a *transient* guest, feeling, etc.); **transitory** refers to that which by its inherent nature must sooner or later pass or end (life is *transitory*); **ephemeral** literally means existing only one day and, by extension, applies to that which is markedly short-lived (*ephemeral* glory); **momentary** implies duration for a moment or an extremely short time (a *momentary* lull in the conversation); **evanescent** applies to that which appears momentarily and fades quickly away (*evanescent* mental images); **fleeting** implies of a thing that it passes swiftly and cannot be held (a *fleeting* thought). —*ANT.* lasting, permanent.

un'a·bridged′ (ũn′á·brĭjd′), *adj.* Not abridged; complete.

un·wield·y (un-wēl′di), *adj.* 1. hard to wield, manage, handle, or deal with, as because of large size or weight, or awkward form. 2. awkward; clumsy.

u·ti·lize (ū′t'l-īz′), *v.t.* [UTILIZED (-īzd′), UTILIZING], [Fr. *utiliser* < *utile,* useful; L. *utilis* < *uti,* to use], to put to use; make use of; get profit or benefit from by using. —*SYN.* see **use**.

vac·u·um (vak′ū-əm; *also, esp. as attrib.,* vak′yoom), *n.* [*pl.* VACUUMS (-əmz), VACUA (-ə)], [L., neut. sing. of *vacuus,* empty], 1. a space with nothing at all in it; completely empty space. 2. *a)* a space, as that inside a vacuum tube, out of which most of the air or gas has been taken, as by pumping; space containing air or gas at a pressure below that of the atmosphere. *b)* the degree to which pressure has been brought below atmospheric pressure. 3. a space left empty by the removal or absence of something usually found in it; void: often figurative. *adj.* 1. of a vacuum. 2. used to make a vacuum. 3. having a vacuum; partially or completely exhausted of air or gas. 4. working by suction or the creation of a partial vacuum. *v.t.* [Colloq.], to clean with a vacuum cleaner.

va·grant (vā′grənt), *n.* [ME. *vagrant;* prob. < OFr. *wa(u)crant,* ppr. of *wa(u)crer,* to wander about, walk; influenced in form by *vagabond* or L. *vagari,* to wander], 1. a person who wanders from place to place or lives a wandering life; rover. 2. a person who wanders from place to place without a regular job, supporting himself by begging, etc.; idle wanderer; vagabond; tramp. 3. in *law,* a tramp, beggar, prostitute, or similar idle or disorderly person whose way of living makes him liable to be arrested and jailed. *adj.* 1. wandering from place to place or living a wandering life; roaming; nomadic. 2. living the life of a vagabond or tramp. 3. of or characteristic of a vagrant. 4. characterized by straggling growth: said of plants. 5. following no fixed direction or course; moving at random; wayward: said of things.
  SYN.—**vagrant** refers to a person without a fixed home who wanders about from place to place, supporting himself by begging, etc., and in legal usage, implies such a person regarded as a public nuisance, subject to arrest; **vagabond,** originally the more derogatory term, implying shiftlessness,

thievery, etc., now often connotes no more than a carefree, roaming existence; **bum, tramp,** and **hobo** are informal equivalents for the preceding, variously discriminated, but **bum** always connotes an idle, dissolute, often alcoholic person who never works, **tramp** connotes a vagrant, whether he lives by begging or by doing odd jobs, and **hobo** is now most commonly restricted to a migratory laborer who follows such seasonal work as crop picking or works on construction jobs, etc. See also **itinerant.**

ver·bal·ize (vūr′b'l-īz′), *v.i.* [VERBALIZED (-īzd′), VER-BALIZING], [< Fr. *verbaliser* (see VERBAL) or < *verbal* + *-ize*], to be wordy, or verbose. *v.t.* **1.** to express in words. **2.** to change (a noun, etc.) into a verb.

vig·i·lant (vij′ə-lənt), *adj.* [Fr.; L. *vigilans*, ppr. of *vigilare*, to watch < *vigil*, awake], characterized by vigilance, or wakefulness; especially, alert to danger; watchful. —*SYN.* see watchful.

vul·can·ize (vul′kən-īz′), *v.t.* [VULCANIZED (-īzd′), VULCANIZING], to subject to vulcanization. *v.i.* to undergo vulcanization.

vul·ner·a·ble (vul′nĕr-ə-b'l), *adj.* [LL. *vulnerabilis*, wounding. likely to injure; also, in pass. sense. vulnerable < L. *vulnerare*, to wound < *vulnus, vulneris*, a wound], **1.** that can be wounded or physically injured. **2.** open to criticism or attack: as, a *vulnerable* reputation. **3.** open to attack or assault by armed forces: as, the Maginot line proved to be *vulnerable.* **4.** in *contract bridge*, liable to an increased penalty if defeated or to an increased bonus if successful: said of a team which has won one game.

war·rant (wôr′ənt, wär′ənt), *n.* [ME. & ONorm.Fr. *warant;* OFr. *garant*, a warrant; OHG. *weren*, a warranty; cf. GUARANTY], **1.** *a)* authorization or sanction, as by a superior or the law. *b)* justification or reasonable grounds for some act, course, statement, or belief. **2.** something that serves as an assurance, or guarantee, of some event or result. **3.** a writing serving as authorization or certification for something; specifically, *a)* authorization in writing for the payment or receipt of money; voucher. *b)* [British], a receipt for goods stored in a warehouse. *c)* in *law*, a writ or order authorizing an officer to make an arrest, seizure, or search, or perform some other designated act. *d)* in *military usage*, the certificate of appointment to the grade of warrant officer: cf. **warrant officer.** *v.t.* **1.** *a)* to give (someone) authorization or sanction to do something. *b)* to authorize (the doing of something). **2.** to serve as justification or reasonable grounds for (an act, belief, etc.): as, my remarks did not *warrant* her tears. **3.** to give formal assurance, or guarantee, to (someone) or for (something); specifically, *a)* to guarantee the quality, quantity, condition, etc. of (goods) to the purchaser. *b)* to guarantee to (the purchaser) that goods sold are as represented. *c)* to guarantee to (the purchaser) the title of goods purchased; assure of indemnification against loss. *d)* in *law*, to guarantee the title of granted property to (the grantee). **4.** [Colloq.], to state with confidence; affirm emphatically: as, I *warrant* he'll be late. —*SYN.* see assert.

writhe (rīth), *v.t.* [WRITHED (rīthd), WRITHED or *archaic* or *poetic* WRITHEN (rith′n), WRITHING], [ME. *writhen;* AS. *writhan*, to twist, wind about; akin to ON. *rītha;* IE. base **wer-*, to bend, twist; cf. WREATH], to cause to twist or turn; contort. *v.i.* **1.** to make twisting or turning movements; contort the body, as in agony; squirm. **2.** to suffer great emotional distress, as from embarrassment, revulsion, etc. *n.* an act of writhing; writhing movement: contortion.

Zn, zinc. *Chem.*